PASSION-BOOK

PASSION-BOOK

Devotions for Household Commemoration of the Holy Season of Passiontide Collected and Reworked from the Historic Treasures of the Orthodox Lutheran Church

Friedrich Lochner

TRANSLATED BY MATTHEW CARVER

Emmanuel Press ✠ Fort Wayne, IN

Published by Emmanuel Press
Fort Wayne, IN
www.emmanuelpress.us

Scripture passages are based on the KJV but adapted to reflect the German of Luther's Bible.

Translated from the combined German volume: *Passions- und Osterbuch: Andachten zur häuslichen Feier der heiligen Passions- und Osterzeit. Aus den älteren Schätzen der rechtgläubigen Kirche gesammelt und bearbeitet von Friedrich Lochner, Pastor der lutherischen Trinitatis-Gemeinde zu Springfield, Ills.* [Passion and Easter Book: Devotions for Household Commemoration of the Holy Seasons of Passiontide and Eastertide, collected and reworked from the historic treasures of the orthodox church by Friedrich Lochner, pastor of the Lutheran Church of the Trinity in Springfield, Illinois.] (St. Louis, Missouri: M. C. Barthel, 1879).

Translation ©2025 Matthew Carver
Design & Layout ©2025 Amanda Carver
Musical Engraving ©2025 David Schotte

All rights reserved. No part of this publication may be reproduced, stored in a retrieval system, or transmitted, in any form or by any means, electronic, mechanical, photocopying, recording, or otherwise, without the prior written permission of Emmanuel Press.

ISBN: 978-1-934328-30-9
Manufactured in the United States of America.

1 2 3 4 5 6 7 8 9 10   30 29 28 27 26 25 24

We hail Thee, Lord, sole Comfort Thou,
In this Thine hour of suff'ring now,
To faithful souls grant steadfastness
And sinners poor, Thy righteousness.

To Thee, eternal Three in One,
Let homage meet by all be done,
Whom by the cross Thou dost restore,
Preserve, and govern evermore.
Amen.

CONTENTS

Dedication xi
Foreword xiii
Translator's Note xix

Devotion 1: Christian and Salutary Contemplation of the Bitter Suffering
    and Death of Our Dear Lord and Savior Jesus Christ 1
Devotion 2: Christ Foretells His Sufferings Again 6
Devotion 3: The High Priests and Scribes Take Counsel against Jesus 10
Devotion 4: Jesus Is Anointed by Mary in Bethany 13
Devotion 5: Judas Makes a Traitorous Pact 18
Devotion 6: Jesus Celebrates the Passover for the Last Time 21
Devotion 7: Christ Institutes the Holy Supper 25
Devotion 8: Christ Washes the Disciples' Feet 30
Devotion 9: Peter and Christ's Conversation concerning the Footwashing 34
Devotion 10: With the Footwashing, Jesus Also Wishes to Give an Example 39
Devotion 11: Jesus Is Troubled at Judas' Hardening 43
Devotion 12: Jesus Reveals His Betrayer 47
Devotion 13: Christ Settles the Disciples' Dispute about Rank 52
Devotion 14: Christ's Further Discourses after Judas' Departure 57
Devotion 15: The Lord Shows His Disciples That the Wedding Party
    Must Now Fast 62
Devotion 16: Christ Goes with His Disciples to the Mount of Olives 67
Devotion 17: Christ Begins to Be Sorrowful in the Garden of Gethsemane 71

Devotion 18: Jesus Wills to Drink the Cup................... 77

Devotion 19: Jesus Wakes the Sleeping Disciples 83

Devotion 20: Christ Goes Confidently to Meet His Enemies.... 88

Devotion 21: Jesus Procures for His Disciples Safe Conduct... 94

Devotion 22: Jesus Suffers Himself to Be Kissed by False Judas 99

Devotion 23: Christ Does Not Wish to Be Defended by the Sword 103

Devotion 24: Jesus Rebukes His Adversaries and Is Forsaken by the Disciples.... 108

Devotion 25: Christ Is Taken Captive and Bound............. 113

Devotion 26: Peter Denies the Lord for the First Time 118

Devotion 27: Jesus Defends His Innocence and Receives a Blow on the Cheek ... 123

Devotion 28: Peter Denies Again, but Repents 128

Devotion 29: Jesus Is Silent at the False Testimony against Him......... 134

Devotion 30: Christ Is Condemned to Death as a Blasphemer............ 139

Devotion 31: Christ, the Son of God, Is Mocked and Mistreated 144

Devotion 32: Christ Is Again Judged by the Sanhedrin....... 148

Devotion 33: Christ Is Delivered to the Gentiles 153

Devotion 34: Judas Comes to a Horrible End 157

Devotion 35: The Chief Priests Take Counsel concerning the Price of Blood 161

Devotion 36: The Jews' Hypocritical Appeal................ 165

Devotion 37: The Jews' Threefold Accusation and Christ's Good Confession 170

Devotion 38: Christ Is Brought to Herod and Ridiculed by Him 176

Devotion 39: Christ Is Equated with the Murderer Barabbas 181

Devotion 40: Jesus Is Scourged and Crowned with Thorns............. 187

Devotion 41: "Ecce homo! Behold, What a Man!".......... 193

Devotion 42: Pilate Is Afraid of the Son of God, but More So of the Jews 198

Devotion 43: Pilate Condemns Jesus, and the Jews Take His Blood
    upon Themselves 204

Devotion 44: Christ Is Led out of Jerusalem Bearing His Cross........... 209

CONTENTS

Devotion 45: Jesus Preaches to the Lamenting Women 215

Devotion 46: Christ Wills Fully to Taste Death for Us 220

Devotion 47: Christ on the Cross 224

Devotion 48: Christ Prays for His Enemies (First Word) 229

Devotion 49: Jesus of Nazareth, the King of the Jews 233

Devotion 50: The Parting of Jesus' Garments 237

Devotion 51: Jesus Takes Care of Those Left Behind (Second Word) 242

Devotion 52: Christ Mocked and Reviled on the Cross 247

Devotion 53: The Conversion of the Thief on the Right (Third Word) 252

Devotion 54: Christ Forsaken by God (Fourth Word) 257

Devotion 55: Jesus' Thirst on the Cross (Fifth Word) 262

Devotion 56: Christ, Dying, Proclaims His Victory (Sixth Word) 266

Devotion 57: Jesus Dies (Seventh Word) 270

Devotion 58: The Miraculous Signs Following Jesus' Death 275

Devotion 59: The Wonderful Effects of the Death of Jesus on Men's Hearts 280

Devotion 60: The Kinsmen and Friends of Jesus at the Cross 285

Devotion 61: Jesus' Side Is Pierced 289

Devotion 62: Joseph Begs for the Body of Jesus 294

Devotion 63: Jesus' Body Is Taken Down from the Cross and Readied for Burial . . 299

Devotion 64: Jesus Is Laid in the Tomb 304

Devotion 65: Jesus Rests in the Tomb during the Sabbath 308

Devotion 66: Jesus' Sepulcher Is Sealed by the Enemies, and a Watch Is Set 312

Index of Hymns & Sources 317

Melody Appendix 321

TO MY ELDERLY MOTHER

in childlike gratitude and reverence

As this my *Passion-book* goes out to the houses and families in which the Lord's death is proclaimed every year in the daily divine service at home, I would like to send it first into your quiet widow's parlor, in which, whenever the holy season of Passiontide appeared during our long years together in the place where I used to serve, you were accustomed to use one or another of the passionals here employed for your own private edification. Though according to His wise counsel the Lord has now finally separated us in place and perhaps also in time, may these devotions, through meditation, worship, and hymn-singing, bring us increasingly closer together in spirit to Golgotha, until we—and if it please God, all our family and friends—shall meet again hereafter at the blessed goal of all the ways of the elect, and shall then know and worship in sight what we have here believed, and in the choir of the perfected righteous, with glorified lips, free from frailty, shall eternally intone our praise to Him "that loved us, and washed us from our sins in His own blood, and hath made us kings and priests unto God and His Father."

FOREWORD

The following Passion devotions were originally designed only for my own private use. According to ancient Christian custom, not only were there special meditations dedicated to the sufferings and death of our Lord Jesus Christ in the public divine services during the holy season of Passiontide, but from time immemorial private devotional hours have also preferably been devoted to such meditations. Thus every year during Passiontide, I have been accustomed to arrange my household devotions accordingly. Yet because Rambach's wonderful meditations on the Passion of Christ seemed to me too detailed to get through the whole Passion History, and because I possessed no older devotional literature of the sort except for Dr. Luther's Passion sermons, and finally, because the manner and language of the earlier Passion preachers gave me more satisfaction and blessing than the more recent ones—therefore I endeavored, with the help of the Altenburg New Testament republished by the Missouri Synod, to produce a passional for my household by synthesizing or combining the parallel parts from the pertinent summaries on the four evangelists, and arranging the excerpts of the Passion accordingly, and choosing for each devotion corresponding hymn stanzas and prayers from my collection of hymnals and prayerbooks. During the blessed use of this private labor over several years, however, I became more and more intimately acquainted with a selection of old passionals, and although none of these could use be used exclusively for my purposes, I nevertheless discovered as time passed that, to my great joy, precisely those which I had arranged for my use were very closely related one to another, and that one author had learned from another, often borrowing whole passages from his predecessors, and that therefore the best material from these passionals could be so combined or interwoven, as the case might be, for shorter devotions, that there was no fear that such use of old Passion treasuries would produce a motley mishmash.

If, accordingly, being encouraged and advised by dear brethren, I have had my *Passion-book* published for the use of godly housefathers and Christians, I am surely indebted to identify my treasure-houses from which I have drawn what I needed for the purpose of meditation and prayer.

The summary meditations are chiefly drawn from the following two works:

1. *Passionalbüchlein oder: Christliche Erklärung der gnadenreichen Historien des bitteren Leidens und Sterbens unseres lieben Herrn und Heilandes Jesu Christi, darinnen aufs kürzeste und deutlichste angezeiget und in gewisse Frage und Antwort gefaßet ist, was aus einer jeden Lection fürnehmlich für Lehren, Trost, Erinnerung und Warnungen zu merken und zu behalten seien. Durch Simonem Gediccum, der heiligen Schrift Doctorn, fürstlich Magdeburgischen Hofprediger, etc.* Leipzig, 1594.

2. *Georgii Renauli, weiland Predigers zu St. Wolffs am Ungerischen See, geistreiche Passionschule, d. i. die ganze Historia des bittern Leidens und Sterbens unsers Herrn und Heilandes Jesu Christi, nach allen vier Evangelien in fünf Abtheilungen verfaßet. Allen frommen Christen zur Unterhaltung ihrer Andacht bei der heiligen Passionszeit lehr- und trostreich erkläret, etc.* Leipzig / Breslau, 1718.

Both authors are faithful witnesses and confessors of the orthodox church.

Dr. Simon Gediccus, born in Wurzen on the 31st of October, 1551, was pastor at St. John's church in Leipzig in 1573; master and, shortly thereafter, deacon at St. Thomas in 1574, and professor of Hebrew, then pastor primarius and consistorialis, in Halle; and thereupon court preacher of the Elector of Brandenburg and provost of Cöln an der Spree. Driven thence by the Reformed, he became pastor and superintendent in Meißen, and finally in Merseburg. Here in 1623 he celebrated his 50th anniversary in the preaching office and in 1624 took part with Gerhard, Meißner, Balduin, and others in a conference of Leipzig theologians in matters of the known controversy of the Gießen and Tübingen theologians. He died on the 5th of October, 1631.

Georg Renaul was, as it seems, a Lutheran preacher in Hungary persecuted by the papists in 1670. His *Passionschule* (Passion-school), which he wrote first for his "poor villagers," he published in its current form as a sweet fruit of the sorrow and exile for the sake of the Word. In the preface of this book, he writes as follows:

FOREWORD

Not many years ago in 1669, when my soul was plucked from death and I saw fit to thank the Lord for His benefit, I joined David in vowing to the Same: "I will take the cup of salvation and preach the name of the Lord!" Howbeit at the time I understood not well the covenant with God itself, let alone meditated often upon it. As long as my dear, faithful God then held me under His fatherly rod in this "school," the great, painful sufferings of our Savior Jesus Christ were like a permanent mirror before the eyes, compared to which all other men's sufferings and sorrows were to be counted scarcely as a cool drop of dew. By this I began to draw from Christ's sufferings so many different teachings and comforts, and pored over many a good and beautiful book, and found betimes precious golden grains of the bloody and salutary merit of Christ, now rich veins of the silver of His most holy innocence, which meanwhile I used for my own benefit; but I could not rightly melt the lumps together until the persecution began, and the heat of tribulation became truly great, even as such gold is best purified when God Himself stokes the fire, so that coal and heat become sufficiently true and plentiful. Then, because I could no longer conceal nor bury this talent lent me by God (lest it some day be required of me), but that I might rather serve my fellow Christians therewith (for he that knoweth to do good and doeth it not, to him it is sin)—in consideration of which, I have now by God's grace employed the grievous time of my troubled exile *ut in otio minime fuerim otiosus, verum in quiete laboriosus* (that I might not be utterly idle in my leisure, but active in quietness).

For assistance here and there, I have also used the passionals of Johann Heermann and Martin Moller already well known to our people through their reprints. The former work, published in 1618, bears the title, *Crux Christi, d. i., die schmerzliche Marterwoche unseres hochverdienten Heilandes Jesu Christi, etc.*; the latter book is titled, according to the edition of Sprotta, 1610: *Martinus Mollerus, Passionsbetrachtungen, oder: wie ein jeder Christ das allerheiligste Leiden und Sterben unseres Herrn Jesu Christi in seinem Herzen betrachten, allerlei schöne Lehren und heilsamen Trost daraus schöpfen und zu einem christlichen Leben und seligem Sterben nützlich gebrauchen soll.* Besides these, a few sentences from Johann Gerhard's Gospel Harmony have been borrowed on a few occasions and, for the sake of shorter composition, a whole meditation—that of the sixty-second devotion from Lassenius' *Passionsbetrachtungen*.

Regarding the prayers, those have been used which were newly published and reworked for home use by the professor, Dr. Schöberlein, having been first published in 1657 in the *Passionsandachten* of Martin Beer, former preacher and professor in Nuremberg. I became acquainted with these devotions when I had already begun the fair copy for print, and made frequent use particularly of those valuable prayers all the more eagerly when I saw to my joy that that learned editor, a recognized liturgical scholar, in his revision followed a similar plan. Otherwise, the prayers have frequently been taken from the aforesaid meditations of Martin Moller and Lassenius, likewise from the excellent prayer-book of Dr. Georg Zeämann, superintendent of Stralsund, which was written during his incarceration in the Ehrenberg fortress in Tyrol at the hands of the papists, and published after his liberation in the year 1632. In addition, some of the prayers from the forty meditations of the Württemberg court chaplain, Johann Andreas Grammlich, first published in 1722 and reprinted in 1865, are also found here.

The Verse prefixed to every Lesson as a sort of motto is, as the Lesson itself or the Meditation on it makes clear, in many cases a prophecy as well. Time and time again we find in the Passion History the words "Then was fulfilled the word of the prophet, which saith . . ."

For those who wish to sing the selected hymn stanzas during their devotion, the musical supplement provides assistance with respect to the less familiar melodies. All the rest of the melodies are found, among other places, in the new edition of the *Choralbuch* extracted from Dr. F. Layriz's *Kern des deutschen Kirchengesangs* and used in many of our congregations, published by L. Volkening (No. 901 N. 4th St., St. Louis, Mo.).

In selecting the Lessons, I have not had in view a specific division of these for the different weeks and days in Lent, since I know from experience that now and then an interruption can occur in their use. I have begun these meditations precisely on Ash Wednesday yearly, sometimes even on the Monday after Estomihi, and used them whenever it was possible in the morning and evening divine service. If I ever finished before the beginning of Holy Week, I selected for those days certain of the devotions for repetition, beginning from Monday after Palm Sunday approximately thus:

FOREWORD

Monday (Morning and Evening)

Devotion 1: Christian and Salutary Contemplation of the Bitter Suffering and Death of Our Dear Lord and Savior Jesus Christ

Devotion 2: Christ Foretells His Sufferings Again

Tuesday

Devotion 3: The High Priests and Scribes Take Counsel against Jesus

Devotion 4: Jesus Is Anointed by Mary in Bethany

Wednesday

Devotion 5: Judas Makes a Traitorous Pact

Devotion 6: Jesus Celebrates the Passover for the Last Time

Maundy Thursday

Devotion 7: Christ Institutes the Holy Supper

Devotion 8: Christ Washes the Disciples' Feet (or one of the two following meditations concerning the footwashing)

Good Friday

Devotion 56: Christ, Dying, Announces His Victory (or Devotion 57: Jesus Dies)

Devotion 63: Jesus' Body Is Taken Down from the Cross and Readied for Burial (or Devotion 64: Jesus Is Laid in the Tomb)

Holy Saturday

Devotion 65: Jesus Rests in the Tomb during the Sabbath.

Devotion 66: Jesus' Sepulcher Is Sealed by the Enemies, and a Watch Is Set

Now let this *Passion-book* go forth from my house at last to other houses, yet further accompanied by the blessing of the Crucified, of whom it will jointly testify, and who once prophesied of His exaltation on the cross, "I, when I am lifted up from the earth, will draw them all unto Me" (John 12:32). If it pleases Him to let this labor find a kind reception, and He grants life and health, the *Passion-book* will in time be followed by an *Easter-book* for use in the days of jubilation from Easter to Whitsunday, seeing the Lord, in the intimations of His sufferings as well as in His Farewell Discourse, continually directs His disciples to the glorious outcome of His sufferings by His resurrection. It is in the pleasant hope that that labor too may be granted me that I have chosen the title given above.

Peace to the house wherein the Lord's death is showed forth until He come!

F. L.

TRANSLATOR'S NOTE

A few words about the provenance of the book and about the translation are in order. The author, Friedrich Lochner, born on September 23, 1822, in Nürnberg, studied in Neuendettelsau, was sent by the Rev. Wilhelm Loehe to the United States in 1845, where he served at various churches, including Trinity Lutheran in Milwaukee, Wisconsin, founded the Teacher's Seminary in that city, and taught at Concordia Theological Seminary in Springfield, Illinois. His German devotional on which the present translation is based was first published in a stand-alone edition in 1877, and then with its counterpart *Osterbuch* (Easter-book) in 1879, with a preface marked "Springfield, Ills., 29 August, 1878."

The approach to the present translation is the same as that used in the previous *Friedrich Lochner: Liturgical Forms and the Shorter Liturgical Works* (Emmanuel Press, 2024). Traditional language is used reflecting that of the time when the original was printed, including the traditional forms of address for God and generally a language in harmony with the Authorized (King James) Version of Holy Scripture, while more modern idiom is used where the reader is addressed. Scriptural quotations are adapted from the Authorized Version in order to convey the sense of the German. For the sake of the reader, some originally omitted Scripture references have been supplied here and there.

The hymnody in this volume, appearing mostly in the form of centos or select stanzas suitably brief for devotional use, is mostly taken from the public domain, especially from Lutheran hymnals. Where this was not possible, translations were sought elsewhere. In several cases, a new translation had to be provided by the present translator (the sources are detailed in the hymn index, which also includes a couple corrections to the German edition). Thanks are hereby expressed to David Schotte for kindly engraving the musical settings at the end.

Matthew Carver
Septuagesima, 2025

DEVOTION 1

Christian and Salutary Contemplation of the Bitter Suffering and Death of Our Dear Lord and Savior Jesus Christ

Mel.: Freu dich sehr, o meine Seele

Boast, O world, of all thy learning,
   Glory in its lofty heights.
But thy carnal knowledge spurning,
   My heart still finds pure delights:
In my Savior's cross and pain,
I find wisdom's highest gain.
   That blest faith His grace hath given
   Seals to me the bliss of heaven.

Come, my Life, my Lord, my Savior,
   Come and teach me as Thou wilt.
Take my heart as Thine forever,
   Thou for me Thy blood hast spilt.
Boundless wisdom, love divine,
Strength omnipotent is Thine;
   Let all earth-born knowledge perish!
   Thee alone my soul shall cherish!

Thus it is written, and thus it behooved Christ to suffer, and to rise from the dead the third day; and that repentance and remission of sins should be preached in His name among all nations, beginning at Jerusalem. And ye are witnesses of all these things.

Luke 24:46–48

He took unto Him the twelve, and said unto them, Behold, we go up to Jerusalem, and all things that are written by the prophets concerning the Son of Man shall be accomplished. For He shall be delivered unto the Gentiles, and shall be mocked and reproached and spitted on, and they shall scourge Him, and put Him to death, and the third day He shall rise again.

Luke 18:31–33

This sermon of Christ's is a brief summary of all Holy Scripture of the Old and New Testaments. For just as the Bible comprises both testaments, so this sermon of the Lord's also contains in it two parts; for the first refers to all the prophets of the Old Testament concerning the sufferings of Christ, while the second shows how all the prophecies would be fulfilled in Jerusalem; which historical account the second part of the Bible—the New Testament—contains, demonstrating in every detail that the sufferings of the Lord happened precisely as was foretold.

But that we may fruitfully commemorate the sufferings and death of our dear Lord and Savior in this time, it should be noted preliminarily that the contemplation of the sufferings of Christ is of four kinds.

First, there is *historical* contemplation. This occurs when we consider how the Passion was prophesied from the beginning of the world, immediately after the lamentable fall of our first parents, and was finally realized and accomplished. For thus it is that Christ crushed the devil's head, that is, his kingdom of death, sin, and hell; thus the devil stings Him in the heel, that is, he torments and puts Him to death. And as these things are foretold and indicated by the most enlightened seers in the Old Testament, so were they also fulfilled, and not the least bit was left out. Therefore everyone should acquaint himself with the history of the Passion as with the Lord's Prayer, so that he is able to remember and relate what Christ did and suffered. This historical contemplation of the sufferings of Christ is the foundation on which faith is grounded.

Second, there is *spiritual* contemplation. This consists of earnest repentance and true faith. For it is not enough to know the mere history, which the devils also know and shudder thereat (James 2:19); but we must apply and appropriate it to ourselves, seeing the whole Passion of the Lord Christ is presented to us as a *mirror of wrath and grace.*

For first we have in the suffering and dying Savior of the world a clear *mirror of wrath,* in which it can be seen more than in all other fearful examples of punishment how vehemently God is angered at and against sin and what a heavy burden the fiery wrath of God is, inasmuch as God so vehemently punishes in His own most beloved Son, in whom He has all pleasure and who is holy and knew no sin, the guilt and sin of others. If this is done in the green wood, what might not be done in the dry? (Luke 23:31). This is of service to us for the knowledge of sins and true penitence, that we may mourn, weep, and lament with St. Peter over our sins and iniquities, and beat our breast with the centurion at Calvary, and turn heartily to God, and henceforth flee and shun sin as the devil himself.

Second, the Passion of Christ is a comforting mirror of grace, wherein we see that God, who is rich in mercy, so deeply loved the accursed world—you, me, and all of us—that He did not spare even His only-begotten Son, but gave Him into the most contemptible death of the cross for our sake and for our good. If God commendeth His love toward us in that, while we were yet sinners, Christ died for us (Rom. 5:8), we will surely be all the more preserved by Him from wrath, having been justified by His blood.

To this *mirror of grace* also belongs the great and unspeakable love of the everlasting Son of God. For since no created thing in heaven and on earth was able to bear the burden of sin and atone for the wrath of God, and accordingly the whole of mankind must perish, the Lord Christ comes, falls humbly at His heavenly Father's feet, offers to obey and bear the punishment in our place, and gives His life as payment for the sins of the whole world.

Third, there is contemplation unto *imitation;* for "Christ hath left us an example, that ye should follow His footsteps" (1 Peter 2:21). And although we are also to follow the patriarchs, prophets, apostles, and other saints of God (Phil. 3:17), yet Christ is the most perfect example, the Example without example, as Basil puts it, whom no one has outdone, and no one shall imitate perfectly. The gracious Savior does not desire that we should imitate Him in His miraculous works, of course. Rather we are to be conformed to His likeness in true faith, prayer, love, patience, humility, and meekness (Matt. 11:29; John 13:15–17). And just as the Lord Christ goes down to meet His death when His hour is come, as seen from the words of our text, so we also are not to recoil at our death, especially when our time and hour are at hand, but simply to approach it cheerfully in true faith and certain confidence in Christ, who is our life.

Fourth, the contemplation of the suffering of Christ is a *spiritual application* of the Passion of Christ to the holy Christian church. For as Christ had His Judas, betrayer, and persecutor, so the church of God is not lacking in these either. The Cainitic and diabolical trial that Christ endured in the Sanhedrin and the judgment hall is reflected by the treatment of the Christian church also, in which slander, blasphemy, and falsehood are offered as the best evidence. As the soldiers cast lots for Christ's garments, the same is done with Scripture and spiritual goods, and as the rogues were masters in rolling dice, so the Enthusiasts are well versed in twisting Scripture. As Christ is stripped, so everyone wishes to cover himself with the cloak of Christ and to have a piece of it. As the title nailed to the cross was written in three languages, so the devil stirs up factions and sects on every side, who join together and attack and despise Scripture, languages, and the liberal arts, which are a fountain of the wisdom of God. These and very many other such spiritual interpretations can be drawn from the History of the Passion.

Prayer

O Lord Jesus Christ, Thou holy and faithful High Priest, who in the time of wrath wast made our Atonement, and didst let the fountain of Thy Blood flow for us on earth: bestow on us Thy grace, that with all Thy dear saints we may comprehend the great work that Thou didst finish on the tree of the cross, that whenever we look upon it, the poisonous serpent of the wilderness may not harm us, but we may follow Thee unscathed to eternal glory.

DEVOTION 1

Mel.: Freu dich sehr, o meine Seele

Dearest Jesus, plant, I pray Thee,
  Thine own wisdom in my heart!
Dwell in me, let naught delay Thee,
  Come, and nevermore depart!
Thou hast suffered death for me
On the cross of Calvary.
  Love divine, let Thy salvation
  Be my sweetest meditation.

At the end, when thoughts of dying
  All thoughts else with fear suspend,
Let mine eyes, the cross espying,
  There my Comforter attend.
Let Thy suff'ring, cross, and pain
In my mind at last remain!
  Grant me this, O Jesus, Savior:
  Let me worship Thee forever.

DEVOTION 2

Christ Foretells His Sufferings Again

Mel.: Jesu Leiden, Pein und Tod

Jesus, I will ponder now
  On Thy holy Passion;
With Thy Spirit me endow
  For such meditation.
Grant that I in love and faith
  May the image cherish
Of Thy suff'ring, pain, and death,
  That I may not perish.

Yet, O Lord, not thus alone
  Make me see Thy Passion,
But its cause to me make known
  And its termination.
Ah! I also and my sin
  Wrought Thy deep affliction;
This indeed the cause hath been
  Of Thy crucifixion.

Sacrifice and meat offering please Thee not, but mine ears hast Thou opened. Thou desirest neither burnt offering nor sin offering. Then said I, Lo, I come: in the book it is written of me, Thy will, O my God, do I gladly, and Thy Law do I have my heart. . . . Thy righteousness do I not hide within my heart, but of Thy salvation do I speak; I conceal not Thy lovingkindness and Thy truth from the great congregation.
Psalm 40:6–8, 10

DEVOTION 2

Now the feast of unleavened bread was nigh, which is called the Passover. And Jesus said unto His disciples, Ye know that after two days is the feast of the Passover, and the Son of Man shall be betrayed, that He may be crucified.

Matthew 26:1–2; Luke 22:1

As the Lord Christ here foretells His sufferings again, He shows at the same time that they shall be accomplished about the time of the *Passover*.

Here, then, we are first to take to heart the *weighty reasons* for which the Lord so often speaks so much of His sufferings to His disciples, and in addition to the place now indicates the time of His crucifixion. By this He would show that He is the omniscient Lord, and that He would freely suffer as the sacrifice acceptable to God and as a sweet savor (Ps. 40:6). In addition, He wishes to testify that His kingdom is a kingdom of the cross and not a kingdom of the world. Furthermore, He wishes to preserve His disciples from the offense of His suffering and death, and to teach us that we are to concern ourselves daily with the contemplation of our own death.

It is therefore comforting that the Lord Christ here indicates that not the Father nor the Holy Ghost, but He, the Mediator, was made Man and thus a sacrifice for our sins, as Scripture here and there testifies. And He was not simply delivered over unto death, but unto the death of the cross, which among both Jews and Gentiles was the most abominable and contemptible death. This death it behooved Him to suffer, that He might atone for the sin that Adam and Eve committed on the tree (1 Peter 2:24), that He might redeem us from the curse and malediction, and procure for us the blessing, forgiveness of sins, righteousness, and eternal life (Gal. 3:13–14), and that by His exaltation on the cross He might draw all men to Himself according to His promise (John 12:32). Therefore He calls to Himself all who are weary and heavy-laden (Matt. 11:28–30) and will not cast out anyone that simply takes refuge in Him (John 6:37). He bows His head as if ready to kiss us, His heart is open to love us, His arms are spread to embrace us: He stretches out His whole body for our redemption. In this we are to be heartily glad and to take comfort, saying with St. Paul, "If God be for us, who can be against us? He that spared not even His own Son, but gave Him up for us all, how should He not with Him give us all things?" (Rom. 8:32).

But because, according to the counsel of God, Christ was to be offered on the cross at the Passover, this should remind us that the Jewish Passover lamb with all its ceremonies was nothing else than a glorious sermon on Christ. As the Passover lamb had to be pure and without blemish and set apart from the flock, so Christ was holy, innocent, unblemished, and set apart from sinners (Isa. 53:5; Heb. 7:26). As the Passover lamb was slaughtered at evening, so Christ was born and slain at the end of the world. As the blood of the lamb had to be smeared on the doorposts, so we are safe from the slaying angel, death, and eternal damnation when our hearts are sprinkled with the blood of Christ. As the Passover lamb had to be roasted in fire and thus consumed, so Christ had to be roasted high on the tree of the cross in the fire of God's wrath against sin and of His unspeakable love toward us, that the meek might eat and be satisfied, and their heart live forever (Ps. 22:26). As the Passover lamb had to be enjoyed with unleavened bread and bitter sauce, so if the sufferings of Christ are to benefit us, we must purge out the leaven in doctrine and life (Matt. 16:6, 12; 1 Cor. 5:5–8), and there must be contrition and sorrow for sin, whereby Christ is consumed in faith, and there must likewise be the holy cross, because the cross brings patience, etc. As the Passover lamb had to be wholly consumed, so the church keeps the doctrine of Christ whole according to Law and Gospel in both Word and Sacrament. As the Passover lamb had to be eaten by the people standing and as if leaving in haste, so we are to be strangers and pilgrims in this valley of sorrow. As the Passover lamb could have no broken bones, so also the Lord Christ (John 19:33–36). As a bunch of hyssop was dipped in the blood of the lamb to sprinkle the posts, so Word and Sacrament are for us the means whereby we come to faith in the power of the Holy Ghost and are made partakers of the benefits of Christ; as David sings, "Purge me with hyssop, that I may be clean; wash me, that I may be white as snow" (Ps. 51:7).

Prayer

O Lord Jesus, who before Thy sufferings didst eat the Passover lamb with Thy disciples, and therein didst testify to the mystery of Thy holy offering on the cross, when in fervent love Thou didst cause Thyself to be roasted in the burning fire of Thy Father's wrath as the true heavenly Passover Lamb, and didst drip with blood: mark the door of my heart with this Thy precious, crimson blood, and grant me Christian patience when like a Passover lamb I too am subjected to all manner of cross and sadness. Bring me through the sorrowful, grievous Holy Week of torments to the joyful Easter Day of the life everlasting. Amen.

Mel.: Herzliebster Jesu, was hast du verbrochen

Now dost Thou go, O Lamb of God, with gladness,
Scorn, blows, and death to suffer for our madness;
  Thus Thou dost long to do in fullest measure
  Thy Father's pleasure.

Now dost Thou seal what was by prophets written,
Now art Thou scorned, tormented, torn, and bitten,
  Now as a curse upon the tree art carried,
  Entombed, and buried.

Lamb, that my God hath slain for my transgression,
Lamb, counting more than life my own salvation,
  O Lamb of God, let me Thy bloodshed's blessing
  E'er be possessing!

DEVOTION 3

The High Priests and Scribes Take Counsel against Jesus

Mel.: O Traurigkeit, o Herzeleid

O treachery!
Hypocrisy!
 O sin and shame aggrieving!
  Jesus men will not endure
  In the land of living!

Sin, death, and hell,
And fear would quell
 The One mankind redeeming,
  And His Godhead would destroy,
 In their wicked scheming.

They take counsel together against me, and devise to take away my life. But I trust in Thee, O Lord, *and I say, Thou art my God.*

Psalm 31:13–14

Then assembled together the chief priests, and the scribes, and the elders of the people, unto the palace of the high priest, who was called Caiaphas, and consulted how they might take Jesus by subtilty and kill Him. But they said, Not on the feast day, lest there be an uproar among the people; for they feared the people.

Matthew 26:3–5; Mark 14:1–2; Luke 22:2

In the council and consultation of the rulers of Jerusalem we are to observe that there are two chief causes of the suffering and cross of Christ. The first is with

God the Father, who ordained it to be so with His Son, that He should be the sacrificial lamb for our sin and die at the time of the Passover (Acts 4:28). The second cause is with the *chief priests, scribes, and elders of the people,* who come together in order that Christ might be crucified and killed, and therefore bring all manner of arguments and conclusions. What? If the heads of the Jewish people agreed with the divine counsel, did they actually not sin, since their will agreed with God's will? Answer: The *impelling causes* produce a great distinction here. God, out of sheer love, looks opposite us to the perfect obedience of His beloved Son for His own glory and our eternal welfare. The Jews, however, are full of hatred and spite, and seek nothing else than that Christ may be rooted out, that they might simply abide in their teaching and supposed worship of God. For this we have an example in Joseph, when he says to his brothers, "Ye meant to do evil with me, but God meant to do good" (Gen. 50:20).

It is also obvious from this that the councils of notable people can err greatly; for here they take counsel against God's decision, desiring by subtilty to take and kill Him of whom God Himself says, "I have set My King upon My holy hill of Zion" (Ps. 2:6). Therefore we ought to adhere to God's Word alone and to "try the spirits, whether they are of God" (1 John 4:1).

Here it is comforting that God arranged, contrary to the counsel of the rulers of the Jews, that His dear Son should be offered as the true Passover Lamb at the time of the Passover, when so many thousands of men were gathered together in Jerusalem, so that His death and accordingly His resurrection might be the more widely known and manifested before all people. "Thus it is written, and thus it behooved the Christ to suffer and to rise again from the dead on the third day, and that in His name repentance and forgiveness of sins should be preached, beginning at Jerusalem. And ye are witnesses of all these things" (Luke 24:46–48).

But as it was for the Lord Christ in His time, so it is for Him still in His dear church. Do not the great lords in the world, both spiritual and secular, in their councils and counsels, that is, in their assemblies and consultations, devise ways to root out true Christians? Do not the Antichrist and his followers seek our life and limb? Do not the ungodly bend the bow and lay their arrow upon the string, that they may privily shoot at the upright? (Ps. 11:2). Do not be alarmed, afflicted

Christian flock! It was so with Christ as well. Draw comfort from the fact that God visited the enemies in their council chamber and with His keen eyes saw what they had in hand, and that He can easily turn and change the game as He wills. Against the Lord no counsel avails. "Take counsel together, and it shall come to naught. Advise ye one another and it shall not stand; for here is Immanuel" (Isa. 8:10).

Prayer

O dear Lord and God, a holy time came when the chief priests and scribes were to have holy thoughts, but oh, what wickedness! They ponder how they may insult the King of Honor, how they may crucify the Lord of Glory! These evildoers fear an uproar on earth, but do not consider that by their bloodthirstiness they make an uproar against the Most High God in heaven. O my Lord Jesus, let me not come into the counsel of the ungodly, nor fall into the wicked company of evildoers! Grant me rather to cling to those who love Thee, that I may be loved in turn by Thee. Amen, Lord Jesus! Amen.

Mel.: Wo Gott der Herr nicht bei uns hält

But now no human wit or might
   His chosen flock affrighteth;
God sitteth in the highest height
   And all men's counsels smiteth;
When craftiest snares and nets they lay,
God goes to work another way,
   And makes a path before us.

Our foes, O God, are in Thy hand,
   Thou knowest their endeavor;
But only give us strength to stand,
   And let us waver never,
Though reason strives with faith, and still
It fears to wholly trust Thy will,
   And sees not Thy salvation.

DEVOTION 4

Jesus Is Anointed by Mary in Bethany

Mel.: Ich ruf zu dir, Herr Jesu Christ

O Jesus Christ, my fairest Light,
  Who in Thy soul dost love me,
With love so measureless of height,
  No end I see above me!
Grant that my heart may warm to Thee
  With love of ardent burning,
  For Thee yearning,
And as Thy property,
  To Thee, Lord, only turning.

My Savior, Thou in love to me
  Hast down to death descended,
And like a murd'rer on the tree
  And thief hast been suspended,
Spit on, despised, and wounded sore;
  The wounds which Thee have riven,
  May I even
Unto my very core
  Such wounds of love be given.

Ah, draw me, Dearest, after Thee,
  And so shall I be hasting!
I'll run, and in my heart will be
  Thy love with rapture tasting;
The gracious words from Thee I'll hear
  Whose blessed consolation
  Brings salvation,
O'ercoming sin and fear
  With ease on each occasion.

Thou wilt not suffer Thine Holy One to be corrupted. — I delight in mercy, and not in sacrifice.

Psalm 16:10; Hosea 6:6

Now when Jesus was in Bethany, they made Him a supper in the house of Simon the leper; and Martha served, but Lazarus was one of them that sat at the table with Him. Then took Mary a pound of ointment of spikenard, very costly, and came and brake the box, and poured it on His head as He sat at meat, and anointed the feet of Jesus, and wiped His feet with her hair, and the house was filled with the odor of the ointment. But when His disciples saw it, they had indignation, saying, To what purpose is this waste? Then saith one of His disciples, Judas Iscariot, Simon's son, which should betray him, Why was not this ointment sold for three hundred pence, and given to the poor? When Jesus understood it, He said unto them, Let her alone. Why trouble ye the woman? for she hath wrought a good work upon Me. For ye have the poor with you always, and whensoever ye will ye may do them good; but Me ye have not always. She hath done what she could; for in that she hath poured this ointment on My body, she is come aforehand to anoint My body to the burying. Truly I say unto you, Wheresoever this gospel shall be preached in the whole world, there shall also this, that this woman hath done, be told for a memorial of her.

Matthew 26:6–13; Mark 14:3–9; John 12:1–8

While a bloody consultation regarding Christ is held in the palace of Caiaphas, He is shown all honor, love, and friendship in Bethany outside Jerusalem. Simon, who had been a leper and was healed by Christ, prepares a feast for Jesus and His disciples, and Lazarus, whom Christ recently raised from dead, is also present, while Martha serves at table as is her wont. Soon her sister Mary also arrives, bringing a glass of costly, sweet-smelling ointment of spikenard, anoints Christ with it according to the custom and usage of the land, and thereby shows what fervent love she has for Him. Therefore Christ in turn comes to her defense when some of the disciples murmur at her, and especially the covetous rogue Judas is heard. And Christ speaks for her and says, "This godly heart troubleth Me not. The poor have ye always, to whom ye may do good always, but Me ye have not much longer visible among you. She hath done it out of love and faith, and therefore wrought a laudable work upon Me, so that she will be remembered among all Christians as long as the world endureth."

Now although the woman here did not understand that Christ, our eternal King and High Priest, was not to see corruption, since He is anointed with the fullness of the Holy Ghost, yet it was arranged by God that she should anoint Him for His burying—that He would not only be buried, but also rise again and live. Kings and princes, when they die, were accustomed to be anointed with precious balm and similar things, by which their body might be preserved many years, lest it decompose. But this woman comes to the Lord beforehand and anoints Him while He is still alive. Now therefore, just as He is our eternal King and High Priest, so we are through Him the chosen generation, the royal priesthood, the people of the possession, anointed with His Holy Spirit. Thus as He received and represented this woman, so He sits on the right hand of God, representing us. When Satan murmurs against us and accuses us, He speaks in our defense. He will also extol our good works which are wrought upon Him in true faith, and will proclaim them in that Day, so that we will be remembered forever.

In the performance of such works, Simon and Mary also serve as an example to us for imitation. Christ at that time was put into exile (John 9:22), no one was to give Him lodging nor have anything to do with Him. But Simon and Mary faithfully hold with Christ and risk everything for Him. Therefore let a Christian not be frightened from keeping and propagating the true divine service, churches, schools, their ministers, and benevolence to the poor, but exercise and demonstrate his faith, love, and confession in these things. Yet alas! Many of them have the nature of Judas, always thinking and saying, "To what purpose is this waste? Why give so much to priests? It could certainly be spent in better ways!" Such people are like the fig tree that bore no fruit when Christ wished to eat of it, for which reason it also withered up.

Prayer

O Lord Jesus, how pleasing the gratitude of this woman was to Thee! How gloriously Thou didst extol her confession! Thou defendest her against the disciples when they murmured, and sayest, She hath wrought a good work upon Me. O my Lord, how would she have better applied her ointment and how wouldest Thou have more deeply gladdened her heart? Help, O Lord, my Savior, that my soul also may acknowledge, like Mary, all that Thou hast wrought upon me, that I too may serve Thy name with praise and glory as is pleasing unto Thee. For because this woman is so grateful to Thee when Thou didst raise her brother merely from temporal death, how much more ought I to be grateful to Thee, my Savior, who deliverest my life from everlasting death, hast won me everlasting righteousness, and hast given me everlasting blessedness?

Oh, Lord Jesus, as Mary hereby commemorated beforehand Thy suffering, so let me now commemorate Thy suffering afterward, and not scorn it, when I, to honor Thee as I am able, give Thee the best that I have, the spikenard of a penitent, grateful love! Grant even through the power of Thy Spirit that my love toward Thee and Thine own may be unadulterated, that I may shatter all the selfishness of my heart and know only Thee alone, love and honor only Thee, and forget my own self and the world for that One, that at Thy cross, on which Thou sufferest for me, I may embrace Thy holy feet with the arms of my longing, and wet them with the tears of my repentance. In the process, keep far from me all temptations of the world and my own flesh, which would fain draw me away from Thee. Protect me from the temptations of Satan, who mocks my love for Thee and would like to pluck from my heart my faith in Thee. Rather, during my whole life, let Thy sufferings, Thy death, and Thy burial be my comfort, my honor, and my joy. Help me to remain steadfast until the end, and let neither death nor life turn me from Thee, that at all times Thou mayest be my Shield and speak in my defense against all my enemies. Preserve my faith, that its fruits may be extolled in that Day before Thy holy angels and all the elect. Let me at last stand among Thy saints in Thy heavenly kingdom, where Thy head is crowned with glory and honor, and love and adore Thee forever and ever. Amen.

DEVOTION 4

Mel.: Der am Kreuz ist meine Liebe (p. 323)
Or: Werde munter, mein Gemüthe

Jesus crucified possesses
  My love's homage evermore.
Sin and Satan, your caresses,
  World, thy pleasures I abhor.
Who your godless way pursue
Will in death their folly rue.
  Jesus crucified possesses
  My love, as my faith confesses.

Jesus crucified possesses
  My love—doth it anger thee,
Scoffer, what my heart confesses?
  Jesus gave Himself for me!
Thus my saving Shield He proves,
Whose example me behooves.
  Jesus crucified possesses
  My love, as my faith confesses.

DEVOTION 5

Judas Makes a Traitorous Pact

Mel.: Christus, der uns selig macht
Or: Jesu Leiden, Pein und Tod

Grant, O Christ, Thou Son of God,
 By Thy bitter Passion,
That we, as Thy pain's reward,
 Joy in Thy salvation,
That we ever weigh the cause
 Of Thy death and suff'ring,
Yea, for this, though poor we are,
 Bring Thee our thank-off'ring!

And when the Midianites, the merchantmen, passed by, they (the sons of Jacob) drew and lifted him (Joseph, their brother) up out of the pit, and sold him to the Ishmaelites for twenty pieces of silver. — And I said unto them, If ye think good, offer up as much as I am worth; if not, forbear. And they weighed as much as I was worth, thirty pieces of silver. Aye, a goodly price that I was prised at of them!
Genesis 37:28; Zechariah 11:12–13

But then entered Satan into Judas, named Iscariot, being of the number of the Twelve. And he went his way and communed with the chief priests and captains, that he might betray Him, and said, What will ye give me? I will deliver Him unto you. When they heard it, they were glad. And they covenanted with him for thirty pieces of silver, and he promised. And from that time he sought opportunity to betray Him without rumor.
Matthew 26:13–16; Mark 14:10–11; Luke 22:3–6

DEVOTION 5

O Judas, is this the reward for the faithfulness and benefits that Christ showed thee? For a handful of coins thou sellest the One who is to be prized higher than heaven and earth? Woe to thee! This deed shall be to thy hurt in body and soul!

Here from this terrible deed of Judas' let every man learn, first, how the devil is such a powerful enemy, who stirs up and drives men to sin, and that "he that committeth sin is of the devil" (1 John 3:8). Therefore we are to resist him, steadfast in the faith. Second, that covetousness is a root of all evil. Behold, Judas lets himself be so taken in by the insatiable devil of covetousness that he betrays his own Lord and Master, who is the Son of God and whose glory he has seen with the other disciples, for thirty pieces of silver. For because the damnable love of money brings great harm, and at the same time ill-gotten goods are kept in a purse full of holes, therefore let every Christian keep himself from this vice, and pray daily with David: O Lord, "incline my heart unto Thy testimonies, and not to covetousness" (Psalm 119:36). Third, let it be learned that many people in the world, out of sheer vainglory and greed for money, hatred and envy, and other inordinate affects, bring themselves and others into all manner of mischief, sorrow, and misery, and lose their life and limb, yea, even their salvation. For because Judas saw that by the anointing of Christ here, a goodly sum had slipped through his fingers, and that he could not attain to worldly honor and great riches with Christ and His Gospel, he sought every opportunity to be rid of Christ, to take revenge on Him, and to obtain great honor, money, and goods with the chief rulers of Jerusalem. Therefore he offered to betray Christ.

This was a bitter suffering for the Lord Christ. But He left us a pattern, that we should walk in His steps and imitate Him and suffer with patience when we have done all good to others and afterward are betrayed and sold and brought into sorrow and misery by them. Chrysostom, the doctor of the church, the veritable "Goldenmouth," had with him a deacon by the name of Severianus, a hypocritical babbler, whom he sometimes caused to preach for him and did him every good at the court of Emperor Arcadius. But afterward, the Empress Eudoxia made so much of this abominable hypocrite that he despised his preceptor and finally drove him into exile and misery, in which the holy man died in the year after the death of Arcadius.

But see that the Lord Christ is the true Joseph, who is sold by his own brothers, as Zechariah prophesied (Zech. 11:12–13). He is sold and betrayed for our sake. It cost a great deal to redeem our souls, for God's only Son Himself is the Ransom, yet He is appraised at only thirty pieces of silver. But it was so resolved that He who was counted as nothing before the world should count a great deal before His heavenly Father, and His death should be a plentiful payment for the sins of the children of men.

Prayer

O Lord Jesus Christ, who art the true Passover Lamb, set apart and sent by Thy heavenly Father, and sold and betrayed to Thy suffering for our sins: help us to believe this from our heart, and always to take comfort in Thy sacrifice; and grant grace that we may keep ourselves from pharisaical counsels and from Judas' covetousness and hardness of heart, that we may so keep the Passover with Thee in this world, and partake of Thy Table, that we may at last also be partakers of the blessed Supper in heaven and appear at the eternal marriage of the Lamb; who livest and reignest with the same Father and the Holy Ghost, ever one God, world without end. Amen.

Mel.: Gott der Vater, wohn uns bei

Holy Ghost, be Thou our Stay,
  Oh, let us perish never!
Cleanse us from our sins, we pray,
  And grant us life forever;
Keep us from the evil one,
  Uphold our faith most holy,
  And let us trust Thee solely,
  With humble hearts, and lowly,
Let us put God's armor on,
  With all true Christians running
  Our heav'nly race, and shunning
  The devil's wiles and cunning.
Amen, amen, this be done;
So sing we, Kyrieleison!

DEVOTION 6

Jesus Celebrates the Passover for the Last Time

Mel.: Auf, Seele, sei gegrüßt

Arise, my soul, prepare!
Thy Savior Christ is there—
  What love He offers!
What longing in Him glows
To hold thee ere He goes
  And for thee suffers.

2. O love without a bound!
The Substance here is found,
  The type fulfilling:
The Bridegroom, even He,
Our own true Lamb to be,
  Surrenders willing.

3. He fashions for our weal
A wondrous festal meal
  Beyond discerning,
To bind us to His death
Which we proclaim by faith
  Till His returning.

When your children shall say unto you, What mean ye by this service? ye shall say, It is the sacrifice of the Lord's Passover, who passed over the houses of the children of Israel in Egypt, when he smote the Egyptians, and delivered our houses. — We have also a Passover Lamb, that is Christ, sacrificed for us.

Exodus 12:26–27; 1 Corinthians 5:7

And the first day of unleavened bread, when the Passover must be killed, the disciples came to Jesus, saying unto Him, Where wilt Thou that we go and prepare for Thee to eat the Passover? And He sent Peter and John, saying, Go ye into the city. Behold, when ye are entered in, there shall a man meet you, bearing a pitcher of water; follow him into the house where he entereth in. And ye shall say unto the goodman of the house, The Master saith unto thee, My time is at hand; I will keep the Passover at thy house with My disciples. Where is the guestchamber, where I shall eat the Passover with my disciples? And he shall shew you a large upper room furnished: there make ready. And they went, and found as He had said unto them: and they made ready the Passover.

And in the evening He came and sat down at table with the twelve apostles. And He said unto them, With desire I have desired to eat this Passover with you before I suffer: For I say unto you, I will not any more eat thereof, until it be fulfilled in the kingdom of God. And He took the cup, gave thanks, and said, Take this, and divide it among yourselves. For I say unto you, I will not drink of the fruit of the vine until the kingdom of God shall come, on that Day when I drink it new with you in My Father's kingdom.

Matthew 26:17–29; Mark 14:12–25; Luke 22:7–18

Here the Lord Christ ate the Passover lamb with His disciples according to the usage of the old covenant with all its ceremonies, as is decreed in the Law, and accordingly did standing, as they that are in haste. Now therefore, when the hour came that they might sit down again, He began to pour out His heart before His apostles, and declared how heartily He had longed for this time, that He might eat this last Passover lamb with them, and thereby conclude the old covenant and begin and confirm the new. But especially, He doubtless taught them how they would see the figure of the Passover lamb, from whence it is named the Pasch, namely, from the passing over, not only that the children of Israel passed out of Egypt through the Red Sea and afterward into the Promised Land, but chiefly that He, Christ, as the true Passover Lamb, who went forth from the Father and had come into the world, would now go to the Father and open heaven to us and bring us into the eternal fatherland through His blood and death, which they must appropriate to themselves with believing hearts.

Yet in the process, He further declares to the disciples that this is to be the *last* Passover lamb. With the Jews, it was the custom, and still is today, that on great feasts, the most notable person among them takes bread, breaks it, and gives it to the others to eat of it, and in the meantime God is thanked by means of a psalm. Here the Lord also keeps this custom. But as He breaks the bread and distributes it, He says, "I will not any more eat thereof, until it be fulfilled in the kingdom of God"; that is, "This is to be the last Passover lamb, namely, My body, which tomorrow shall be given up on the cross, and My blood, which shall be shed. This shall henceforth be distributed to Christians through bread and wine, that they may remember Me therein, that is, that they may believe firmly and certainly that I have given My body for them, and shed My blood for them, that they may have forgiveness of sins and be saved." After this word, the Lord takes the cup of thanksgiving, also according to the custom of the Jews, speaks His prayer, drinks to the disciples, and says again, "I will not drink of the fruit of the vine until the kingdom of God shall come, on that Day when I drink it new with you in My Father's kingdom"; that is, "until sin is atoned for by My death, death and the devil are overcome, and My Christian church is begotten through My Gospel."

Here, therefore, the old covenant ends and the new begins. For the Lord Jesus keeps the feast of the Jews, but says that it is to be the last (the farewell), so that just as formerly, the Passover lamb has been eaten for 1,543 years and a memorial of the deliverance out of Egypt has been kept, so from this time on, from generation to generation, the body and blood of Christ shall be eaten and drunk in the Supper. Herein we have a memorial not of a temporal deliverance and redemption, but of a blessed and everlasting redemption from the power of the devil, sin, death, and hell achieved by Christ Jesus, the true Passover Lamb, to continue until God shall one day cause our Passovers and Easters of the new covenant to have an end, and we will celebrate without ceasing the heavenly Easter in the kingdom of God—which end cannot be long now, seeing our Easter has already lasted far longer than the Jews' Passover lasted.

Prayer

O my Lord Jesus, why didst Thou so heartily desire to eat the last Passover with Thy disciples and to institute a new covenant? Thou didst so heartily desire it that the redemption of mankind might be brought near, and by Thy death life, salvation, and blessedness might be obtained for me and all men! O my Lord Jesus, if Thou didst have such deep longing for My salvation that it should cause Thee so much anguish and sorrow, so much pain and toil, and finally death, how much more wilt Thou long for it now, when Thou hast surmounted all anguish, and death can no longer have dominion over Thee! O Lord, grant me Thy grace, that I may take thought for myself and not neglect my salvation, nor make a mockery of it with willful, intentional sin. Help me rather to long more and more for Thee, my Passover Lamb sacrificed for me, and for Thy consolation, that in true faith my soul may partake of Thee and be satisfied, until I shall see Thee face to face in Thy Father's kingdom, and sit at table with Abraham, Isaac, and Jacob, yea, with Thee and all Thy saints, and celebrate the eternal Passover! Amen.

Mel.: Herr Gott, dich loben alle wir

This day from Egypt forth we go,
And Pharaoh's bondage off we throw;
  The Paschal Lamb, the Lord Divine
  This day we eat in bread and wine.

We also take the manna sweet,
Which Moses bade God's people eat,
  Nor suffer leaven sour therein,
  That we may live all free from sin.

The vengeful Angel passes o'er,
No firstborn dies behind our door,
  Upon our lintel Jesus' blood
  Has been applied, our shield holds good.

DEVOTION 7

Christ Institutes the Holy Supper

Mel.: Jesus Christus, unser Heiland

Jesus Christ, our blessed Savior,
Turned away God's wrath forever;
  By His bitter grief and woe
  He saved us from the evil foe.

As His pledge of love undying
He, this precious food supplying,
  Gives His body with the bread
  And with the wine the blood He shed.

Praise the Father, God in heaven,
Who such precious food hath given,
  And for sins which thou hast done
  Gave into death His only Son.

What He ordaineth is laudable and glorious; and His righteousness endureth forever. He hath founded a memorial of His wonders, even the gracious and merciful Lord. *He giveth meat to them that fear Him, and He is ever mindful of His covenant. [And He maketh them to know His covenant.]*

Psalm 111:3–5 [25:14]

And whilst they ate, in the night in which He was betrayed, the Lord Jesus took bread, gave thanks, and brake it, and gave it to the disciples, saying, "Take, eat, this is My body, which is given for you; this do for My remembrance." In the same manner also He took the cup after supper, gave thanks, gave it to them, and said: "Drink ye all of it; this cup is the new testament in My blood, which is shed for you and for many for the forgiveness of sins. This do, as oft as ye do it, for My remembrance." And they all drank of it.

Matthew 26:26–28; Mark 14:22–24; Luke 22:19–20

The Lord Christ, having eaten the Jewish Passover lamb with His disciples, and the time having come to be parted from them, considers first His dearest friends, makes His testament, and appoints to them His goods. For so great is His love that in the sorrowful night when He is betrayed and great anguish of heart and death stand before Him, His heart as it were turns away from itself and toward His own, and is wholly occupied with assuring them of the forgiveness of sins, the love and grace of His Father, and the comforting future of eternal life.

O wondrous testament! He who makes it, the *Founder and Testator,* is no apostle or angel or any other creature, but the Lord of heaven and earth, the God-Man, the True, All-wise, and Almighty. The *goods* which He bequeaths in this testament are not gold and silver, costly jewels and sumptuous garments and such things; but what Christ regarded as most precious and most valuable, that He gave, even His holy and true body and His precious blood, and in these goods has given us remission of sins and pledged us eternal life. For so His words read: "This is My body, which is given for you." And: "This is My blood, the new testament, which is shed for you for the forgiveness of sins." And where there is forgiveness of sins, there is also eternal life. How it happens that there, under the blessed bread, Christ gives us His true body to eat, and under the blessed wine His true blood to drink—do not worry yourself about that. Leave it to the presumptuous, who usually like to seek after lofty things unnecessarily and to their own destruction. Cling simply to the words of Christ, which, being the words of the testament of the highest Lord of all, are clear and certain.

The *heirs* and *friends* of this testament are those who believe in Christ, none excluded. They keep His testament and use it according to His institution for His remembrance until He comes. He desires us as faithful brothers and sisters to come together often for His remembrance, and to eat and drink there what is best of all, and to talk with one another of matters in which the heart may deeply rejoice, as St. Paul explains when He writes: "As often as ye eat of this bread and drink of the cup of the Lord, ye shall show the Lord's death till He come" (1 Cor. 11:26). We are to thank and praise Him for His boundless love (thus the Sacrament is called the *Eucharist* or Thanksgiving) and to comfort afflicted and troubled consciences, to strengthen the weakly believing, and to confirm the faithful against all the doctrines of devils, additions of men, hypocrisy, and lies. Is this then not a joyful collation or meal where the commandment of God and remembrance of Christ are kept and divine matters are treated, even the salvation and blessedness of the soul? Woe to those who despise it!

But in these things alone does *the right use* of this testament consist. That in the papacy it was turned into the sacrifice of the Mass and a mere work of merit, and that the cup was withheld from the laity, is a blasphemous abuse and a malicious alteration of Christ's testament. So also the Sacramentarians do wrong, who teach according to their reason that the Sacrament is not the true body and blood of Christ, but only *a sign and a signification* of His body and blood. The Christians of the early church kept this *right* use in the midst of their distresses and afflictions. If God sent war, famine, pestilence, and persecution, the Christians made haste to live in repentance, lamented their sins, prayed for grace, and received the most worthy Sacrament, that they might comfort their heart and conscience and endure with patience in anguish and distress. If a husband lost his wife or a wife her husband, the survivor went with family and friends to the Sacrament, not with a mind to assist the deceased, as the hopeless papists have turned such occasions into utter purgatory masses, but that they might receive a certain sign that God the Father would still be gracious for the sake of His Son Jesus Christ.

Whoever uses this Sacrament *worthily* becomes a partaker of all the goods of Christ and will at last have everlasting life. Therefore, in accordance with St. Paul's words, *a man is to examine himself* to see whether he is worthy, for whoever eats the body of Christ and drinks His blood unworthily is guilty of the body and blood of Christ and eats and drinks judgment to himself by not discerning the body and blood of the Lord. But he eats and drinks worthily who eats and drinks in faith in the words, "given and shed for you for the forgiveness of sins." Therefore, if you find that you are weak in faith, cold in love, wavering in hope, impatient in cross, inclined to all sins, and would like to be strong in faith, fervent in love, strong in hope, patient in cross, and free from your sins, if you would like to be godly, humble, merciful, peaceable, just, generous, sober, gentle, faithful, and true, then you are prepared in the best possible way. The greater the hunger and thirst for righteousness, the better you are prepared. For this heavenly food calls for a hungry soul. The full have no place here. Mary sings in the Magnificat: "He filleth the hungry with good things, and the rich He leaveth empty." Go therefore in faith and brotherly love with contrition and sorrow for your sins, with a good resolution to avoid sin and every occasion thereof, with thanksgiving to God, and look well that you also follow the Sacrament with fruits, as the elements of the Sacrament, bread and wine, suggest, and you will certainly find God's blessing and Christ's help and assistance, grace and mercy upon thee, and finally, everlasting life.

Prayer

Dearest Lord Jesus! Who would doubt the forgiveness of his sins? Who would doubt the love of the Father? Who would not in the midst of dying have certain hope of everlasting life? For as truly as we eat under the blessed bread Thy true body given for us, and drink under the blessed wine Thy true blood shed for us, so truly are all our sins forgiven, so certainly will Thy heavenly Father accept and receive us with loving grace. Oh, Lord Jesus, vouchsafe to me this request, that, just as Thou hast commanded us to keep Thy Holy Supper often and therein to remember Thy countless benefits, so prepare my and my brothers' and sisters' souls by Thy Holy Spirit, that as often as I approach these heavenly mysteries with them, I may worthily appear there and in true repentance, confident faith, and heartfelt humility receive Thy holy body and Thy holy blood. Oh, Lord Jesus, make me worthy and mercifully quicken me! Amen, Lord Jesus! Amen.

DEVOTION 7

Mel.: Meins Herzens Jesu, meine Lust*
Or: Es ist gewisslich an der Zeit

Lord, I believe in simple trust,
  Strength in my weakness give me,
For I am naught but sinful dust,
  Nor of Thy Word bereave me!
Thy Baptism, Supper, and Thy Word,
My consolation are, O Lord,
  For they contain my treasure.

Grant that we worthily receive
  Thy Supper, Lord, our Savior,
That for our sins we truly grieve,
  And prove by our behavior
That we obtained Thy saving grace,
And trust in it throughout our days;
  Then will our life be godly.

For Thy consoling Supper, Lord,
  Be praised throughout all ages!
Preserve it, for with one accord
  The world against it rages.
Grant that Thy body and Thy blood
May be my comfort and sweet food
  In my last moments. Amen.

---

* Melody: No. 15: "Herr Jesu Christ, du hast bereit," in the appendix to Dr. F. Layritz's *Evangelisch-Lutherisches Choralbuch für Kirche und Haus* (St. Louis, 1874).

DEVOTION 8

Christ Washes the Disciples' Feet

Mel.: Ich ruf zu dir, Herr Jesu Christ

Thou ever hast had love for me
  And to Thyself didst move me;
When still I did no good for Thee,
  E'en then did Thy heart love me:
O let Thy love, almighty Lord!
  Continue here to guide me,
  Close beside me
Aid ever to afford,
  Whatever may betide me!

Thy love let be my joy in woe,
  In frailty, strength to stay me;
And when my course is run below,
  And down to rest I lay me,
Then let Thy loving faithfulness
  Lord Jesus, stay beside me,
  Strength provide me,
Until all joy and bliss
  In heaven be supplied me.

Thou shalt also make a laver of brass, and his foot also of brass . . . and thou shalt put water therein, that Aaron and his sons may wash their hands and their feet thereat, when they go into the tabernacle of the institution, or when they come near to the altar to minister with a fire of the LORD, *that they die not. This shall be a perpetual manner to him and to his seed among their generations. — He shall purify and purge the sons of Levi as gold and silver; then shall they offer unto the* LORD *a meat offering in righteousness.*

Exodus 30:18–21; Malachi 3:3

DEVOTION 8

Now before the feast of the Passover, that is, on the same night when Jesus knew that His hour was come that He should go out of this world unto the Father, having loved His own, He loved them unto the end. And after supper, the devil having now put into the heart of Judas Iscariot, Simon's son, to betray Him, Jesus knowing that the Father had given all things into His hands, and that He was come from God, and went to God: He rose from the supper, laid aside His garments, and took a towel and girded Himself. After that He poured water into a basin, began to wash the disciples' feet, and dried them with the towel wherewith He was girded.

John 13:1–5

Here is a wondrous account of how Christ washed the disciples' feet with His own hands after the Last Supper, at which not only we men but also the angels in heaven ought justly to marvel, and with particular delight behold and hear the everlasting and almighty Son of God in this work. For we are not to think that this event is of little import to us, since it is described only by St. John in the thirteenth chapter and omitted by the other three evangelists; for John was so careful to record this event precisely because it was omitted by the others. For he composed his Gospel last and was usually most careful to record what Matthew, Mark, and Luke had either touched on only with a few words or else reported not at all. Therefore we are to pay particular attention to this account of the footwashing.

From the words above, then, we learn, first, with what thoughts the Lord Jesus was occupied during the Last Supper, when He now wished to prepare Himself promptly for this work. For when He had eaten the Passover lamb with His disciples and then instituted His Holy Supper, He was considering and pondering the fact that now the hour was at hand when His suffering would begin, but that it would have a blessed end, since by death He would pass out of this world to the Father and into His glory. Therefore He did not cast away the yoke nor let Himself be moved by any occurrence, not even by Judas' betrayal. No, by no means! Rather, just as He began to love His own, so He loved them to the end, and in exceptional love for both God and us He completed the work of His suffering. From this, then, we are to take to heart the fact that our dearest Savior *voluntarily and sincerely* offered Himself as a sacrifice for us. For although He knew that the hour of His death was at hand and that Judas had decided, at the instigation of the devil, to betray Him and to offer Him up on the chopping block, yet He chose not to make haste nor to flee that death, and that out of great and fervent love which bound Him as it were with bonds, so that He willingly and gladly awaited agony and death, that our redemption might not only be begun, but also brought to the desired conclusion. This is what it means that He loved His own to the end. But this gives us the powerful consolation that Christ defends our cause to the blessed end. For just as He did not cut off the great work of our redemption at its very beginning, but brought it to completion, so through the Word and Sacrament He will also graciously bring to completion His gracious work which He began in us in Holy Baptism. Therefore St. Paul writes: "I am confident of this, that He which hath begun the good work in you will also perform it until the Day of Jesus Christ" (Phil. 1:6).

Second, we see here the unfathomable humility of the Lord Jesus. In the hot lands of the Orient, there is a custom, when receiving a dear guest, of washing his feet with fragrant waters before sitting at table. Such did Abraham to the three men who were his guests in Hain Mamre; likewise, Lot, and Abigail to those sent by David. It was also customary among the children of Israel that, when they were to celebrate notable banquets and meals, as the Feast of the Passover was with its Passover lamb, they first washed and cleansed themselves thoroughly. Therefore they no longer needed more than footwashing, because in the hot lands of the Orient, they went about barefoot; hence Christ afterwards says: "He who is washed needeth not save to wash his feet, but he is wholly clean" (John 13:10).

Now, since Christ also lives according to this custom and undertakes this footwashing for His disciples, He displays a humility at which heaven and earth stand in awe. Of this Simon of Cascia justly writes: "See here the signs of deepest condescension, that the divine Majesty stoops down to the feet of the apostles, and God kneels before men, Holiness before sinners, Righteousness before the unrighteous, Immortality before the mortal, the Creator before the creature, the Sun before the stars, the Light before the darkness, the Day before the hours. On His knees, the King of all kings and Lord of all lords washes them, so that the condescension of no creature can be greater than that of the Redeemer's was."

Prayer

O dear Lord Jesus, how deep is Thy humility! My tongue cannot express and my heart cannot sufficiently comprehend Thy lowliness. How fervent is Thy love also! Yea, truly, as Thou didst love Thine own, Thou didst love them to the end. Thou provest this here in very deed. Surely Thou art He of whom Moses says in wonder: "Behold, how (the Lord) loveth the people!" (Deut. 33:3). Therefore I am certain that no devil or death can separate me from Thy tender love, and that Thou wilt perform until Thy Day the good work which Thou hast begun in me; for Thy grace and truth abound upon us forever, and Thy mercy endureth forever and ever among them that fear Thee. Oh, help me in turn to love Thee with all my heart until the end! Amen.

Mel.: Wer nur den lieben Gott läßt walten

O Lord of heav'n and earth Most Holy!
   How comes this servant form to Thee?
How do I see Thee bent so lowly,
   How emptied of th' authority
Which else doth all the world contain,
Since Thou dost Lord of lords remain?

The Master His disciples cleanses
   And washes clean their filthy feet—
Mere mortals, filled with all offenses,
   For whom such honor is not meet;
How shall I such humility
Explain, which so astoundeth me?

   Yet this can only hint at slightly
      Thy greater humbleness and loss,
   Who can that virtue measure rightly,
      That brought Thee even to the cross.
   Now dost Thou only water pour,
   Then shalt Thou shed Thy blood and more!

DEVOTION 9

Peter and Christ's Conversation concerning the Footwashing

Mel.: O du Liebe meiner Liebe

Lord, great debts my deeds have earnèd,
  More than I have pow'r to count!
I from Thee away have turnèd,
  Thy Law's accusations mount,
Saying judgment must befall me;
  Yea, it saith I merit not,
That Thy child I should dare call me,
  Since I have perversely wrought.

Yet how can I be despairing?
  If I am a child of hell,
See Thy Child who suffered, bearing
  All my sins and stripes as well.
Jesus' blood cries grace and favor!
  Grace, it cries, for righteousness!
Oh, Lord, in this bloody laver
  Wash my sin-polluted dress!

Behold, I was shapen in iniquity; and in sin did my mother conceive me. Behold, Thou desirest truth in the inward parts: and in the hidden part Thou shalt make me to know wisdom. Purge me with hyssop, and I shall be clean: wash me, and I shall be whiter than snow.

Psalm 51:5–7

DEVOTION 9

Then cometh Jesus to Simon Peter: and Peter saith unto Him, Lord, dost Thou wash my feet? Jesus answered and said unto him, What I do thou knowest not now; but thou shalt know hereafter. Peter saith unto Him, Thou shalt never wash my feet. Jesus answered him, If I wash thee not, thou hast no part with Me. Simon Peter saith unto him, Lord, not my feet only, but also my hands and my head. Jesus saith to him, He that is washed needeth not save to wash his feet, but is clean every whit: and ye are clean, but not all. For He knew who should betray Him; therefore said He, Ye are not all clean.

John 13:6–11

This conversation of Christ's with Peter, which begins because the latter at first refuses to let Him wash his feet, shows us three things.

First, it reminds us that in the works of God, we are to take our reason captive to the *obedience of faith*. Peter errs here in thinking that Christ is here performing an unwise and foolish work, and in undue cleverness criticizing Him for it—that He, as the Lord and Master, should wash the feet of His disciples. Whatever God does, performs, speaks, establishes or ordains, commands or forbids, "it is honorable and glorious" (Ps. 111:3). Therefore true, pious Christians do well not to dispute a great deal about such matters, asking why our Lord God undertakes this or that, why He does it thus and so. For all such thoughts and words, which attempt to resist and withstand God and His work, are of no avail, but are harmful, as seen in our first parents, when Eve was seduced by the serpent into speculating why God had forbidden them to eat of the tree of the knowledge of good and evil.

Second, we hear here from the words of Christ *what great need we poor men had* of our Savior's service, that we should be washed and purified from all our sins; for we are wholly and thoroughly unclean and polluted, since we are by nature wholly unclean, conceived and born in sin, and thereafter stained with all manner of sins in thought, word, and deed. Therefore Christ came, emptied Himself of His majesty, and took on the form of a servant, as He Himself says: "The Son of Man came not to be served, but to serve, and to give His life a ransom for many" (Matt. 20:28). Thus He washed us and purified us with His holy, precious blood from all sin and unrighteousness. "The blood of Jesus Christ (God's) Son cleanseth us from all sin" (1 John 1:7).

To that end, He has also prepared for us a special *washing*, in which He mightily performs this salutary work and cleansing in us, namely, *Holy Baptism*, in which not the uncleanness of the body, but that of the soul, is removed and we can be wholly clean in the sight of God. For thus writes St. Paul in Ephesians 5:25–27: "Christ loved the church and gave Himself for her, that He might sanctify her, and He hath purified her by the washing in the Word, that He might present her to Himself a church that is glorious, having no spot or wrinkle or any such thing, that she may be holy and blameless." But because through the frailty of the corrupted flesh and blood we fall again into sin after receiving Baptism, therefore, to purify and pacify our conscience and to preserve us in the purity of our Baptism, He has given Absolution and the Sacrament. We are to apply and appropriate to ourselves this purification of the Lord through Baptism, Absolution, and the Sacrament in true faith, through which hearts are purified.

For this faithful service, we ought to give our Savior eternal *praise* and *thanks*, and watch out lest we lie again in the filth of sin. For then it could be no help to us that we were cleansed before in Holy Baptism and that God wishes to cleanse us again and again by Word and Sacrament. Such people are like swine, which after their washing wallow again in the muck (2 Peter 2:22). Therefore we are to conduct our life soberly by the help of the Holy Spirit, and pray God through Christ that we may be delivered of what is still sinful in it, that we may be purified and sanctified vessels of use to the glory of the Householder and prepared for every good work (2 Tim. 2:21).

Third, we are reminded by the words of Christ, "Ye are clean, but not all of you," that the *Christian church* here on earth will never be so pure that *hypocrites* cannot also be found in the flock. For the company of the apostles was certainly a chosen flock, yet the traitor Judas was among them. Likewise, while there were only eight persons in Noah's ark as the totality of the whole world and the true church of God, yet the ungodly scoffer Ham was still found among them. The holy patriarch Jacob's household was the true, genuine church of God on earth in his time, but what wicked scoundrels are found therein! Yet Jacob's house must be allowed to pass as God's church and people on account of the few godly and elect persons who were in it. We ought to take note of this in opposition to all the Anabaptists and other Enthusiasts, who invent for themselves a church in the

DEVOTION 9

world the likes of which no church on earth has ever been, nor shall ever be until the Last Day.

Prayer

O Lord Jesus, Thou didst wash the unclean feet of Thy disciples and thereby wouldst portray to them the spiritual cleansing of their sinful souls, even as Thy words intend which Thou speakest to resistant Peter: "Unless I wash thee in a spiritual manner from thy sins, thou hast no part in Me, and canst now no longer be My disciple, nor one day My fellow-heir in the kingdom of God." O Lord Jesus, let me not make many words like Peter, but let me acknowledge the uncleanness of my heart and say with David, "Behold, O Lord, I am begotten of sinful seed, and in sin did my mother conceive me" (Ps. 51:5). Alas, alas! I am one of those of whom Job (14:4) says, "Who shall find a clean man among those where there is none clean?" Therefore, O my Lord Jesus, behold, I hasten to Thee and pray Thee humbly, blot out mine iniquities and cleanse me from my sins with Thy precious blood. Wash me, that I may be white as snow. Let me hear joy and gladness, that the bones which Thou hast broken may rejoice. Hide Thy face from my sins, and blot out all mine iniquities. Create in me a clean heart, O God, and give me a new, certain spirit. Cast me not away from Thy presence, and take not Thy Holy Spirit from me. O Lord Jesus, let me have and retain a part in Thee, and lead me in by the heavenly door! Amen, Lord Jesus! Amen.

Mel.: Auf meinen lieben Gott

O Jesus, Source of grace!
I seek Thy loving face,
  Upon Thine invitation,
  With deep humiliation;
Oh, let Thy blood me cover,
And wash my soul all over!

(continued)

Through Thy so spotless blood,
That precious, healing flood,
  Purge off all sin and sadness,
  And fill my heart with gladness;
Lord, hear Thou my confession,
And blot out my transgression!

Lord, strengthen Thou my heart;
To me such grace impart,
  That naught which may await me,
  From Thee may separate me;
Let me with Thee, my Savior,
United be forever.

DEVOTION 10

With the Footwashing, Jesus Also Wishes to Give an Example

Mel.: Gott des Himmels und der Erden

Love, who hast for me endurèd
  All the pains of death and hell;
Love, whose contest hath procurèd
  Endless joys and life as well:
Love, I give myself to Thee,
Thine for all eternity!

Love, my Life, Pow'r, and Salvation,
  Light and Spirit, Truth and Word!
Love, who borest condemnation,
  My soul's comfort to afford:
Love, I give myself to Thee,
Thine for all eternity!

Love, who to Thy yoke hast bound me
  And my mind and senses taught;
Love, who in Thyself hast drowned me
  Till mine eyes for heaven sought:
Love, I give myself to Thee,
Thine for all eternity!

Even my friend, in whom I trusted, which did eat of my bread, hath trodden me underfoot.

Psalm 41:9

When Jesus had washed their feet, He took His garments and was set down again, and said unto them, Know ye what I have done to you? Ye call Me Master and Lord: and ye say rightly therein, for so I am. If I then, your Lord and Master, have washed your feet, ye also ought to wash one another's feet. For I have given you an example, that ye should do as I have done to you. Truly, truly, I say unto you, The servant is not greater than his lord; neither the apostle greater than he that sent him. If ye know these things, blessed are ye if ye do them. I speak not of you all: I know whom I have chosen: but that the Scripture may be fulfilled, He that eateth bread with Me hath lifted up his heel against Me. Now I tell you before it come, that, when it is come to pass, ye may believe that I am He. Truly, truly, I say unto you, He that receiveth whomsoever I send receiveth Me; and he that receiveth Me receiveth Him that sent me.

John 13:12–20

Since Christ says here, "I have given you an example, that ye should do as I have done to you," namely, that you also should wash one another's feet, therefore in the papacy, a yearly procession was made of it, wherein the pope and his bishops would wash the feet of twelve men on Maundy Thursday. But this is apery and hypocritical footwashing; for the commandment of Christ has nothing at all to do with the mere *work* of footwashing. Otherwise, not only must twelve men's feet be washed, but everyone's. And people would be far better served by being given a full bath and having their whole body washed. With this example, Christ has a far different meaning.

First, it is an example of *humility* which we are to follow. No one is to think, "Why should I do something to please this or that person? He is not my equal, he is of far too little account." Here the Lord says, "Look at Me! I am a kind of Lord and Master whose equal is not to be found, yet you see what I do. Whosoever is greatest among you, let him be the servant of the others." Therefore let every Christian beware of pride and arrogance, look diligently in this clear mirror of the humility of the Son of God, and think thus: "Since the eternal, divine Majesty from heaven humbled Himself so deeply, and did not hesitate and was not ashamed to wash His disciples' feet, dear God! who am I, that I should wish to exalt myself so highly or despise others around me? Get thee gone from me, thou arrogant, fiendish devil, with thy darts and whisperings!"

Thus we should justly be warned by this mirror of Christ's humility against the Roman, Antichristian pope, who out of insatiable, cursed vainglory, as Daniel and Paul prophesied, lifts himself up and exalts himself over and against all that is comprehended by God and divine service, and sits in the temple as an earthly god, where all potentates are to lie at his feet and kiss his slippers. This is to suggest that the Lord said not, "Ye other disciples ought to be humble and wash one another's feet," but, "Thou, Peter, art excepted, for thou shalt be pope, and wash no man's feet, yea, rather thou shalt live sumptuously, nor suffer thy feet ever to be kissed by any but the mighty on earth." Of this Christ spoke not a word, but rather earnestly desires that St. Peter, no less than all other disciples, wash the others' feet, and in his whole life behave humbly, even as he also endeavored to do. For he cannot suffer the centurion, Cornelius, to fall down before him, but it is simply an abomination to the humble apostle of Christ, and he says, "Stand up, for I also am a man" (Acts 10:26). Yet the son of perdition, the miserable pope of Rome, actually claims before God and all the world that he is a follower of Peter, while trampling underfoot Christ's preaching of humility. Cannot a child of seven years see that the papacy of Rome is established by the devil?

Second, this footwashing is to be an example of *love* to us, showing how the Lord Christ's heartfelt love compelled Him to such deep humility. How earnestly He desires this following in love is shown by His words, when He says immediately afterward to the disciples, "A new commandment give I unto you, that ye love one another, even as I have loved you; whereby every man shall know that ye are My disciples." Oh, let us then love not only in word, but in deed and in truth! Yea, just as Christ serves the apostles, so you also, out of unfeigned love, ought to be of service to your neighbor by counsel and action, both bodily and spiritually—and not only to your faithful, intimate friend, who stands constantly with you in all your troubles and tribulations, but also to your enemy, as your Redeemer does here to His betrayer, Judas. This He bids you do with clear words, "Love your enemies, bless them that curse you, do good to them that hate you," etc. (Matt. 5:44). Blessed are you if you do so, it says in the text.

Finally, we are also and especially warned against *despising the holy preaching office.* For although Judas, one of the Twelve, trampled Christ underfoot, as Christ adduces here from Psalm 41, we are not therefore to discard the whole preaching office. For those who occupy this office are legates and messengers in Christ's stead; he that receives them receives Christ Himself, as He affirms here. They are therefore ungodly Epicureans who immediately condemn the whole estate and ordinance of God, saying, "Such are they all!" No, God always preserves for Himself a holy seed. And the preaching office, the estate of rulers, and the estate of the household, are certainly to be maintained as Christian, as in the past, so also now, even if some wicked villains are sometimes found in these estates and offices; whom God will certainly judge and punish.

Prayer

O Lord God, heavenly Father, we Thy children call upon Thee, beseeching Thee with penitent hearts to take away our sins that we may be clean, and to make us teachable students of Thy beloved Son, our Lord and Master, that we may learn from Him true humility and love, follow His example, and show all manner of service and works of Christian love to one another, that on the Last Day we may appear before Thy dear Son in all readiness and enter with Him into the pure, holy city of God and the heavenly fatherland. Amen.

Mel.: Herzliebster Jesu, was hast du verbrochen

Herewith a good example hath been given,
That ye should mark it and to good be driven:
 "As I have done to you, My brothers truly,
 Ye should do duly."

Let me consider this with all conviction,
And should some Judas cause me some affliction,
 Let me repay his malice with all kindness,
 Nor curse in blindness.

Let me receive all people Christian namèd,
Nor of such humble service be ashamèd,
 But in Thy name do good to those before Thee,
 Lord, I implore Thee!

DEVOTION 11

Jesus Is Troubled at Judas' Hardening

Mel.: Christus, der ist mein Leben

Abide, O dearest Jesus,
  Among us with Thy grace,
That Satan may not harm us,
  Nor we to sin give place.

Abide with Thy protection
  Among us, Lord, our Strength,
Lest world and Satan fell us,
  And overcome at length.

Abide, O faithful Savior,
  Among us with Thy love;
Grant steadfastness, and help us
  To reach our home above.

Even my friend, in whom I trusted, which did eat of my bread, hath trodden me underfoot. — If mine enemy had reproached me, then I would bear it: and if he that hated me did magnify himself against me, then I would hide myself from him. But thou art mine equal, my guide, and mine acquaintance; we who took sweet counsel together, we walked unto the house of God in company.

Psalm 41:9; 55:13–15

When Jesus had thus said, He was troubled in spirit, and testified, and said, Truly, truly, I say unto you, One of you shall betray Me. Behold, the hand of him that betrayeth Me is with Me on the table. Then the disciples began to be sorrowful, and looked one on another, doubting of whom He spake.

Matthew 26:21–22; Mark 14:18–19; Luke 22:21; John 13:21–22

When the Lord Jesus has concluded His beautiful sermon on the washing of feet, and cannot by His service and kindness keep Judas back from his wicked undertaking, He is troubled in spirit. For since He is not only true God, but also true Man, it stirs His heart, and Judas' ungodly plot causes Him such painful grief that He again pours out His troubled heart to the disciples, and as not long before He spoke of him somewhat obscurely from Psalm 41, now He speaks somewhat more clearly and plainly.

But the reason why Christ is so troubled over Judas here that His whole body trembles, as Cyril writes, is easy to understand. This trembling and dread struck Him (1) on account of the great *ingratitude* of Judas, for the world certainly saw nothing more unjust than when one of the chosen witnesses betrayed his God, Maker, Lord, and Master, whom he was rather supposed to proclaim; (2) on account of the terrible *punishment* that would come upon the traitor, for he became *Iscariot,* "a man of rooting out and destruction," on whom Christ's suffering and death would be lost; (3) on account of the horrifying *offense,* for by this, Judas brought great shame upon the holy apostolate, ministry, and preaching office, in which the majesty of God is supposed to give light and shine, and thus offended men.

Now, that *Christ's disciples* were also very troubled at these words of Christ and looked at one another in fear to see whether anyone turned pale, this is an example for us that we should be especially sad and troubled when anyone in our midst suffers a serious fall. For when the hand of God is withdrawn, it is all over for us and there is none too great or high among us for the devil to lay a pitfall for him. After all, he invades the company of the apostles here and accomplishes so much that the miserable Judas becomes a faithless traitor and a guide for the enemies of Jesus Christ. Therefore it is of utmost necessity for us that we pray and sigh that we may not fall into temptation, that God would not take His Holy Spirit from us, but would grant us strength and might to resist the devil, who walketh about as a roaring lion, seeking whom he may devour. But it should especially be a heartfelt sorrow to us when we hear and experience that people fall away from the pure doctrine for the sake of their belly, or will not surrender to it, even though they have been convinced of its truth in their heart, simply because covetousness has so blinded and disgraced them that, for some temporal gain, they wittingly endorse the lie and thus betray and sell Christ and His truth for money and goods.

Further, *preachers* and *hearers* are also to be reminded of their *duty.* For *teachers* and *preachers* are to terrify people away from sin with great frequency according to Christ's example, and not to be silent dogs or soft treaders, much less to set pillows under people's heads. "Cry confidently, forbear not," it says in Isaiah 58:1, "lift up your voice like a trumpet and declare to My people their transgression, and to the house of Jacob their sin." And St. Paul writes in 1 Timothy 5:20: "Them that sin rebuke before all, that others also may fear." Likewise in 2 Timothy 4:1–2: "I charge thee therefore before God and the Lord Jesus Christ, who shall come to judge the quick and the dead . . . Preach the word; be instant in season, out of season; reprove, rebuke, exhort with all longsuffering and doctrine." Yet the ministers of God are to learn from the Lord Jesus to keep this modesty so that they do not instantly name people by name, since the Lord here does not name His betrayer. The rebuke is to be of a fatherly nature and to come from a well-meaning heart, that all may sense and mark that it is meant well and faithfully. Christ directed all His sermons toward correction and salvation as the necessity and occasion of those present demanded. In turn, *hearers* are to not to perceive and regard such sermons of rebuke as sermons of shame, if fitting propriety is maintained and it does not break out into unfitting words of vituperation—as the dear disciples here regard it as no sermon of shame when the Lord suggests to them that there is a traitor in their midst. For this is the work and office of the Holy Spirit, who will not and does not desire to forbear to rebuke the world, as Christ says. This rebuking, however, happens through the Word and the called ministers thereof.

Prayer

O dearest Savior, Thou wast sorely troubled when Thou didst see Judas, Thy betrayer sitting at table with Thee, and didst perceive that now no reminder, admonition, nor warning would affect him, but that he would carry out the wickedness already conceived, and would thereby cast himself into utter and eternal destruction. This afflicted Thee, Lord Jesus, this caused Thee pain in Thy heart. Let me, I pray Thee, also be heartily and painfully troubled when in this corrupt world I am made to see Thy holy name profaned, Thine honor diminished, and Thy will left undone and despised by the children of men out of pure malice. But as Thou, faithful Lord Jesus, didst not leave the hardening of Judas unattended, but didst rebuke him for it, at first discreetly, yet afterward openly, so grant me also such heartfelt boldness that, wherever I have fitting occasion to bring to my neighbor's awareness his transgression and iniquities, I may not neglect to do so, but without premeditated hatred and spite, and only for Thy glory and for his good, may show him where he is doing wrong and sinning against Thee, that I may save his soul from death and pull him out of the pit of destruction, and that one day we may both by grace inherit eternal salvation. Amen.

Mel.: O Gott, du frommer Gott

O God, forsake me not!
  Take not Thy Spirit from me
And suffer not the might
  Of sin to overcome me.
Increase my feeble faith,
  Which Thou Thyself hast wrought.
Be Thou my Strength and Pow'r—
  O God, forsake me not!

O God, forsake me not!
  Lord, hear my supplication!
In ev'ry evil hour
  Help me o'ercome temptation;
And when the Prince of hell
  My conscience seeks to blot,
Be Thou not far from me—
  O God, forsake me not!

DEVOTION 12

Jesus Reveals His Betrayer

Mel.: Wer nur den lieben Gott läßt walten

Lord, am I one who loves Thee truly,
  Who clings to Thee in times of woe?
Who is to Thee devoted wholly,
  And in Thy ways alone doth go?
Am I the one? The truth display:
O Light of life, say yes or nay!

Am I the one who 'gainst Thee liveth,
  Who coldly turns his back to Thee?
Am I the child that with Thee striveth,
  That loves and hears Thine enemy?
Am I the one? The truth display:
O Light of life, say yes or nay!

Have I become a Judas-brother,
  Who hath for money sold his Lord?
Is now the murd'rous foe my father,
  Am I among the wicked horde?
Am I the one? The truth display:
O Light of life, say yea or nay!

Let his days be few; and let another take his office. . . . He desired the curse, so shall it also come unto him; he delighted not in the blessing, so shall it also abide far from him. And he put on the curse like as his garment, and it came into his bowels like water, and like oil into his bones. So let it be unto him as a garment that he weareth, and for a girdle wherewith he is girded continually.

Psalm 109:8, 17–19

And they began to inquire among themselves which of them it was that should do this, and to say unto Him one by one, Lord, is it I? He answered and said, It is one of the Twelve that dippeth with Me in the dish, the same shall betray Me. The Son of Man indeed goeth, as it is was determined and written of Him; but woe unto that man by whom the Son of Man is betrayed! It were better for him if that man had never been born. Then Judas, which betrayed Him, answered and said, Master, is it I? He said unto him, Thou sayest it.

Now there was among His disciples who sat at table one leaning on Jesus' bosom, whom Jesus loved. Simon Peter therefore beckoned to him that he should ask who it should be of whom He spake. He then lying on Jesus' breast saith unto Him, Lord, who is it? Jesus answered, He it is, to whom I shall give a sop, when I have dipped it. And He dipped the sop and gave it to Judas Iscariot, the son of Simon. And after the sop Satan entered into him. Then said Jesus unto him, That thou doest, do quickly. Now no man at the table knew for what intent He spake this unto him. For some of them thought, because Judas had the bag, that Jesus had said unto him, Buy those things that we have need of against the feast; or, that he should give something to the poor. He then having received the sop went immediately out. And it was night.

Matthew 26:22–25; Mark 14:18–21; Luke 22:22–23; John 13:23–30

The question of the disciples, "Is it I?" reveals their *honest, upright heart,* for they were not conscious of such betrayal. But this also shows their *fearful* heart; for although they were not conscious of this frightful sin, they were worried out of mistrust in their own heart that they themselves might somehow have committed this sin unconsciously, since the heart of man is corrupt and filled with mischief. Conversely, Judas' question displays his *shameless and brazen* heart; for he had sold himself to the high priests for money, lay in wait for the opportunity to betray Jesus, and carried in his heart the devil of murder; yet he is so brazen as to sit among the apostles in good humor, as though the words of Christ concerning His betrayer had nothing to do with him; yea, he is so shameless, he even asks the omniscient Jesus to His face, "Is it I, Rabbi?"

But we see here how Judas fell deeper and deeper into sin and hardened himself against God's Word; for just as in the godly, faith and the fear of God are accustomed to grow, so in the children of wickedness, ungodliness and unbelief have their increase and growth, as it is written in Proverbs 4:18–19: "The path of the righteous gleameth as a light that goeth forth and shineth unto the fullness of the day; but the way of the ungodly is as darkness and they know not where they shall fall." Accordingly, when the evangelist says here that after the sop, Satan entered into Judas, it does not mean that he had not been in him before, since it was reported above that he had entered into Judas Iscariot, nor that the sop which the Lord gave him was so harmful and wicked. Rather the evangelist John means to indicate that Judas devoted himself more and more deeply to his ungodly intent, and that the devil raged far more vehemently and powerfully with the suggestion and performance of betrayal than ever before, and that Judas also cast to the wind all the Lord's admonition and entirely despised the riches of the goodness, patience, and longsuffering of Christ, so that with seeing eyes he did not see, and with hearing ears he did not hear. For because he despised all Christ's admonitions and warnings, and willfully followed the devil, the Lord withdrew His hand from him and forsook him, and thus his heart was hardened.

This, then, is the right way to understand Christ's saying, "The Son of Man goeth, as it is written of Him" (i.e., Ps. 41:9–10) "and was determined of Him" (that is, in the counsel of the eternal divine Majesty; Acts 4:28); "but woe unto that man by whom the Son of Man is betrayed!" etc. So although Judas' betrayal was also foreseen in the counsel of God and foretold in the Word of God, it was performed neither secretly nor openly by God, but Judas betrayed the Messiah without any divine impulse, only by the instigation of Satan and his own will. Thus the cause of this sin and hardening of Judas is not God's foresight and prior announcement, but the only cause is the wicked will of the devil and of Judas.

"Thou art not a God whom ungodliness pleaseth; he that is wicked abideth not before Thee," it says in Psalm 5:4. And James 1:13 testifies that God is not a tempter unto evil. Therefore Judas is by no means to be excused by the fact that his betrayal was foreseen in the counsel of God and announced beforehand in the Word of God, nor that by his betrayal the salutary sufferings of Christ and thus the salvation of mankind was advanced. For as his betrayal was the work of him and of

Satan alone, so the outcome thereof was the work and intention of God alone. Although God according to His judgment and fatherly will toward us ordained that His dear Son should be the ransom for our sins and for those of the whole world, yet the traitor's intention was in no way that we men should be saved, but rather out of malice and despicable greed he hoped to deliver Christ to the high priests and to scrape money from His hide. It was in this case as it was with Joseph, as the type of the Lord Christ, who says to his brothers, "Ye meant to do evil with me, but God meant to do good, that He might do as it is now this day, to save much people" (Gen. 50:20). Our God is a God who can direct and govern according to His eternal wisdom and omnipotence the wicked endeavors of the devil and his minions in other ways, so that they serve the glory of His name and the good of the church.

A similar sense is also met in the words of Christ, "That thou doest, do quickly." For these words are not to be understood as an imperative, as though the Lord encouraged him to sin—no, by no means! Rather, it is a retention of the treachery and announcement of the punishment. As when a father says to his wayward son, "My son, since I can draw thee by neither good words nor bad, simply go thy way to the gallows as thou wilt; God will certainly find thee." St. Augustine writes about this passage, "Christ said this more out of longing according to His suffering than out of consent to the treachery." And in another place: "Christ does not command the error to be committed, but hereby announces to Judas his evil, which attains to the good of us Christians and believers; for what would be more harmful to Judas and better for us, than that Christ should be betrayed by him?"

Finally, Judas' example is to be a *warning* to us, that we may guard ourselves against the children and works of darkness. Judas was a child of the night and of darkness; therefore he rushes out into the night to carry out his ungodly work in the darkness; for "he that doeth evil hateth the light" (John 3:20). In the process, he came into eternal darkness, where there is wailing and gnashing of teeth. But we as the children of the Light are to put on the weapons of the Light and to cling to Christ, the Light of the Gentiles; then in His Light shall we see the Light everlasting.

Prayer

"Lord, is it I?" Now I too come to Thee, O my Jesus, and ask Thee, "Lord, is it I?" Even if my heart tells me it is not I, and would persuade me who and what I am, yet I ask Thee, O Knower of hearts, "Is it I?" Although my own conscience is aware of nothing, yet I do not count myself justified, but ask Thee, all-knowing Jesus, "Is it I?" Yet here I turn my question into a frank confession, and say to Thee, my meek and gentle Savior: Lord, is it I? Have mercy upon me! I confess unto Thee with contrition and sorrow that it is I who have betrayed Thee in my life, not once, but often and much. For as often as I committed knowing and intentional sins, so often have I been Thy betrayer. It is I, who with Judas loved the riches of this world. It is I, who ate bread with Thee and yet trampled Thee underfoot. How can I tell all the betrayals which I have committed against Thee in the time of my life? Oh, turn to me, and I will be turned, and let me not be hardened with Judas, nor afterward doubt Thy grace; but help me to be truly freed from the vile service of this world and thus from the betrayal of Thee, and to give myself to Thee as wholly Thine own from henceforth. From now on, O Lord Jesus, I will come before Thee every evening and in earnest examination of my heart I will ask Thee, "Lord, is it I?" Who have I been through the course of this day? Search me then on every occasion, O God, and know my heart; try me, and know what my intention is, and see whether I am in the evil way, and lead me in the right way for Thy faithfulness and truth. Amen.

Mel.: Das Jesulein soll doch mein Trost
Or: Was mein Gott will das gscheh allzeit

Be true to God, O man, and keep
   Within His cov'nant rooted;
Rely on this foundation deep,
   To Him alone devoted.
Recall how He
Laid claim to thee,
   His Word with water blending,
A binding oath,
Conferring both
   His love and grace unending.

Be true to God, who evermore
   Is faithful, kind, and gracious,
And as His vassal wage the war,
   Nor suffer sin rapacious
To steal the rein
Of thy campaign;
   Yet if thy heart be riven,
Do not forestall;
Confess thy fall,
   And fight as one forgiven.

DEVOTION 13

Christ Settles the Disciples' Dispute about Rank

Mel.: Christus, der uns selig macht
Or: Jesu Leiden, Pein und Tod

Christ, who doth us blessèd make,
  Humblest form hath taken,
Mending what we men did break,
  Long in sin forsaken;
God low bendeth for His bride,
  Highest bliss supplying,
Life hath "Eloi, Eloi!" cried,
  Giving life by dying.

In His body physical
  Is the fullness dwelling
Of the Godhead powerful;
  Yet He, freely willing,
Himself empties wondrously
  Of His powers holy,
And in all humility,
  Is a servant lowly.

And this doth the highest Good
  To bring us to heaven;
By His suff'ring, death, and blood
  Wrath divine was riven;
Man, who robbed to be divine,
  God must pay for solely;
Therefore now in us shall shine
  His own image holy.

DEVOTION 13

Behold My servant: I uphold him; and Mine elect, in whom my soul delighteth. . . . He shall not cry, nor call out, neither shall his voice be heard in the streets. The bruised reed shall he not break, and the smoking flax shall he not quench. He shall teach justice to be held in truth.

Isaiah 42:1–3

And when Judas was gone out, there was a strife among them which of them should be accounted the greatest. And He said unto them, The kings of the world exercise lordship, and they that have authority are called gracious lords. But ye shall not be so: but the greatest among you, let him be as the youngest; and the chiefest, as a servant. For whether is the greatest, he that sitteth at table, or he that serveth? Is it not he that sitteth at table? But I am among you as a servant. And ye are they which have continued with Me in My temptations. And I will appoint unto you a kingdom, as My Father hath appointed unto Me; that ye may eat and drink at My table in My kingdom, and sit on thrones judging the twelve tribes of Israel.

Luke 22:24–30

Here is an account of the unfitting quarrel of the disciples concerning seniority, and how Christ settled the dispute.

After the Lord finally instituted and celebrated His Holy Supper with them, the apostles, in their vainglory, strove one with another for the primacy and seniority in the kingdom of Christ, which they expected to be a worldly kingdom. This reminds us again of the corruption of mankind, and that nothing good dwelleth in our flesh, and hence no man can cancel out Psalm 32:6: "For this (i.e., forgiveness of sins) shall every saint pray unto Thee in due season." In particular, we see that vainglory, which has done very great harm since the beginning of the world, is inborn in us. It was this shameful fault that brought Satan and his angels to their fall, thrust our first parents out of Eden, cast Korah, Dathan, and Abiram with their retinue into the pit of hell, raised up the two greatest deceivers, the pope and Mahomet, destroyed countless kingdoms, principalities, lands, and peoples, and still wreaks sorrow and heartache today in every estate. We are to acknowledge this wickedness of our nature, to pray God to remove it, and to humble ourselves under His mighty hand, that He may exalt us in His time (1 Peter 5:6).

But because the disciples are still weak in knowledge, especially since they do not rightly understand what the kingdom of Christ is, the Lord silences their quarrel in the kindest way and instructs them in the goodness of that better country (Heb. 11:16) by showing them the distinction between the dominion of the world and the servanthood of the church, presenting His own example as a pattern, and promising and pledging them an eternal reward in His kingdom.

The Lord confirms this *distinction of office* between servants of the church and rulers of the world, saying that as the worldly rule and govern and in so doing are to bear their great honorific titles of office, so the clergy are to be servants, even as the Lord here stills the strife and quarreling of His disciples with three weighty arguments. He takes the first from the distinction between the spiritual and secular estates, which are not to be opposed to each other, but to be in harmony with each other, as Moses and Aaron were, yet distinct and unmingled. The second He takes from the dignity of the Christian church. For the Christian church, which the apostles are to serve, is greater than they, so it is incongruous for preachers to wish to exercise dominion over the people (1 Peter 5:3). The third He takes from His own example, when He says, "'I am among you as a servant'; therefore ye ought justly to be ashamed that ye seek after dominion and do not rather follow My example."

Next, it is especially comforting that the Lord Christ pledges to His servants a *glorious reward*. For first, He appoints to us, instead of the kingdom of the world, the kingdom of His Father, even as the Father appointed it to Him, so that all who believe in Him may not perish, but have everlasting life (John 3:16). Second, He pledges to us, instead of the worldly table of princes, that we shall sit at His lordly table in that kingdom, and enjoy eternal joy and majesty. Third, He comforts us with the fact that, instead of dominion over others, we are to have the power to judge all the world either unto heaven or unto hell, so that whatsoever is bound on earth shall also be bound in heaven, and whatsoever is loosed on earth shall also be loosed in heaven (Matt. 16:19). The servants of God shall be regarded in the sight of the world as the abomination of the land, the "offscouring" (1 Cor. 4:13) from which the land must be purged; they are granted neither possession nor inheritance, often not even the place where they live and breathe; as Cardinal Cajetan said to Dr. Luther, "Where wilt thou dwell safely?" Rather, they are to await an everlasting kingdom, where no man shall be able to exile, excommunicate, or banish them. They are often made to eat meager portions, the bread and water of affliction, as did Micah (1 Kings 22:27), but hereafter they shall sit at the princely table of the eternal Son of God, where there shall be pleasures at His right hand forevermore (Ps. 16:11). They must also suffer themselves to be judged by all men, and to be a song (Ezek. 33:32), but hereafter they shall judge the world. Daniel took comfort in this, saying, "They that teach shall shine as the brightness of heaven, and as the stars forever and ever" (Dan. 12:3). Christ says, "Rejoice, and be of good cheer, for it shall be greatly rewarded you in heaven" (Matt. 5:12). St. Paul extols, "There is laid up for me the crown of righteousness" (2 Tim. 4:8). St. Peter writes to the elders, "Ye shall receive the crown of glory" (1 Peter 5:4); and it says in Revelation, "Be thou faithful unto death, and I will give thee the crown of life" (Rev. 2:10).

Prayer

O Lord Jesus, what a wicked dispute this strife of Thy disciples was! Thou wast afflicted and they afflicted Thee yet more. Thou didst exhort them to humility, but wicked pride and arrogance exercised dominion over them. The love-pledge of Thy body and blood that they received shortly before should have bound them together in brotherly love and kindness; instead, utter hatred, envy, and bitterness was felt among them. And Thou, dearest Lord Jesus, bearest them with great patience, with gracious meekness, and with loving gentleness. When they strive, Thou teachest them; when they quarrel, Thou quietest them. They seek only what is earthly, and Thou leadest them from the earthly to the heavenly, from the temporal to the eternal, from the perishable kingdoms of the world to the imperishable kingdom of heaven! O Lord Jesus, I cry and groan to Thee: have patience with me also whenever I err and am mistaken, whenever I stumble and sin! O Lord, when I sin, let me not go on sinning, but let me quickly turn and repent. Grant that I may stamp out in myself all wrathful inclinations, all carnal arrogance and haughty pride. Instead of these, accustom me to lovingkindness, gentleness, and humility. In all persecutions, in all cross, and in all tribulation otherwise let me persevere steadfast with Thee and be faithful to Thee even unto death; then shalt Thou grant me the crown of life. Yes, grant me that crown of life, O Jesus, Son of God! Amen.

Mel.: Christus, der uns selig macht
Or: Jesu Leiden, Pein und Tod

Thou, made poor, enrichest me,
  Thou, a servant lowly,
Makest servants be like Thee,
  Sinners, like the Holy.
Thou canst calm our heaving breath
  By Thy soul's great sadness;
Lord, Thy suff'ring and Thy death
  Bring me life and gladness.

Rise, my spirit! Risen be,
  Jesus is arisen.
He received good gifts for me,
  Rising from His prison.
Whither He before me goes,
  He will surely raise me.
Here I suffer deathly throes,
  Life with Him awaits me.

DEVOTION 14

Christ's Further Discourses after Judas' Departure

Mel.: Jesus, meine Zuversicht

Son of God and Mary sweet,
  Prophet, Priest, and King forever,
Mediator, Mercy-seat,
  Crucified and living Savior:
Let my faith Thee know and claim,
And Thee my dear Jesus name!

All salvation's in Thy hand,
  Savior of all sinners lowly!
In Thy death life's door doth stand,
  Who hast death defeated wholly.
Let Thy suff'ring, pain, and death
Be my merit and my faith.

By his knowledge shall he, My servant, the righteous, justify many; for he beareth their iniquities.

Isaiah 53:11

Then Jesus said, Now is the Son of Man glorified, and God is glorified in Him. If God be glorified in Him, God shall also glorify Him in Himself, and shall straightway glorify Him.

    Little children, yet a little while I am with you. Ye shall seek Me, and as I said unto the Jews, Whither I go, ye cannot come. And now I say to you, A new commandment I give unto you, that ye love one another as I have loved you, so that ye love *one another. By this shall all men know that ye are My disciples, if ye have love one to another.*

Simon Peter saith unto Him, Lord, whither goest Thou? Jesus answered him, Whither I go, thou canst not follow me now; but thou shalt follow me afterwards. Peter saith unto Him, Lord, why cannot I follow Thee now? I will lay down my life for Thee. Jesus answered him, Wilt thou lay down thy life for Me? Truly, truly, I say unto thee, The cock shall not crow till thou hast denied me thrice. Simon, Simon, behold, Satan hath desired to have you, that he may sift you as wheat. But I have prayed for thee, that thy faith fail not. And when thou art converted, strengthen thy brethren. And he said unto Him, Lord, I am ready to go with Thee, both into prison, and to death. And He said, I tell thee, Peter, the cock shall not crow this day before that thou shalt thrice deny that thou knowest Me.

Luke 22:31–34; John 13:31–38

This is, as it were, the swan-song of the Lord Christ. For although He spoke tenderly with His disciples at all times, yet He does so with increasing longing the closer He comes to His death. Here He preaches of His glorification, and holds quite a pleasant conversation with His disciples, especially with Peter.

When He calls His death a glorification of the Father and of the Son, He is praising the fruit of His death. The Father is glorified in Christ because the Son renders to Him perfect obedience, and accordingly brings the world to His knowledge, worship, and praise. The Son of God, our faithful Brother and Immanuel, is glorified by His suffering, death, and resurrection, since He has proved Himself the Victor over sin, death, the devil, and hell, and obtained and restored to us eternal glory and majesty. And although God's glory and majesty are perceived in all created things, it is to be seen in nothing more clearly than in the death and resurrection of Christ alone, whereby sin is blotted out and life and blessedness are restored. God glorifies His *righteousness* in that He does not connive or overlook our sin, inasmuch as He has caused our sin to be atoned for by the innocent death of His Son; His *mercy*, in that He is moved to give His Son into the *death* of the cross; His *truth, faith, and fidelity*, in that He fulfills the prophecies concerning the blood and death of Christ; His *wisdom*, in that He satisfies righteousness and yet also remembers mercy; His *omnipotence*, in that

Christ, in our flesh and blood which He assumed, has mightily overcome His and our enemies.

Now therefore, as Christ by His death was glorified, and also thereby glorified and honored His Father, so through Him we also are glorified and made glorious in our death. For by it we are completely released from sin and clothed in perfect righteousness, holiness, life, and blessedness. If we could see through tribulation and death with the eyes of faith, we would truly perceive the glory and majesty of the children of God lying hidden under the cross and death, and would say with good cheer, "I reckon that the sufferings of this age are not worthy to be compared with the glory which shall be revealed in us" (Rom. 8:18). "Our affliction, which is momentary and light, worketh an exceeding and immeasurably eternal weight of glory for us, who look not at what is seen, but at what is unseen: for what is seen is temporal; but what is unseen is eternal" (2 Cor. 4:17–18). Therefore, as Christ turned His eyes from the present cross and death to that glorification and took comfort therein, so we are to look in distress and death at that which God has prepared for them that love Him.

Further, the Lord says, "A new commandment I give unto you, that ye love one another as I have loved you." The meaning is: "I do not wish to burden you with many statutes, like Moses in the old covenant, but all the statutes of the new covenant are to be this, that ye love one another. Therefore it is a new commandment of the new covenant, set apart from all others." However, it is called a new commandment not as though Moses had not also given any commandments concerning love; but because the nature of that love is established on a new *example,* namely, on the Lord Christ. For this reason, whoever wishes to know and learn how one is to love one's neighbor, let him look not merely to Moses, who also teaches that one is to love one's neighbor as oneself, but to *Christ,* where he will find what it is to love rightly. For Christ loves us not as Himself; He loves us more highly and more deeply, since He gives His own life and limb for us, as He says later, "No man hath greater love than this, that he lay down his life for his friends" (John 15:13). This is a new example of love; therefore it is also to be called a new commandment, since we are also to conform our love to this example.

Finally, we are also to learn from Christ's conversation with Peter, who wishes that he may go with Him into prison and into death, that we should avoid self-security and presumption, and that Satan desires nothing more fondly than to sift Christ's disciples, and all of us, and to shake us to and fro in the sieve of temptation and tribulation, so that no corn of wheat remains in the sieve, but all must fly and fall out. God is also accustomed to sift His own, that He may purge His threshing-floor and finally gather the wheat into His barn. Yet He does not act so mercilessly with the sieve, but soberly, so that no more than the dust and tares fall through, and the grains of wheat are beautified and purified. As He says, "I will sift the house of Israel among all nations, like as a man sifteth with a sieve, and not the least grain shall fall upon the earth" (Amos 9:9).

How comforting it is that Christ here assures Peter that, although Satan will sift Peter and bring thrice him to deny the Lord, yet with His prayer for Peter He has made sure that Peter will *be converted* and preserved in the true faith unto salvation. However, Christ prayed not for Peter and the other holy apostles alone that their faith should not fail, but for those also who would believe on Him through their word, that they might be saved, as He says afterward (John 17:20). Christ "is at the right hand of God, and maketh intercession for us," writes St. Paul (Rom. 8:34). And John writes: "My little children, these things write I unto you, that ye sin not. And if any man sin, we have an Advocate with the Father, Jesus Christ, who is righteous, and He is the Propitiation for our sins; and not for ours only, but also for the sins of the whole world" (1 John 1:1–2).

Prayer

O Lord Jesus, Thou callest Thy suffering a glorification, Thy shame and reconciliation an honor! Thanks be to Thee that Thou hast also glorified me by the Gospel, and I can acknowledge and confess Thee in faith as my Lord, who by Thy death and resurrection art become my Righteousness. But because Thou also knewest for certain that, when Thou hadst glorified Thy Father by Thy suffering here below, He would also glorify Thee, therefore also make me, I pray Thee, certain that, if as Thy member I shall suffer with Thee here below, I will also be exalted to glory with Thee there; and together with this hope, implant in my cold, insensible heart true brotherly love.

DEVOTION 14

What kind, comforting words Thou speakest not only to Peter but also to me! O Lord Jesus, I may have suffered and endured somewhat in Thy Word before now, for although flesh and blood have shown themselves to be quite weak, yet Thou hast come to my aid with Thy Spirit and prayer, so that I have overcome; for which I also heartily give Thee praise and thanks. But I know all the same that I have not yet overcome all things, but that Satan will still pursue me with his sieve, that I might fall, yea, that I might deny Thee. But lest this ever happen to me, I pray Thee, Lord Jesus, deign to intercede for me, that my faith fail not, but rather grow and burn within me till my end. But if an exceptional trial should ever be imposed on me, and I should be overwhelmed by Satan and suffer a fall, I pray Thee, Lord Jesus, let me not die therein, nor perish, but help me up again, that I may repent in the time of grace and obtain forgiveness of my sins, and then also have heartfelt compassion on my brothers and sisters who are overtaken out of weakness and the devil's craft, and strengthen and comfort them, that they may not despair of Thy grace, but with me and other penitent sinners have eternal salvation! Amen.

Mel.: Machs mit mir, Gott, nach deiner Güt

Lord Jesus, to my soul attend,
  And in my life forever
I will mine eyes upon Thee bend,
  And turn them from Thee never.
Against the tempter's craft and might
Defend me! So shall all be right.

Lord Jesus, who didst suffer all,
  And bear, like us, temptation,
And if I in temptation fall,
  For me mak'st intercession:
Attend me in temptation's hour,
And save me thence with godly pow'r.

DEVOTION 15

The Lord Shows His Disciples That the Wedding Party Must Now Fast

Mel.: Lasset uns mit Jesu ziehen*

Let us suffer here with Jesus,
  To His image e'er conform;
Heaven's glory soon will please us,
  Sunshine follow on the storm.
Though we sow in tears of sorrow,
  We shall reap with heav'nly joy;
  And the fears that now annoy
Shall be laughter on the morrow.
  Christ, I suffer here with Thee;
  There, oh, share Thy joy with me!

Let us also die with Jesus.
  His death from the second death,
From our soul's destruction, frees us,
  Quickens us with life's glad breath.
Let us mortify, while living,
  Flesh and blood and die to sin;
  And the grave that shuts us in
Shall but prove the gate to heaven.
  Jesus, here I die to Thee,
  There to live eternally.

The visions and prophecies shall be sealed up, and the Most Holy anointed.

Daniel 9:24

---

* See Dr. F. Layritz, *Anhang zum Evangelisch-Lutherischen Choralbuch für Kirche und Haus* (St. Louis, MO, 1874), no. 24b.

DEVOTION 15

And He said unto them, When I sent you without purse, and scrip, and shoes, lacked ye any thing? And they said, Nothing. Then said He unto them, But now, he that hath a purse, let him take it, and likewise his scrip. And he that hath no sword, let him sell his garment, and buy one. For I say unto you, that there must yet be accomplished in Me this that is written: He was numbered with the transgressors. For the things that are written concerning Me have an end. And they said, Lord, behold, here are two swords. And He said unto them, It is enough.

Luke 22:35–38

Here the Lord Christ shows His disciples that He spared them at the beginning and wished to impose on them no more than they could bear. For when they were first sent forth to preach the Holy Gospel, they suffered no trouble where they went (Matt. 10:8–13; Luke 10:4–8). But now He announces to them that it shall be otherwise, and they shall be treated differently, so that they will certainly need a sword, that they may stand and defend themselves soon, when all shall be fulfilled that the Scripture prophesies of Him. However, the Lord Christ does not mean a *physical* or earthly sword, as the disciples understood it, who therefore bring forth two fishing knives; but the *spiritual* sword, which is the Word of God and true faith, with which we can extinguish all the fiery darts and attacks of the evil one.

From this we learn first that *our Lord God is accustomed to spare young preachers and rulers heavy tribulations in the beginning, when they are still somewhat new and untried.* For He is a wise Lord, who knows well when it is the right time to bring us into the school of the holy cross and to examine us therein, or to cast us into the smelting furnace of fire and prove and test us. He gives us to understand this in Matthew 9:14–15, when the disciples of John were impatient, because the Lord Christ was too gentle with His disciples, whereas they were treated so severely and strictly by their own master with fasting and many other burdens, and He answered them, "How can the wedding party mourn as long as the Bridegroom is with them? But when the days will come that the Bridegroom shall be taken from them, then shall they fast."

Second, we also learn here that *we are to be equipped with the sword of the Spirit,* and to arm ourselves well with God's Word against all tribulations. For in this latter age of the world, shortly before the Last Day, the devil rages and raves more fiercely than he has ever done before, since he sees that he has little time left (Matt. 24:24; Rev. 12:12). Augustine says, "The more days pass, the more sorrows amass. Let it be not promised any man what the Gospel promiseth not. Holy Scripture promiseth us in this world nothing else than sorrow, oppression, anguish, multiplication of pains, excess of temptations. For this chiefly we are to be equipped, that we may not fall thereto as those unready." Therefore put on the armor of God! (Eph. 6:11ff.). And again Augustine says, "Just as a wise and cautious government prepares for war in time of peace, and in every way readies itself for it, so also we ought in time of peace to take up the teaching of wisdom, which will be hard to discern in time of sorrow. For in time of need, the armor and weapons which were not sought in time of peace are not soon found."

Further, we are reminded of *our own folly and of our incomprehension in spiritual matters,* when the disciples take the words of Christ to mean physical swords, and by these would oppose the Father's counsel for the contemptible death of the cross of His Son, of which He had just now told them, and in so doing think that, with their two fishing knives, they will oppose a throng that will then come with torches, lamps, swords, and staves to seize the Lord. God says that we are to be strong in quietness and confidence (Isa. 30:15) and to possess our souls in patience (Luke 21:19), nor does God wish His Gospel to be helped by the sword, for His kingdom is not of this world (John 18:36) and the weapons of our warfare are not carnal, but spiritual (2 Cor. 10:4–5).

Here we can see how what to think of the spiritual and secular sword of *the Roman Antichrist* and his way of dealing with Scripture. For just as the disciples here bring forth two swords, saying, "Lord, behold, here are two swords," and the Lord says to this, "It is enough," the pope claims that two swords are entrusted to him, the spiritual and the secular sword. Here, however, everyone sees that this is not the meaning at all, since the disciples are rather being tenderly rebuked in Christ's words, as though the Lord would say, "Ye would not understand Me. Leave off with your questions. I see well that ye are still carnally minded. Enough hath been said of this business." For in like manner scholars are otherwise accustomed to respond to those who after much instruction do not rightly understand, and to say, *"Satis est,"* that is, It is well, it is enough.

Finally, it is comforting that Christ is "numbered with the transgressors" according to the prophecy of Isaiah 53:12, for by this He obtained our being numbered with the children of God—all who believe in Him (John 1:12). Likewise, when He adds, "For the things that are written concerning Me have an end," He gives us the consolation that not only have the prophecies of Christ's sufferings, death, resurrection, and whole kingdom been fulfilled, but "all the promises of God in Him are yea and Amen" (2 Cor. 1:20), and He "is the End of the Law; every one that believeth in Him is righteous" (Rom. 10:4). What the prophets and apostles accordingly foretold concerning the resurrection of our flesh, the Last Judgment, and eternal life, will and shall certainly also be fulfilled and accomplished. "We see," says Augustine, "that many things are fulfilled, from which we hope and without all doubt know that what remains to be fulfilled yet shall be. Likewise, as the former came, so shall the latter also come, which the unbelieving did not think would come. For it is God the Lord who promised both and foretold that both should come." And Cyprian says, "Behold, that which was said before comes to pass, and because that which was foretold comes to pass and is accomplished, very well, so shall all that has been promised certainly follow as well!"

Prayer

Yes, dearest Lord Jesus! All the things that the holy prophets wrote concerning Thy bitter sufferings and Thy contemptible death have an end. It was written that Thou shouldest be handed over to the Gentiles; and this hath an end. It was written that Thou shouldest be scourged and put to death; and this hath an end. Yet, O blessed end with which all evil is ended and all good is begun! For now, the wrath of God hath an end, and the grace of God upon us is begun. Now the curse hath an end and the blessing is begun. Death hath an end and life is begun. Damnation hath an end and our salvation is begun. O desired end! O joyous beginning! For this, O Lord Jesus, who art the Beginning and the End, be praise and glory given to Thee both now and forever, world without end! Amen.

Mel.: Freu dich sehr, o meine Seele

Now shall be that word fulfillèd,—
  Word that told of wrath on high.
What, then, hath the Savior willèd,
  Earth to tread, alone to die?
Look upon the Son of God
Fainting 'neath the scorner's rod,
  Every wound His body grieving
  To your hearts in faith receiving.

Thousand times to Thee be chanted,
  Dearest Jesus, hymns divine!
Death and hell have been supplanted;
  Savior, now indeed I'm Thine,
And Thou art the joy I've won;
May I see Thee, blessèd Son,
  Soon in glory undefeated;
  Come! Thy suff'rings are completed.

DEVOTION 16

Christ Goes with His Disciples to the Mount of Olives

Mel.: So gehst du nun, mein Jesu, hin

So, Lord, Thou goest forth to die,
  For me the cross enduring;
For me a sinner willingly
  A blest release procuring.
Go forth, my Lord—
Be Thou adored;
  Thee may I follow weeping!
A flood of grief
Without relief,
  Watch o'er Thy sorrows keeping.

Lord Jesus, I, yes, I should bear
  Sin's price in pain and sadness,
In soul and body, flesh and hair
  I should be of all gladness
Fore'er deprived
And sore aggrieved,
  But Thou the debt dost sever;
Thy blood and death
Bring me by faith
  To God the Father's favor.

Awake, O sword, against My shepherd, and against the man that is My fellow, saith the L*ord* *of hosts: smite the shepherd, and the sheep shall be scattered.*

Zechariah 13:7

And when they had spoken an hymn, Jesus went forth, as He was wont, over the brook Kidron, to the Mount of Olives; and His disciples also followed Him. Then saith He unto them, All ye shall be offended because of Me this night; for it is written, I will smite the Shepherd, and the sheep of the flock shall be scattered. But after I am risen again, I will go before you into Galilee. But Peter answered and said unto Him, Though all men shall be offended because of Thee, yet will I never be offended. Jesus saith unto Him, Truly, I say unto thee, That this day, even in this night, before the cock crow twice, thou shalt deny Me thrice. But he spake further, Yea, though I should die with Thee, yet will I not deny Thee. Likewise also said all the disciples.
Matthew 26:30–35; Mark 14:27–31; Luke 22:39; John 18:1

This is the beginning of the second act or scene of the Passion of the Lord, when Christ talked on the way to the Mount of Olives from the city of Jerusalem, which He left with His disciples about midnight.

Just as David, the grandfather of Christ according to the flesh, once had to make recompense for his own sins and go into exile, when he was driven from the land and people by his wayward son Absalom (2 Sam. 15:23), so here, 1,080 years later, the Lord walks the same road over the brook Kidron, surrounded by others' sins, and withdraws from the earthly Jerusalem, that He may bring us into the eternal. Neither is it without special cause that the evangelist also reports here that, when Christ would begin His grievous sufferings, He went over the brook Kidron to the Mount of Olives. This is reported not only for the sake of the *history*, but also for the sake of the *mysteries* which are found in the sufferings of Christ. For just as *Kidron* means a veritable "black brook," and was dark by virtue of the mud and filth and blood of sacrificed animals which were brought there from the city and Temple, so Christ had now to enter into the dark valley of death (Ps. 23:4), where the streams of Belial terrified Him (Ps. 18:4), and had to drink of the brook in the way (Ps. 110:7), in which the wrath of God and the filth of sin collected, so that His eyes flowed with tears to redeem us from the filth of sins and eternal darkness.

DEVOTION 16

After His sorrowful walk, Christ again gives His disciples warning, when He says sadly, "All ye (none excepted) shall be offended because of Me this night," with which He reminds them of the prophecy of Zechariah 13:7, because He, as the Knower of hearts, sees that they still trusted and built on their own powers, and He also comforted them by saying that He would not remain in death, but would rise again and as the Good Shepherd would gather up His scattered sheep. But the disciples refused to believe this saying about the offense especially, and Peter particularly uses presumptuous words when he did not take his own weakness to heart, puts himself before all, and makes himself suspect, and in addition contradicts Christ and wishes to call Him a liar, when it would have better become him to have said, "If God wills! God help me! etc., then I will not be offended in Thee." We are therefore to guard ourselves against self-security and presumption, and not put anything under our power without God's help. Whom God's hand holds not at all, the same must fall, however bold and brazen he may act. "Therefore let him that thinketh he standeth take heed lest he fall" (1 Cor. 10:12).

Prayer

O my dearest Lord Jesus, with what sorrow Thou didst go out from Jerusalem over the troubled, gloomy, black brook of Kidron to the courtyard of Gethsemane in the Mount of Olives, to the press of Thy cross and Thine agony, when Thou didst drink to the dregs the dark cup of Thy Father's wrath, that Thou mightest win for me a blessed entrance into everlasting life and the glad draft of heavenly glory. Strengthen me, that I may gladly follow Thee here with a little, sorrowful draft. Grant patience to all Thy disciples, who find themselves under the press of persecution or sadness and whose hearts are ready to burst in a thousand pieces. Oh, how many tears are pressed out for Thy people in this dark and wicked time! Help us to wrestle valiantly in true faith, love, and patience. Preserve me from self-security and presumption. Let me remember how soon I may fail and fall, and so be vigilant and cautious in all my doing. But if I should ever be surprised and made to fall by Satan and my own flesh and blood, oh, then cast me not suddenly away from Thee, but hasten to help me, and lift me up again! Seek Thy lost sheep, I pray Thee, Arch-shepherd of my soul, and bring me quickly again to the flock of Thy faithful. Protect and defend me, that I may not fall prey to the enemy forever. And since Thou, dearest Savior, after Thou hadst eaten supper and spoken a hymn with Thy disciples, didst go out from sinful Jerusalem into the deepening night, take me with Thee also, I pray Thee! Take me with Thee also, that in the night of this latter day I may go out of the sinful Babylon of the Antichrist and the world estranged from God, and not walk in the counsel of the ungodly, nor stand in the way of sinners. Take me with Thee, O my Lord Jesus, who didst go over the brook Kidron, and let me always remember that, though I do not know the hour, yet I shall certainly go over the black brook of death. Oh, take me with Thee to the Mount of Olives to watch and pray with Thee there. Let Thy mortal anguish which Thou didst endure for me, and the holy blood which Thou didst sweat for me, comfort me, that in Thy strength I may pass through death into life. Amen, Lord Jesus! Amen.

Mel.: Herzlich thut mich verlangen

World, go with all thy gladness,
   Depart, ye pleasures vain!
Thy Lord must suffer sadness,
   The Off'ring for all men.
Away, ye wicked passions,
   Christ bears our agony!
How can true, humble Christians
   Behold this joyfully?

See how His soul is grieving,
   He groans as death impends,
The cup of wrath receiving
   That God the Father sends!
See how for our salvation
   With death He wrestles now,
His bloody perspiration
   That presses through His brow.

The world with all its gladness
   May go its way to hell;
With Christ in grief and sadness
   And by His cross I'd dwell.
O Jesus, Thy love burneth,
   To death it bids Thee fly;
Therefore my heart, too, yearneth
   To its own self to die!

DEVOTION 17

Christ Begins to Be Sorrowful in the Garden of Gethsemane

Mel.: Christus, der uns selig macht

Now my soul, it is the time!
  Late the evening groweth,
Up the mount with Jesus climb
  Where the olive floweth;
Since at life's beginning came
  Death within a garden,
Here begins the end of shame,
  Here begins our pardon.

All men's sin, and all of mine
  Jesus doth inherit,
God doth make His Son divine
  On His back to bear it.
God's great wrath, sin's heavy load,
  Death with plagues incessant,
All aggrieve the Son of God—
  These His guests unpleasant!

Be not far from me; for anguish is nigh; for there is no helper here. — The bonds of death compass me, and the floods of Belial make me afraid. The bonds of hell compass me about: the cords of death overwhelm me. When I have distress, I call upon the L*ORD*, *and cry unto my God.*

Psalm 22:11; 18:4–6

Then came Jesus with them unto a courtyard, which was named Gethsemane, where was a garden, into the which Jesus entered, and His disciples. And Judas also, which betrayed Him, knew the place, for Jesus oft-times resorted thither with His disciples. And Jesus said unto them, Sit ye here, till that I go yonder and pray.

And He took with Him Peter and James and John, the two sons of Zebedee, and began to be sorrowful and sore amazed and very heavy, and said unto them, My soul is troubled even unto death; tarry ye here, and watch with Me, that ye fall not into temptation.

Matthew 26:36–38; Mark 14:32–34; Luke 22:40; John 18:1–2

He that hath ears to hear, let him hear! Behold, the Lord and Captain of life, Christ Jesus, before whom heaven and earth and all that stirs and moves must tremble and travail, begins to be sore amazed and very heavy. All the parts of His body, from the soles of His feet to the crown of His head, shake and shiver like an aspen leaf for sheer toil of anguish. He thinks not otherwise than that He has been forsaken by all creatures, yea, by His heavenly Father. He feels this strong blow to the heart, so that He must break forth in the moving lament, "My soul is troubled even unto death!"

Now therefore, as this sorrow of His soul is a clear testimony that Christ was a true, natural Man who also felt sorrow as any other child of man, yet without sin, since He did not sin in His sorrowing, heaviness, and sadness, nor was He moved to sin as other men, so here we also hear of the extreme humiliation of the eternal Son of God. Matthew and Mark use a special word that means not merely to be sorrowful or troubled in a usual way, but to be so overtaken by great sorrow, and so afflicted, anguished, and distressed, that like a man in despair, one does not know what to do—where a man's heart is so oppressed that he is entirely unmoving, his hands drop, and his legs will bear him up no longer. Such unspeakable sorrow and heartache was described by David in Psalm 22:11. Now therefore, when we see that Christ is doubled over and twisted like a poor worm, whereas the holy martyrs went with all boldness and confidence to their death, we are to know that it is a far different case with the Lord Christ than with the holy martyrs. For when the fearless blood-witnesses are so steadfast, courageous, and confident, it is because all their sin has been taken from them and they have been reconciled with God through Christ. But Christ is so sorrowful and afflicted here because the Father has now entered into judgment with His Son, and cast all our sins upon Him, who was made our Mediator and appointed to pay for our sins Himself (Isa. 53:6). It was not so much that Christ recoiled at death as that He was afflicted by other and indeed weightier reasons. The first of these is that He felt the wrath of God, who is a consuming fire; the second, that He was a little while forsaken by God (Ps. 8:5); the third, that His bitter sufferings and death would not be applied to the greatest portion of mankind, but lost to them; the fourth, that His people, the Jews, of which He was born according to the flesh, committed such terrible sin, and by impenitence fell into great sorrow and misery some forty years later.

For this reason, we are to learn here what a heavy weight sin is. As Bernard says, "I would never have been able to believe that sin is such an unbearable, heavy burden if I had not seen in the Son of God how heavily it affected Him to bear sin." How often Satan, the master of a thousand arts, deceives you, how your own thoroughly corrupted flesh and blood deceive you, which cause you to imagine that sin is not such a serious matter, that the wrath of God is not so unbearable, yea, that hell is not so fiery as it is heated and made to blaze up in the pulpit! Therefore let us pray with St. David in Psalm 119:120 that God would put His fear in our heart, that we may rightly acknowledge our sin, fear God's wrath, and by the grace of God guard ourselves against sin, and continually think, "If it was so exhausting for the Son of God to pay for others' sin, how much more heavily will it affect us to bear our own sin, at which the ungodly shall cry for great anguish, yet in vain, 'O ye mountains, fall on us! O ye hills, cover us!'"

However, from this sorrowing of the Lord Christ, with which His sufferings began in the Garden of Gethsemane, we may draw two different comforts: First, this account gives us the sweet comfort that just as in the garden the first Adam introduced sin and everything unwholesome, so also in the garden the second Adam, Christ Jesus, by His obedience took away sin and everything unwholesome, and merited for us eternal righteousness and blessedness. Augustine says, "It was fitting that divine mercy stooped down in the place where human pride was brought to so great a fall."

And for this reason He also appeared in the form of a gardener after His resurrection (John 20:15), that He might be the true Gardener of the paradise of His church, who brings us the precious fruit from the promised fatherland of heaven. Second, we have here a comfort against the terror of death. For Christ with His fear, trembling, and heaviness, and great sorrowfulness, merited for us the fact that death may no longer frighten us with its terrible form, but must be for us a gentle sleep and further us to our blessedness (John 5:24; 8:51).

In the same manner, we can derive many profitable *reminders* from this account. First, we have an admirable reminder that Christians also suffer in the Garden, yet with a distinction. For here, the Lord Christ brings all His disciples with Him into the Garden; yet He leaves eight of them outside the Garden, but took with Him the other three (that is, Peter, James, and John, who were more courageous, and who before saw the glory of Christ in the raising of Jairus' daughter and on Mount Tabor) further into the Garden and closer to the place where the contest with death and the wrath of God should begin, since they were able to endure more than the others. Therefore the Lord Christ, according to His wise counsel and consideration, brings certain men into the school of the cross rather than others. One comes closer to the heat than the other; for He is faithful and will not suffer us to be tempted above our ability (1 Cor. 10:13). Second, we have a reminder here that in anguish and distress, we may seek some place apart, as Christ did here, or enter into a chamber, shut the door, and seek God in prayer. Third, we are also to be reminded here not to judge hastily and condemn unseasonably when we see that the prospect of death makes someone so troubled, sorrowful, and distressed, or when a godly heart in pain or in its last hour curls up like a poor worm on account of the great sorrows and the anguish of death, since even the Lord was sorrowful, sore amazed, and very heavy; only let a man not speak blasphemy or despair of God. Agag, the King of the Amalekites, went confidently to Samuel and said, "So must the bitterness of death be driven away" (1 Sam. 15:32), but he was not therefore saved. As little as a tree is torn down without a great noise, or a house without rumbling and clamor, there is no less sorrow and anguish when the body and soul are to part. Therefore it is necessary to watch and pray, that the heart may always be directed toward God. This is the contemplation of death with which we ought always to be busied.

DEVOTION 17

Prayer

O Jesus, only Joy of my soul, shall Thy soul be troubled? O Jesus, Prince of life, shall Thy soul be troubled even unto death, yea, even unto death, so that Thou art surrounded by the heaviest sorrow, and sorrow and anguish overwhelm Thee? O Lord Jesus, all this happened to Thee for my sake. Thou art sorrowful that I may not be sorrowful forever in hell. Thou art sore amazed, that I may not be sore amazed in sin. Thou art heavy, that I may rejoice forever. Thy soul is afflicted even unto death, that my soul may feel gladness and rejoice in Thee, my God. O Lord Jesus, give me Thy grace, and grant that the frequent reminder of Thy mortal anguish may be the comfort of my heart in my own anguish. Let me drive away all the tribulations of Satan and overcome all the fear of death and be preserved—till I, released from all sorrow, amazement, and heaviness, may for Thy sorrow, amazement, and heaviness finally thank Thee in heaven, and joyfully glorify Thee, when I come to Thee and taste the heavenly joy. Amen, Lord Jesus! Amen.

Mel.: O Jesu, du mein Bräutigam

When I consider, Christ my Lord,
What anguish over Thee was poured,
  When unto death Thy soul was grieved,
  Thy sweat the form of blood received:

Then all my bones are sore oppressed,
My heart recoils within my breast.
  Yet if I look to Thee, I see
  Thou didst it all in love for me;

On Thee Thou took'st my every sin,
God's wrath and chast'ning and disdain,
  In death Thou gav'st Thyself for me,
  And poured Thy blood unstintingly.

(continued)

Didst buy me by Thy wounds so red
From sin and death and hellish dread;
  It doth my conscience comfort bring,
  And comforts me, so that I sing:

My thanks and praise, O Christ, to Thee,
That Thou didst suffer death for me!
  Thy bitter death, Thy suff'ring pain,
  Alone my life and bliss remain.

DEVOTION 18

Jesus Wills to Drink the Cup

Mel.: Herzliebster Jesu, was hast du verbrochen

Come and behold, come with your hearts attending
Christ's suff'ring, pain, and sorrows without ending.
  Surely alone God's winepress He is treading,
  His lifeblood shedding.

See how our sins by such great pains are thwarted,
On Olivet, He, like a worm contorted,
  Writhes in such anguish, drops of grief expressing,
  Blood's form possessing.

God here Himself collapses in the garden,
Angels must bear Him up, who bears our burden,
  All creatures see their Maker fall asunder;
  Mark well this wonder!

All sins by us and Adam e'er committed
On Jesus' blameless back must all be fitted;
  That burning anger which was our unmaking
  Here He is taking.

I am poured out like water, all my bones are out of joint; my heart is in my body like molten wax. My strength is dried up like a potsherd, and my tongue cleaveth to my gums; and Thou layest me into the dust of death. — Yea, thou hast made labor for me in thy sins and hast made toil for me in thine iniquities. I, even I, blot out thy transgressions for mine own sake, and remember not thy sins.

Psalm 22:14–15; Isaiah 43:24–25

And He was withdrawn from them about a stone's cast, and kneeled down, fell on His face to the ground, and prayed that, if it were possible, the hour might pass from Him, and said, Abba, Father, all things are possible unto Thee; take away this cup from Me: nevertheless not what I will, but what Thou wilt. And He came unto the disciples, and found them asleep, and said unto Peter, Simon, sleepest thou? Couldest not thou watch with Me one hour? Watch ye and pray, that ye fall not into temptation; the spirit indeed is willing, but the flesh is weak. And the second time He went away again, and prayed, and spake, O My Father, if be not possible that this cup may pass away from Me, except I drink it, Thy will be done. And He came and found them asleep again; for their eyes were full of sleep, neither wist they what to answer Him. And He left them, and went away again, and prayed the third time the same words, saying, Father, if Thou be willing, remove this cup from Me; nevertheless not My will, but Thine, be done.

And there appeared an angel unto Him from heaven, strengthening Him. And it came to pass that, being in an agony with death, He prayed more earnestly. And His sweat was as it were drops of blood falling down to the ground.

Matthew 26:39–44; Mark 14:35–40; Luke 22:41–44

Punished by the Lord in His wrath, Jerusalem cries in the Lamentations of the prophet Jeremiah 1:12, "Behold, and see if there be any sorrow like unto my sorrow, which is done unto me. For the Lord hath filled me with affliction in the day of His fierce anger." So and yet more the Lord Christ laments here also, inasmuch as the Lord cast on Him the iniquities of all men, and all the fierce anger of God presses Him. But we are to consider His affliction yet further, and take to heart the doctrine, comfort, and exhortation which this view provides.

First, we see further here that Christ, in His terrible anguish, *falls down with His holy face to the ground*. For He was made for us the roasted barley bread that tumbled into the camp of the infernal Midianites (Judges 7:13). By His utter humiliation, He atoned for our pride and vainglory, and raised us up again out of the dust of death (Ps. 113:7).

Second, we see that He would gladly be spared the bitter cup, and *prays three times* that God would remove it from Him, yet only if it were God's will. From this we learn not only how great and beyond measure the anguish of His soul was, but also that Christ, in whose person two distinct natures are united, yet without confusion, also has two wills, namely, a divine will and a human, yet such that in His humiliation, there was no conflict between these *two wills,* but the human will piously surrendered to the divine, even as the whole orthodox church opposed to the Monothelites* this testimony concerning the will of Christ.

From this we also learn how we are rightly to pray so that we may be comforted and heard. Our prayer must be made diligently, as Christ here makes His prayer thrice, and calls this praying "seeking and knocking" (Mark 10:46–52); likewise, it must be done wisely, for as here Christ places His will into that of the Father, so also we are not to prescribe to the Lord God the time nor the manner and measure when and how He is to help, but to submit always to His gracious and fatherly will, as David did (2 Sam. 15:25–26) and as the Son of God also teaches us in the Lord's Prayer: "Thy will be done on earth as it is in heaven." In this manner, then, the prayer of a righteous man can accomplish much. If it is not always answered according to our will, yet it is answered for our blessedness, and we are strengthened and comforted thereby, so that we can overcome all things and nothing can separate us from the love of God, which is in Christ Jesus. By a faithful and insistent prayer, we can roll the mountain of anguish from our heart and cast it into the sea; or as Macarius says, "Even if the devil were the same as the strong mountains, yet they shall be consumed by prayer as wax by fire."

Third, we see that *Christ repeatedly rises from prayer,* at once goes to His disciples, then leaves them, weeps and laments, does not know where to go for anguish, goes back and forth, paces the length and breadth of the garden in black of night, makes the disciples speak, seeks eagerly for relief in His conversation with them, bids them watch and pray, curls up like a worm in grief and sorrow and is eager to find some place of rest, as a man who feels great pains of body can

---

* The Monothelites, a sect that arose in the 7th century, taught that there were two natures in Christ, but that the will of the human nature was wholly absorbed into the will of the divine nature, and Christ therefore has only one will, namely, the divine. Their teaching was rejected at the ecclesial assembly at Constantinople in the year 680.

change his place of slumber ten or twelve times in an hour, seeking a new place of rest and finding none.

Fourth, we see that *an angel from heaven must strengthen the Lord Christ.* No doubt the angel spoke approximately thus: "O Jesus, Son of God, this suffering is not against the will of Thy Father in heaven, but Thou hast Thyself helped and ordained, and with Thy Father and the Holy Ghost decreed and decided, that Thou shouldest and wouldest suffer to redeem mankind, for which thing the holy patriarchs, kings, and prophets hoped and waited with great longing. And through Thy suffering there is prepared for Thee an eternal glory and majesty, and Thou shalt sit on the right hand of Thy Father and be Judge of the quick and the dead." This strengthening through the angel shows again how great the anguish of the Lord Christ was, that such strengthening was necessary, and how the Lord thereby made Himself lower than the angels. But with this He merited for us the right to be comforted by the presence and help of the holy angels, even as they often visited the Lord's prisoners in prison and set them free (Acts 5:18–19; 12:6–11) or else mightily comforted them (Acts 27:23–24). Prudentius writes that the angels sometimes attended so diligently to the service of the suffering martyrs that they even wiped and mended their stripes and wounds. But often God also sends us an angel in a good man who strengthens and comforts us.

Fifth, we see that *Jesus even wrestles with death.* Before His eyes He sees the whole murderous kingdom of hell opposing Him. The great dragon intends simply to devour Him, the bonds of death compass Him, and the floods of Belial make Him afraid. Hell spreads its fire-spouting jaws before Him to swallow Him whole. All the wicked spirits with their poisonous arrows of tribulation turn all their external might upon Him to overwhelm Him.

Lastly, we see that amid such wrestling with death, *His sweat becomes as drops of blood falling upon the ground.* Usually in great terror and anxiety, the humors of the body flow from the outer limbs to the heart, as the fountain of life, seeking to give it help and assistance; therefore the faces of terrified and troubled men grow visibly pale, and they do not know what to do. In addition, the sweat of one who is anguished and fearful breaks forth, yea, blood springs forth, when the conscience awakes, as is reported of Aristobulus. This sweat of blood was therefore a depletion of all His powers, so that all His energy drained away, and

DEVOTION 18

thus all His strength was dried up as a potsherd, and His tongue cleaved to His gums. In this sweat, however, we see the great, fervent, and burning zeal of duty to His office (Isa. 43:24). When He sweats blood, it is therein that our redemption and atonement consists (Heb. 9:12–13). And when His blood freely runs out of Him and falls upon the ground, it is in this that we have an overflowing and perfectly complete satisfaction. For "with the Lord there is . . . plenteous redemption" (Ps. 130:7). Therefore, whenever we feel the fear of death in our heart, so that we also labor and sweat on the Mount of Olives and in the vineyard of the Lord, where God embraces and kisses us so fervently that our heart bursts and trembles in our body, then we are to remember Christ's bloody sweat of anguish and sing with the church in the Litany: "By Thy mortal agony and bloody sweat, help us, dear Lord God!"

Prayer

O Lord Jesus, how deeply Thou didst humble Thyself! O Lord Jesus, what weakness overcomes Thee! Thou art the Lord, our Strength, and an angel must strengthen Thee! Thou art the God of all comfort, and an angel must comfort Thee! An angel strengthens the Lord of angels! A creature comforts its Creator! The Lord, who sustains, governs, and quickens all things suffers Himself to be quickened by His minister! O Lord Jesus, Thou wouldst not have needed to do this if Thy divine power had only shown itself a little and manifested itself. But it rests, and Thou sufferest Thyself to be strengthened, comforted, and quickened, all to the end that I might have eternal strength, eternal rest, eternal comfort, eternal quickening in Thee and through Thee. O Lord Jesus, I beseech Thee: for the sake of Thine anguish, Thy sore amazement, and Thy dereliction never leave me! Assist me when I fall into anguish, sadness, and oppressive sorrow. But especially be with me when my final distress comes upon me and I must wrestle with bitter death. Send to me then, I pray Thee, Thy minister as an angel of God, to speak to my anguished heart a comforting word, and to assure me of the blessed glory to come! In my final throes of death let Thy heavenly seraphim encamp round about my bed, that they may drive from me all tribulations of darkness, and joyfully take up my soul, sprinkled with Thy precious blood, and bear it to

Thee in heaven. O Lord Jesus, for the sake of Thy struggle with death and Thy bloody sweat have mercy upon me now and forever! Amen, Lord Jesus! Amen.

Mel.: Wer weiß, wie nahe mir mein Ende

Now death draws nigh, the fight impendeth,
  Whereat my soul is sore afraid;
Yet, soul, take heart! For Christ amendeth
  Thy struggle by the one He made.
O Christ, Thy mortal agony
Let in my dying strengthen me!

The host of sin, the Judge's sternness,
  The flames of hell, death's fearful brood,
Oppress me like a gaping furnace—
  My Jesus bears them for my good.
O Christ, Thy mortal agony
Let in my death deliver me!

DEVOTION 19

Jesus Wakes the Sleeping Disciples

Mel.: O du Liebe meiner Liebe*
Or: O Durchbrecher aller Bande

O Thou Love wherewith I'm lovèd,
  Source of all my happiness;
Thou, O Love, by mercy movèd,
  Tak'st upon Thee my distress:
As a lamb led to the slaughter
  Goest to the cross's tree,
Seal'st Thy love with blood and water,
  Bear'st the world's iniquity.

Love, so strikingly displayèd
  In Thy tears and bloody sweat;
Love, by sinful men betrayèd,
  Dragged before the judgment-seat;
Love, who for my soul's salvation
  Willingly didst shed Thy blood:
Through Thy death and bitter Passion
  I am reconciled to God.

I wait to see if any man might pity me, but there is no man; and for comforters, but I find none.

Psalm 69:20

---

* Melody no. 26 or 27 in the appendix to the St. Louis *Evang.-Luth. Choralbuch.*

And He rose up from prayer, and came to His disciples, and found them sleeping for sorrow, and said unto them, Ah! Will ye sleep now and take your rest? Why sleep ye? It is enough, the hour is come, and the Son of Man is betrayed into the hands of sinners. Rise up, let us go; lo, he that betrayeth Me is at hand. But pray, that ye fall not into temptation.

Matthew 26:45–46; Mark 14:41–42; Luke 22:45–46

Behold, when the Lord is in His greatest sorrow of heart, His disciples are snoring and sleeping. He comes three times and visits them, but He always finds them sleeping, as though no trouble were at hand. He complains to them of His misery, but there is no compassion, no consolation. When the enemies are already on the way and danger is most near, they are at their most self-secure and sleep on without any care. They would have even been caught asleep by the soldiers if Christ had not forcefully roused them and warned them of harm. The Lord might well lament here and say, "I wait to see if any man might pity Me, but there is no man; and for comforters, but I find none" (Ps. 69:20).

Here we have, first, an example of *sleeping friends*. When trouble has reached its height, behold, sometimes even your best friends—those on whom you would have built towers and to whose purse you would have entrusted your heart—are found asleep. Those with whom you have lived in happy estate on the friendliest terms shut their eyes in your trials and act as if they had never known you all their life. Though you cry to them with a loud voice, complain to them of your troubles, and ask for comfort and deliverance, you cannot wake them or move them to pity. Think of holy Job. When he fell into his heavy cross of home and heart, and by God's permission was plundered by Satan and stricken and afflicted with black boils all over his body from head to toe, then his friends kept faith no better than a dog keeps a fast. They blamed him, saying that he must have a secret crime in his heart, for which reason the Lord of Sabaoth is punishing him so vehemently. His own wife came and mocked him, saying, "Cleavest thou yet firmly to thy godliness? Yea, bless God and die! Thou doest admirably, praisest and servest God, and art brought low as a result!"—as Luther says of the subject in his marginal gloss. Oh, how this heartache must have pained the most aggrieved man! Therefore Augustine says, "This woman was the devil's helper, not the man's comforter. She should have spoken comfort to him, but she afflicted his troubled soul even more." Therefore, "trust not in princes; they are men, and cannot help" (Ps. 146:3). But it is good to trust in God. If all men, yea, all creatures, sleep through your salvation and welfare, the Lord your God nevertheless keeps a vigilant eye on you. As King David says, "Behold, the Keeper of Israel neither sleepeth nor slumbereth" (Ps. 121:4). After all, the Lord Jesus cannot forget the apostles in His direst need, but goes to them three times and visits them. Yea, when danger is at hand, He wakes and warns them.

Thus we have here, above all else, a clear image and example of great *blindness and self-security*. When the highest danger is at hand, and Judas is on the way with his murderous band, the disciples are having their best and deepest sleep. So (and yet more so) do you also do, O mad world, drunk with all wickedness! The closer the distress, the more self-secure you are. Though the messengers of God cry before our eyes and ears, "Rise, thou that sleepest, and Christ shall shine upon thee," yea, though the righteous Judge in heaven Himself lifts up the rod of His anger and strikes us with all manner of civic and domestic punishment, most regard it little or not at all, and many as a result grow even more brazen and unruly from day to day. It is with us as it was with the people before the flood; although Noah told them of the punishment drawing near, they regarded it as if a goose were honking at them. They thought, "The old fool is raving. How can the whole world be drowned? Where would so much water be procured?" Yea, when he built an ark and finally went in with his family that he might "receive his life for a prey" (Jer. 38:2), they went on in their ungodly sinfulness, supposing there was no danger. Oh, think how it was with Jerusalem! Did not Jesus preach to them Himself with words and tears? Did not the Roman soldiers all gather their engines of war and whet their swords? Yet the Jews went on living in such self-security until they went to their graves with bloody heads. In truth, we do not do much better today. Do not many, with the foolish virgins, think that they have plenty of time, and the Bridegroom will not come for a long time yet? The end of the world is at the door, yea, we know not what moment the evening of our death might fall. Yet many a man would swear an oath that there are still thousands of years till it comes to that. Although the traitor Judas and his evil throng are already on the way, indeed, at the threshold, we spend the day like senseless beasts, thinking there is no God who will punish the wicked, no devil who will torment them. Our great negligence and self-security powerfully teaches us one of these two things: Either we are already delivered over to the murderous hands of the enemy and do not know it, or since we are preserved among so many a danger, we are far too ungrateful to Him who thus preserves us.

Therefore, in spiritual and heavenly matters, where the glory of God and our salvation are concerned, we should not sleep in self-security as the world does, but rather be ourselves roused to every good by the very alert cunning and malice of the enemies! For as the dear apostles here slumber and sleep, Judas and his band are awake and are not lacking in diligence Because they are industrious and diligent in their enterprise and to the end of causing our harm, oh, then we should be all the more attentive, active, and cautious to work out our salvation with fear and trembling!

Prayer

Dearest Lord Jesus, Thou didst take Thy disciples with Thee to watch with Thee, but they sleep. Thou didst take Thy disciples with Thee to pray with Thee, but they sleep. Thou art sorrowful and sore amazed, Thou dost weep and lament, Thou dost sweat and bleed, and Thy soul is greatly troubled, but Thy disciples sleep and are slothfully at rest. O Lord Jesus, it might well have been the same with me if I had been with Thee, for I feel within me great negligence in my Christian faith, great slothfulness in my prayer, and great self-security amid the great danger to my soul. The spirit is willing, and I feel a Christian impulse in my mind, yet the flesh is active, trying to hinder me in the good that I would do. Therefore open the eyes of my heart, my Lord Jesus, that I may always watch and pray! My adversary, the devil, walketh about as a roaring lion, seeking whom he may devour, including my own soul. Oh, in what great danger I am, whether I go or stay, stand or sit, sleep or wake! Therefore, my Lord Jesus, as my enemy seeks diligently to harm me, let me be diligent and careful to guard myself against him. Grant me, I pray, by constant vigilance and vigilant caution to work out my salvation with fear and trembling. Amen, Lord Jesus! Amen.

DEVOTION 19

Mel.: Straf mich nicht in deinem Zorn

Rise, my soul, to watch and pray,
  From thy sleep awaken;
Be not by the evil day
  Unawares o'ertaken.
For the foe,
Well we know,
  Oft his harvest reapeth
  While the Christian sleepeth.

Watch against the devil's snares
  Lest asleep he find thee;
For indeed no pains he spares
  To deceive and blind thee.
Satan's prey
Oft are they
  Who secure are sleeping
  And no watch are keeping.

Therefore let us watch and pray,
  Ever without ceasing
For we know, with every day
  Dangers are increasing,
And the end
Doth impend;
  When the trumpet calleth,
  Earth in ruins falleth.

DEVOTION 20

Christ Goes Confidently to Meet His Enemies

Mel.: Es ist gewisslich an der Zeit

Hold in remembrance Christ the Lord,
  Thy ever precious Savior;
Who came from heav'n, incarnate Word,
  To be thy Brother ever.
Forget it not: 'twas for thy good
That He took on thy flesh and blood:
  O bless His love forever!

Hold in remembrance Christ the Lord,
  And all His bitter suff'ring;
He died for thee, thee to afford
  Salvation by His off'ring,
From sin, death, devil set thee free,
  From hell and every misery!
  O bless His love forever!

Hold in remembrance Christ the Lord!
  Who shall return from heaven,
By whom then shall the just reward
  To quick and dead be given.
Think how thou wilt escape from woe,
And with Him to His kingdom go:
  O bless His love forever!

For, lo, they lie in wait for my soul: the mighty are gathered against me; not for my transgression, nor for my sin, O LORD. *They run and prepare themselves without*

DEVOTION 20

my fault: awake to help me, and behold.... The God of my mercy shall prevent me: God shall let me see my desire upon mine enemies.

Psalm 59:3-4, 10

And while He yet spake, lo, Judas, one of the Twelve, having received a band of men and officers from the chief priests and Pharisees, the elders and scribes, went before the band with lanterns and torches, swords and staves. Now the betrayer had given them a token, saying, Whomsoever I shall kiss, that same is He; take Him, and lead Him away safely. Jesus therefore, knowing all things that should come upon Him, went forth, and said unto them, Whom seek ye? They answered Him, Jesus of Nazareth. Jesus said unto them, I am He. And Judas also, which betrayed Him, stood with them. As soon then as He had said unto them, I am He, they drew back and fell to the ground.

Matthew 26:47-48; Mark 14:43-44; Luke 22:47; John 18:3-6

As Joseph, the son of Jacob, did not remain in the pit into which his envious brothers had cast him, but was pulled out again at the counsel of Judah, and handed over to the Ishmaelites for money, so is it also here with our Redeemer. As soon as Jesus is pulled from His painful pit of anguish and mortal agony, and speaks with His disciples and exhorts them to pray, behold, Judas comes with a throng of armed soldiers, whom he has given a sign by which they are to recognize Christ and not to seize another, since (according to Ignatius' report) St. James looked very similar to Christ, saying, "Whomsoever I shall kiss, that same is He; take Him, and lead Him away safely (if He escapes you, I will be held responsible, and I can certainly not lose the money)." Here see that the religious as well as the secular are enemies of Christ and His church. For although Judas promised to hand over Christ to the Pharisees without drawing attention, yet because he knew that Peter and certain others were bold men, he dealt with the chief priests so that, along with the clergy and their servants, he might also have a troop of soldiers from the garrison of the Romans. And although it was then the time of the full moon, they nevertheless come with torches and lamps, that the Lord might not conceal Himself among the foliage and olive trees in the garden.

Accordingly, although Christ humbled Himself very deeply, He gloriously reveals His divine majesty here, and this serves admirably for our instruction and consolation.

First, Jesus lets His divine *omniscience* be seen, in that He knew the coming of the betrayer and "all things that should come upon Him." But He knew this on account of the union of divine and human natures in His person, even according to the assumed humanity, as Damascenus also says: "The soul of the Lord Christ, as it is personally united with the everlasting Son of God, has knowledge of all things—not by grace, but because of the personal union." Again: "The soul has communion with the operating Deity, understands, knows, and governs all things, not as a mere human soul, but as it is personally united with the Son of God and is the Son of God's own soul." This is also comforting to us here, since we see that Christ, who knows all that shall come upon Him, willingly goes to the garden to meet His enemies. Our first parents went unwillingly from the garden after they had sinned, so that the cherub with a sword was made to guard the door. Therefore this second Adam now comes and atones for our disobedience. If Christ had not with a good will heartily and gladly suffered for us, we would not have been served or saved thereby (Ps. 40:8–9; Heb. 10:9–10). But now Christ's sacrifice is our sanctification, because He took our place so utterly willingly and gladly.

Second, the Lord in His humiliation here reveals His divine *wisdom*. For although Judas and his whole throng, as children of this world, have organized their enterprise with all cunning, so that they thought it would not fail them in the slightest, yet the omniscient Lord turns them all into dullards and fools, so that they do not recognize Him, even though most of them have seen Him before, and also have their torches and lamps in the clear moonlight. Judas himself is so blinded that he did not know his own Master, with whom he had now traveled for more than three years, though He spoke to him and to them all. For Christ held their eyes so that they could not now recognize Him whom they had certainly known by sight before, even as the Syrians that laid siege to Samaria to seize the prophet Elijah, were smitten with blindness (2 Kings 6:18–20). Likewise, when the Nazarenes, the fellow countrymen of the Lord, wished to cast Him off the rock, He went through the midst of them, so that they could not see Him (Luke 4:30), and when the Jews wished to stone Him, He blinded their eyes, so that they did not see Him, and He passed through their midst (John 8:59). Therefore we have here a powerful consolation, that Christ, our Lord, is wiser and understands more than all our enemies. So we are not to be greatly afraid of our enemies; God has the power and knowledge to destroy them easily. It is written, "He covereth me in His tabernacle in the evil day, He hideth me secretly in His tent" (Ps. 27:5); "How great is Thy goodness, O God, which Thou hast laid up for them that fear Thee, and showest to them that confess Thee before men. Thou hidest them secretly with Thee from the pride of every man; Thou coverest them in Thy tabernacle from the striving tongues" (Ps. 31:19–20); "Under the shadow of Thy wings do I take refuge, until the calamity be overpast" (Ps. 57:1); and the like. How often St. Athanasius was protected, so that his enemies sought and encountered him, and yet did not recognize him!

Third, Christ also lets His majestic power and omnipotence be seen here, which He demonstrates by casting the troop of armed soldiers to the ground with a word. He says to them, "Whom seek ye?" They answer, "Jesus of Nazareth." Hereupon He says no more than, "I am He!" At once they fall backward, as though they are struck by a thunderbolt. Mark this, O tyrannical enemies of the church! For Christ our Protector, it is only the matter of a little word, and you must fall to ruin! When God wishes to terrify the snorting Pharisee Saul in his wicked enterprise, He calls from heaven, "I am Jesus, whom thou persecutest!" (Acts 9:5). Be terrified here also, O impenitent vessels of wrath! For if Christ can give such a mighty force to His words in the state of His humiliation, what shall not happen on the Last Day? If Christ Jesus with these gentle words struck the enemies to the ground, oh, how shall the ungodly be able to endure His threats when He addresses them in His wrath? "If He was able to show such power to His enemies," says Augustine, "when He was about to be killed, what shall He not do now that He reigns in heaven? If His Word was so powerful when He was to be judged, what shall happen when He comes as the appointed Judge of the world and thunders against the kindling of hell, 'Depart from Me, ye evildoers! Go, ye accursed, into the everlasting fire!'" Therefore, "Kiss the Son, lest He be angry, and ye perish in the way, for His anger shall shortly be kindled. But blessed are all they that trust in Him" (Ps. 2:12). For Jesus also has a comforting, "I am He," which He speaks to all believers in Christ. "Fear not, . . . I am the LORD thy God, the Holy One in Israel, thy Savior," He says through the prophet Isaiah (43:1, 3). When Christ walks in the midst of the sea, He says to His frightened disciples, "I am He!" and at once they are so heartened by His words that Peter says, "Lord, if it be Thou, then bid me come to Thee" (Matt. 14:27–28). Likewise, "I am the Way and the Truth and the Life" (John 14:6). "See My hands and feet, I am Myself He" (Luke 24:39). "I am the Alpha and Omega, the Beginning and the Ending. Fear not, I am the First and the Last, and the Living One. I was dead, and behold, I am alive from everlasting to everlasting, and I have the keys of hell and of death" (Rev. 1:8, 17–18).

Prayer

O Lord Jesus, what a powerful comfort and instructive reminder I find in the fact that Thou, as the omniscient Lord, didst go forth to meet Thy betrayer and didst reveal Thyself to Thine enemies, whom Thou layest upon the ground in a moment with the little word, "I am He!" as if with a powerful thunderclap from heaven! Grant me such patience and such a fearless heart in all manner of cross and tribulation, that I too may go forth to meet my enemies confidently, especially when it is a matter of doctrine and confession. Let Thy word, "I am He!" be a heartfelt comfort to me also as it was long ago to Thy friends Abraham and Moses. Oh, Lord, be with me when I pray, and speak Thy powerful word of life in my heart: "I am He who commanded you to pray and promised to hear you." When I walk in the midst of the dark valley, be with me, that I may fear no evil, and say to my heart: "I am He! Fear not, I will strengthen you, I will help you, I will uphold you by the right hand of My righteousness. Behold, they shall all be put to shame that are angry with you. I am your Light, your Salvation, the Strength of your life. Under My protection you shall be secure against all the gates of hell." And at last when I am to bid this world farewell by temporal death, call to my heart also with this word: "I am He! I am the Way and the Truth, the Resurrection and the Life! I have redeemed you with My precious blood and won you heaven! I am yours, and you shall be with Me forever!" Amen.

DEVOTION 20

Mel.: Erhalt uns, Herr, bei deinem Wort

Thine honor rescue, righteous Lord!
Hear Zion's sighs and help afford;
  Destroy the wiles of mighty foes,
  Who now Thy Word and truth oppose.

Preserve Thy little flock in peace,
Nor let Thy boundless mercy cease;
  Let it to all the world appear
  Thy holy church indeed is here.

That Thou art with us, loud proclaim
Who putt'st each enemy to shame;
  Dost all their haughtiness suppress,
  And help Thine own in their distress.

DEVOTION 21

Jesus Procures for His Disciples Safe Conduct

Mel.: Wer nur den lieben Gott läßt walten

It is Thy cause, my dearest Savior,
  To keep Thy faithful who believe,
Thy loyal love displaying ever
  To weak and feeble souls that grieve.
This heartens me; I trust anew—
Thou faithful art, and all wilt do.

Myself to lose, I have the power;
  Myself to save, I lack the might;
Thou must direct me every hour,
  Or I shall never reach the Light.
Then guide me, Lord! I trust anew—
Thou faithful art, and all wilt do.

Thou to the Father speakest for me,
  Thou represent'st me, and Thine own;
And, till Thou comest in Thy glory
  Thou as my faithful Priest wilt groan.
We'll see and praise Thee, heav'nly Son—
Thou faithful art, and all hast done!

I have trodden the winepress alone; and of the peoples no man is with me. — Chastisement lieth upon him, that we might have peace.

Isaiah 63:3; 53:5

DEVOTION 21

Then asked He them again, Whom seek ye? But they said, Jesus of Nazareth. Jesus answered, I have told you that I am He; if therefore ye seek Me, let these go their way; that the word might be fulfilled, which He spake, I have lost none of them which Thou gavest Me.

John 18:7–9

After the enemies, cast down to the ground together with their leader, Judas, rose again, Christ asked them a second time, "Whom seek ye?" But they answered again, "Jesus of Nazareth." Here we see how great the wickedness of man's heart is, that it either does not regard punishment or instantly forgets it, as we see here in Judas and his retinue. They fall to the ground as if they had been struck by a thunderbolt, yet they do not convert. In the same way, King Pharaoh in Egypt was somewhat humble while the punishment afflicted him and his land, but as soon as the punishment withdrew, he grew even worse and was more hardened. So it often goes with many:

> When God lifted the curse,
> The sick man grew worse.

Often we are visited with poverty, famine, pestilence, and other punishments. As long as the affliction lies on our neck, we are godly, but when God gives us a little air again, we return into the world and grow increasingly worse with the ungodly (2 Tim. 3:13). Therefore, when we are judged, we are chastened by the Lord, that we may not be condemned with the world, even as Paul, when he was on the way to Damascus, experiences the power of Christ, falls on his face, and asks for grace (Acts 9:4–6).

When the enemies answered Christ's question and said that they sought Jesus of Nazareth, we also see here how the enemies seek Christ, namely, not with prayer, sighing, and supplication, but with torches, swords, and staves—not to know Him from His Word, but to destroy Him along with the Word. Therefore they find Him to their destruction and not their salvation. But as for us, let us seek Christ aright, and we shall find Him to our salvation, as the church and the Christ-believing soul says: "I will rise and go about the city, in the streets and the broad ways, and will seek Him whom my soul loveth" (Song of Songs 3:2). And the Son of God, who is the Wisdom of the Father, answers, "Blessed is the man that hearkeneth unto Me, watching daily at My gates, waiting at the posts of My door. For whoso findeth Me findeth Life, and shall obtain favor of the Lord" (Prov. 8:34–35). But where Christ and His doctrine are found, there let a man hold Him fast, and say with Jacob, "I will not let Thee go, except Thou bless me" (Gen. 32:26).

Now, when the Lord Christ hears this answer from the enemies, He says, "If therefore ye seek Me, let these go their way!" We are to regard these words first as the answer of His prayer on behalf of His disciples and all who would believe in Him through their words, since the evangelist adds, "That the word might be fulfilled, which He spake, I have lost none of them which Thou gavest Me," whereby St. John refers back to the last prayer of Christ (John 17:12). Accordingly, although these words no doubt refer to the physical preservation of the disciples only, it is nevertheless certain that if they had fallen with Him into the enemies' hands, they would not only have been lost physically but also spiritually and eternally, as is clear to a certain extent from Peter's example, who in his anguish later denied his Master thrice. But second, we must also regard these words of Christ's as *a further revelation of His divine power and majesty*, since these words, "Let these go!" are by no means said *as a plea* but strictly *as an imperative*. With them, Christ provides the apostles a free path of escape; for if the enemies were not restrained by the power of these words, not one of the apostles would get away unscathed. For the throng came not to seek Jesus only, but really "to clear out the whole nest." And what Christ did once in the garden, He still does daily. He drives back the bloody counsels of His enemies and prepares for those who teach His church a season of peace, that they may be able to spread the teaching of the Gospel. As with these words He built a wall around the disciples, He still continually builds "a wall of fire" about His church (Zech. 2:5). "How shall He who then showed such care for so few disciples not protect the countless faithful?" says Cyril. And since His prayer and command were so powerful and efficacious then that the enemies could not harm one hair of the apostles, how shall Christ's intercession at the right hand of His Father, where He has assumed all power and authority in heaven and on earth, and His writ of safe conduct which He has issued ("Touch not Mine anointed, and aggrieve not My prophets"), not have their mighty effect? Therefore we are not to lose heart in persecutions or in trials. Nothing can happen to us apart from God's will and permission. Christ says, "But the very hairs of your head are all numbered" (Matt. 10:30), and Paul in the shipwreck is undaunted, and encourages his companions (Acts 27:34–36). We can exhibit no greater cunning to the devil than to acquit ourselves manfully in the cross, and not to show ourselves the least bit timid because of it.

Finally, we also have *the* consolation that Christ alone is the true good Shepherd who laid down His life for us. For here He does not desire that any of His apostles should endure His suffering with Him. He has trodden the winepress alone, and of the peoples no man is with Him (Isa. 63:3). Thus He has truly obtained and accomplished for us a full and perfect redemption, which for the apostles or any other saints would have been impossible to do. For Christ alone is true God and Man. Our eternal redemption demanded that for the sin of all the world, one should suffer who is simultaneously true God and Man, that it might be a divine suffering, which the Son of God performs in His assumed human nature, as Paul says, "The Son of God loved me and gave Himself for me" (Gal. 2:20). Hence the suffering and the death of Christ have this virtue: If God takes and lays on the scale the sins of the whole world and on the other scale the good works and sufferings of all saints on earth, they are far too light and cannot balance the sin; but if the high, precious merits of Christ are set there, the scale is so heavy that it far, far outbalances all the sins and transgressions of men, since Christ alone is true God and Man, as Luther admirable expounds in his book on the councils from the ancient writer Damascenus. Let us therefore take comfort with the holy apostles Peter, Paul, and John, and other saints of God, and all believing Christians, in the fact that the eternal Son of God has redeemed us, that the Captain of Life and the Lord of Glory has been crucified for us, that we are bought by His blood, and that the blood of the Son of God cleanses us from all sins.

Prayer

O Lord Jesus, again Thou carest more for Thy disciples than for Thyself, obtaining for them safe conduct and delivering them out of the hands of Thine enemies while having no regard for Thyself! Be also my Hope and Strength, a Help in my great troubles. Thou hast provided us also with a strong writ of safe conduct in Thy Word, where Thou sayest that Thine anointed must not be touched, nor Thy prophets aggrieved, that Thou wilt build a wall of fire round about Jerusalem, and no hair on our head shall perish apart from Thy will. I take hearty comfort in Thy promise, which has the power of an oath, and I leave my cause entirely in Thy care. O Lord Jesus, protect me also, and keep me in Thy safe conduct when the enemies of my soul wish to attack me, the devil to prevail against me, everlasting death to snatch me away, sin to condemn me, and hell to swallow me up! O my Lord Jesus, deliver me out of their hand, and declare to all my fierce enemies Thy mighty word of power: "Let this man go! Let this man go; for My grace is stronger than His sin. Let this man go, for I have bought him all for Myself with My precious blood. Let this man go, for I have graven him upon My hand, out of which no man shall snatch him. Yes, Lord Jesus, let me never be separated, sundered, or snatched away from Thee! Amen.

Mel.: Jesu, meine Freude

Under Jesus' shelter,
From the storm and welter
  Of all foes I'm free;
Satan may come prowling,
All the world be scowling;
  Jesus helpeth me.
Let them crash
And smite and flash!
   Let both sin and hell deride me!
   Jesus still will hide me.

Th' ancient worm may glower,
Jaws of death may lower,
  Fear may fill the land;
Rage, O world, with groaning;
Here, my hymns intoning,
  In sure peace I stand!
God's decree
Defendeth me;
   Earth and hell shall silent crumble,
   Much though now they rumble.

DEVOTION 22

Jesus Suffers Himself to Be Kissed by False Judas

Mel.: Der am Kreuz ist meine Liebe (p. 323)
Or: Werde munter, mein Gemüthe

Ah, how is my heart afflicted,
  When I think, O dearest Lord,
Of the sorrows unrestricted
  On Thy heart and soul outpoured,
Which, when Judas in the night
Came with sinners into sight,
  On th' appointed Mount before Thee,
  O my Savior, then came o'er Thee!

Thy disciples all too clearly
  Did Thy godly pow'r perceive,
And above three years quite nearly
  What Thou daily didst achieve—
Thee they heard and witnessed well;
One, alas! did greed compel
  As a traitor to betray Thee,
  And in wicked hands to lay Thee.

Even my friend, in whom I trusted, which did eat of my bread, hath trodden me underfoot. — If it were mine enemy that reproached me, then I would have borne it, and if he that hated me did magnify himself against me, I would have hid myself from him. But thou art my companion, my caretaker, and mine acquaintance. We were friendly one with another, we walked unto the house of God in company.

Psalm 41:9; 55:12–14

And Judas drew near unto Jesus, to kiss Him, and as soon as he was come to Him, he said, Hail, Rabbi; and kissed Him. And Jesus said unto him, My friend, wherefore art thou come? Judas, betrayest thou the Son of Man with a kiss? Then came they, and laid hands on Jesus, and took Him.

Matthew 26:49–50; Mark 14:45–46; Luke 22:47–48

O shameful malice and wicked cunning of Judas, who betrays his Lord with a kiss, perverting the sign of love, peace, and reverence into a token of malice, and as Jerome says, giving the sign of friendship with the poison of the devil! But with such treachery, as seen here in Judas, likewise in Joab (2 Sam. 3:27; 20:9–10) the world is now filled.

> Judas' kiss is born anew,
> Kindly word, and pledge untrue;
>   Smile at me and hand me o'er—
>   'Tis what worldlings now adore.

Therefore we are to keep ourselves from such treachery and deceitfulness, and to be honest. For God destroyeth "them that speak leasing; the Lord abhorreth the bloody and deceitful man" (Ps. 5:6). We are also to make sure that we do not, like Judas, persecute Christ and His church under false pretense, or associate with those hypocrites of whom God laments, "This people draweth nigh unto Me with their mouth, and honoreth Me with their lips, but their heart is far from Me" (Isa. 29:13; Matt. 15:8), for this is also to betray Christ with a kiss.

Yet we see how things become increasingly worse for disloyal Judas, now that Satan has entered into him, and he heads speedily toward destruction. For he not only traitorously kisses Christ, but at the same time also says with sweet words and actions, "Hail, Rabbi," as if he would say, "Behold, dear Master, these men are here to take Thee captive. Now therefore, because I cannot deliver Thee, I will take my leave of Thee, and because it is altogether hard for me to part from Thee, therefore let me kiss Thee once more."

Such shameful infidelity and devilish hypocrisy Christ now bears with great longsuffering, not only letting Himself be kissed by false Judas, but even saying to him, "My friend, wherefore art thou come? Judas, betrayest thou the Son of Man with a kiss?" Thus tenderly He now holds the betrayer's wrong before his eyes, as if to say, "Thinkest thou I do not mark thy treachery and falsehood, who now makest as if to give Me a parting kiss, seeing thou hast led this throng thyself to offer Me up on the chopping-block? O Judas, thou who betrayest the Son of Man with a kiss, alas! thou shouldest have thought on thy name, that as the Messiah I am born of the tribe of *Judah,* and am come into the world for the sake of all men. Thy name should have been for thee a constant reminder of the Savior of the world, that thou shouldest believe in Him and be a true *confessor,* as was Judas Maccabaeus, good Judas Thaddaeus, and others besides, and here thou comest and betrayest Him!" It is as if the Lord should say to us today, "Dear Christians, think from whom ye have your name *Christian!* Despise ye the riches of His goodness and forbearance and longsuffering, not knowing that the goodness of God leadeth you to repentance? God willeth not that any should perish, but that all should come to repentance" (Rom. 2:4; 2 Peter 3:9).

Now, this took place for our *consolation,* for Christ willed to endure Judas' false kiss that He might atone for all those sins when we pretend to holiness outwardly and yet harbor in our heart a wicked resolve to sin, and for all hypocrisy, which is inborn in us, and that He might merit forgiveness and the Holy Ghost for the penitent, that He might kiss us Himself with the kiss of His mouth (Song of Songs 1:1) and that we in turn might kiss the Son by faith (Ps. 2:12).

Second, this also happened as an *example* to us, that we might not withhold our cheeks from the false kiss of Judas, and nevertheless not cease to admonish to repentance those who give it.

Prayer

O Lord Jesus, innocent Lamb of God, how shamefully Thou art betrayed with a kiss by Judas, that false heart, under a show of great friendship, and delivered up to the slaughter! O patient Lamb of God, how utterly free Thou art from any trace of wrath, anger, or revenge, offering Thy gracious mouth to the false betrayer, calling Him Thy friend, and giving Him a tender greeting!

O Lord Jesus, keep my soul, that I may not offer Thee the kiss of malice and mischief. Grant that I may love Thee not only in word but also in deed, and hence follow Thine example left for me here. Let me not be one of those who draw nigh unto Thee with their mouth and their heart is far from Thee. O Lord Jesus, Thou knowest that I believe in Thee! Thou knowest that my soul loves Thee! Therefore I fall at Thy feet and kiss them like the great sinner, Mary Magdalene. I mourn my sins bitterly and sigh from the depths of my heart. Kiss me in turn, Lord Jesus, with the kiss of Thy mouth, and quicken my troubled soul with Thy comfort. Speak kindly to my soul, and I will be obedient to Thy mouth, and Thy Word shall be the joy and comfort of my heart. Yea, Lord, I will also kiss Thy hands and thank Thee continually for Thy goodness; I will sing praise unto Thee for all Thy benefits to me, and will give glory not unto me, but unto Thy holy name! Amen.

Mel.: Freu dich sehr, o meine Seele

Be thou faithful in believing,
  Build thy house on solid ground;
Let no doubts or thoughts deceiving
  This baptismal gift confound.
Then, in the o'erflowing wave,
God is with thee, strong to save.
  Lost art thou, by God deserted,
  If thou falsely hast converted.

Be thou faithful, that within thee
  E'er thy heart to truth incline;
To a truthful heart let win thee
  Joab's kiss and Judas' sign.
Falsehood be thy baneful foe;
Let thy heart thy mouth o'erflow.
  In thy faith be wise and clever,
  Nor yet false or lying ever.

DEVOTION 23

Christ Does Not Wish to Be Defended by the Sword

Mel.: Schmücke dich, o liebe Seele

'Twas Thy love for man, O Savior,
Moved Thee to such kind behavior,
   And Thy faithful heart did press Thee,
   In our very flesh to dress Thee
And enwind Thee in our weakness,
Bearing cross and tomb in meekness.
   O the wondrous love that drove Thee!
   Faithful love for man did move Thee!

Oh, how high Thy pity holy,
That Thou for the lowliest lowly
   Thine own priceless life hast given,
   To the vilest death wast driven,
Into sinners' hands wast handed,
To release us debtors branded,
   Thus the blessing us procuring,
   As a curse our death enduring!

For Thou shalt make him a little while forsaken of God, but with glory and honor wilt Thou crown him. — (But one in a certain place testified, saying, . . . Thou madest Him a little while lower than the angels; with glory and honor hast Thou crowned Him. . . . But Him, who was made a little while lacking of the angels, we see that it is Jesus, by the suffering of death crowned with glory and honor; that He by the grace of God should taste death for every man.)

                                                              Psalm 8:5; Hebrews 2:6–7, 9

When they which were about Him saw what would follow, they said unto Him, Lord, shall we smite with the sword? Then Simon Peter having a sword drew it, and smote the servant of the high priest, and cut off his right ear. And the servant's name was Malchus. But Jesus answered and said, Suffer ye them thus far. And He said unto Peter, Put up thy sword into the sheath, for whosoever taketh the sword shall perish by the sword. Thinkest thou that I cannot pray to My Father that He might send Me more than twelve legions of angels? Shall I not drink the cup which My Father hath given Me? But how then shall the Scriptures be fulfilled. Thus it must be. And He touched his ear, and healed him.

Matthew 26:51–54; Mark 14:47; Luke 22:49–51; John 18:10–11

When the sword of the heavenly Father's wrath begins to smite the Shepherd (Zech. 13:7; Matt. 26:13; Mark 14:27), the disciples wish to defend Him with the physical sword, thinking in this to do a good work, since they had of course boasted on the way that they would fight for Christ to the death. Although they only now ask Christ whether they are to strike back, yet Peter, in great fervor, cannot wait, but immediately strikes with the sword and cuts off the ear of Malchus, the servant of the high priest. And though the disciples' enterprise and Peter's work are well intended, yet Christ not unfittingly rebukes Peter and the other disciples, for their pledge was utter presumption, their love for Christ without understanding, their zeal without reason, their example unlike that of Moses, their defense foolish. It was time not for swordfighting but for suffering.

From these words of Christ, therefore, we see first that *personal vengeance* is forbidden. Indeed, a private person is not permitted even to avenge the impropriety done to another or to the general public. But someone might say, "Are you saying that a Christian may not use the sword in self-defense?" In this case, the theologians give this Christian counsel: It is better for him to stop with good words and to try all means and ways, that bloodshed may be avoided as much as possible; for it is a heavy sin and burden to have a man upon one's soul. But if he must perform this miserable act of self-defense, he is to do it without wrath or vengeance in his heart, not to harm his neighbor, but to defend and preserve his life and limb. If it cannot be otherwise, and a man is waylaid in a field or forest or by night, when he cannot call the authorities for protection nor preserve himself in any other way, he is to remember that Holy Scripture and the Law in this case permit self-defense: "If a thief be found breaking in, and be smitten that he die, no judgment of blood shall be given for him" (Ex. 22:2). Yet we are not to go beyond the preserving of our life. We are not to seek revenge nor to injure others, if we are able to escape without risk to our life, as St. Augustine teaches.

Second, we have here a confirmation of *secular authority*, as that into whose hand God has given the sword for vengeance upon evildoers (Gen. 9:6; Rom. 13:4). But authorities are to use their God-given power rightly, for whoever becomes a tyrant and uses the sword for his own desire contrary to God's Word and kills the innocent, is threatened by Christ's word no less than his subjects, and Christ says that he will perish by the sword, as happened to Ahab and his wife, and others besides.

Third, Christ teaches us here that He wishes neither Himself nor His Gospel to be defended *by force*. Therefore we are not to take up arms under the appearance of religion and to cause havoc and bloodshed; for the kingdom of Christ is not of this world, so it is not to be propagated by the swords and arms of this world. It is certainly committed to Christian rulers to be nurses and nourishers of the church, since God has often used their power and arms for the protection and defense of the church. But when preachers and subjects try to fight for the Gospel with the sword, it commonly turns out badly, and other things are commonly sought in the process, and the Gospel is made to lend its name to the cause. Rather, we are to look to God, who will be our fiery wall, as the holy doctor Basil beautifully said when the emperor in his day wished to take the Gospel from his subjects by force: "There shall no man endeavor to draw the sword against the emperor for this cause; for he has other means by which he may do the emperor far greater harm and damage, namely, the Word of God, prayer, and sighing to God. These are the true weapons with which we can do the greatest harm to the enemies of the Gospel." And in short, if it has been committed to Peter to put up his sword into his sheath, it in no way means that he is to save it for use in the future and to keep it with him, as the papists expound this text, claiming this is now fulfilled when the so-called successors of Peter, the pope with his bishops, wield both swords. Rather, by this word of Christ's the sword is taken entirely away from Peter. "The weapons of our warfare are not carnal" (2 Cor. 10:4).

Fourth, we are to learn from Christ His heartfelt *love and benevolence,* when He heals the ear of Malchus and does all good to the one who is helping to take Him and bring Him to His death. Anyone can love his faithful friends and kinsmen; but loving and supporting one's enemies—only godly Christians do this, as Tertullian says. Of course, flesh and blood find it quite difficult to return love and benefaction to those who show us all annoyance and reluctance. But how can it be avoided? The Lord desires that His enemies too should be loved and good be done to them, and confirms this with His own example. "Blessed are the peacemakers, for they shall be called children of God" (Matt. 5:9).

Prayer

O Lord Jesus, Prince of Peace, help me not only to know this teaching which Thou gavest to Thy disciples here, but also to live accordingly, and in time of persecution not to act with too great fervency, nor as a private person to exercise judgment for myself, lest Thy Holy Gospel fall into disrepute or I be burdened with a heavy conscience or shameful reputation, as though Thy Word taught people to be rebellious, and I suffer justly as an evildoer, a seditious man, or one who had infringed on another's office. Rather, as Thou, my Lord Jesus, didst at this time gladly and willingly drink the cup of the cross which Thy Father poured for Thee, grant that I may gladly take, willingly taste, and patiently drink my own cup of suffering, especially in grief and persecution for the sake of the Word. Let me meanwhile be mindful that, as Thou didst love Thine enemy Malchus, Thou wilt all the more readily receive me, who am Thy friend, and that my cross shall not last forever, but my persecution shall be followed by Thy help, and my death by Thy life. O my soul, whenever you are troubled, cheer yourself with this exceedingly glorious comfort, and consider what bliss you will receive one day when among many thousand legions of angels you will have the fullness of joy and be given to drink of pleasures as a river! Therefore, my soul, be patient; the cross is temporary, joy abides forever. Amen.

DEVOTION 23

Mel.: Kommt her zu mir, spricht Gottes Sohn

Requite not evil deeds in wrath,
Pursue in love the narrow path,
  Heed not the world's seduction;
Revenge and glory yield to God,
Stray not to byways lush and broad—
  For there is all destruction.

But ye, beyond this world's annoy,
In Christ shall find your endless joy—
  On this, then, fix your thinking;
No mortal tongue can realize
What pleasures and eternal prize
  He'll cause thee to be drinking!

For what the God of changeless truth
Confirms by Spirit and by oath,
  Must come, and ye shall see it.
Whoso will trust His proffered grace
Shall in His kingdom find a place
  Through Jesus Christ. So be it!

DEVOTION 24

Jesus Rebukes His Adversaries and Is Forsaken by the Disciples

Mel.: Wie wohl ist mir, o Freund der Seelen

Where is a shepherd truer, fonder
  Than Thou, O Christ, my Savior true?
Not only seeking them that wander,
  Not only mending wounds anew—
No, Thou Thy priceless life hast offered,
And for Thy sheep chastisement suffered,
  Atonement making perfectly!
Where is a greater love and favor?
Thou hast laid down Thy life, dear Savior,
  And with salvation crownèd me.

Thou, Shepherd, smitten and offended,
  Thy flock was scattered on the plain,
Yet when Thy days of suff'ring ended,
  The call of grace went forth again:
That all might seek that pasture ever
That from Thy side, O risen Savior,
  And from Thy holy wounds outflows;
Here is refreshment for the ailing,
For troubled hearts the balm availing,
  A rest where restless souls repose!

Awake, O sword, against My shepherd, and against the man that is My fellow, saith the L*ord* *of hosts: smite the shepherd, and the sheep shall be scattered, and I will turn mine hand upon the little ones.*

Zechariah 13:7

DEVOTION 24

In that same hour said Jesus unto the chief priests, and captains of the Temple, and the elders, which were come to Him, Ye be come out as against a robber with swords and staves for to take Me. I sat daily with you teaching in the Temple, and ye stretched forth no hands against Me. But this is your hour, and the power of darkness, that the Scriptures might be fulfilled. And all this was done, that the Scriptures of the Prophets might be fulfilled. Then all the disciples forsook Him, and fled. And there followed Him a certain young man, having a linen cloth cast about his naked body, and the young men laid hold on him, but he left the linen cloth, and fled from them naked.

Matthew 26:55–56; Mark 14:48–52; Luke 22:52–53

After the Lord had rebuked His disciples' impropriety and healed the ear of Malchus, He rebuked the impropriety and wickedness of His adversaries also in wishing to come against Him as against a robber, with swords and staves, to take Him by dark of night, whereas they saw Him daily in the Temple carrying out His office. Although Christ gladly and willingly bore this disgrace for our sake, and was willing to be numbered among evildoers, that we might be numbered among the righteous, yet He is unwilling to let the actions of His adversaries be accounted *right*, and says particularly, "As children of the darkness ye do only works of darkness, and this is done unto Me that the Scriptures might be fulfilled, which told these things beforehand; not that they commanded you to do them, but God hath so ordained, and the Scriptures have foretold that, because ye are wicked, ye would do this evil thing." Therefore Christ teaches us here that we should be patient and show love to our enemies when they hate and persecute us, and nevertheless not to hold our peace at their impropriety, nor to consent to it, but to preserve our innocence in a lawful manner to the glory of God and to the good of our neighbor, so that even our adversaries may realize that they are committing works of darkness and, since they are not converted, becoming utter devils, for Satan is the prince of darkness. Accordingly, Christian love and patience does not conflict with a responsibility to be innocent and a denouncing of the contrary.

In this way David (Ps. 7:4–6; 26:1), Elijah (1 Kings 18:17–18), Stephen (Acts 7:1ff.), and Paul (Acts 23:1ff.) all rebuked their enemies.

But when the Shepherd is smitten, the sheep are scattered. For behold, all the disciples forsake Him and flee, that the Word of the Lord may be fulfilled, when He said, "Behold, the hour cometh, yea, is now come, that ye shall be scattered, every man to his own, and shall leave Me alone" (John 16:32). The fact that Christ is so shamefully forsaken by all His disciples not only serves as a sad example of human weakness and inconstancy, but was also very troubling for the Lord. Yet it all had to be so according to God's counsel (Zech. 13:7), for He was to tread the winepress of wrath alone (Isa. 63:3), and to merit for us the power not to be forsaken in any distress, particularly when we are conformed to the likeness of His image, and must lament with David, "My dear ones and My friends stand aloof from My sore; and My kinsmen stand afar off" (Ps. 38:11). Yet although the disciples committed a great sin in this flight, Christ did not cast them away, but after His resurrection sought them out as lost sheep and restored them again, giving us the sweet comfort that our gracious God will not deal with us according to our sins, nor reward us according to our iniquities (Ps. 103:10), but rather He says, "What shall I make of thee, Ephraim? Shall I protect thee, Israel? Shall I not justly make thee as Admah and prepare thee as Zeboim? But mine heart intendeth otherwise, my mercy is kindled greatly, so that I will not execute the fierceness of mine anger, nor return to destroy Ephraim; for I am God, and not a man; the Holy One in the midst of thee" (Hosea 11:8–9).

The evangelist Mark makes particular mention of a young man who was compelled to flee naked, to show how the enemies of Christ at that time raged without moderation, sparing not even a poor, unknown young man, who, wakened by the bright lights and noises, ran half-naked out of bed. But this incident reminds us that while we must all suffer for Christ, there is a distinction. The apostles are forced to flee and go into hiding, and they keep their garments, but the young man even loses his tunic in the matter and escapes naked and bare. Yet the apostles, who now depart, afterward forfeit their very skin and bodies. Therefore we are not to worry why God treats us this way, even as we always think that our cross is the greatest and ask why others seem largely to avoid crosses, and say in effect, "What about this man?" (John 21:21). One man is banished and goes into exile, another loses all his goods, a third is deprived of life and limb, as God appoints for each man, to whom alone we are to commit it. Sometimes, even the innocent children and young men must pay (1 Sam. 22:18–19; Matt. 2:16). In short, we must all through much tribulation enter into the kingdom of God (Acts 14:22). Each of us men has his measure and allotted portion to which we are to take heed.

Prayer

O Lord Jesus, Thou wast forsaken by all Thy disciples after they had boasted that they would follow Thee into death, for Thou wast to suffer alone and to tread the winepress of Thy Father's wrath with no man to help Thee. Thy disciples all fled from Thee, that I might receive free access to Thee and Thy Father, and in no cross be left helpless or comfortless, but especially, that I might not be forsaken eternally. Oh, how utterly vain it is to trust in the help of man! Cursed shall he be that trusteth in man, and maketh flesh his arm! Therefore be my Help and my Refuge in trouble, for vain is the help of man. In the day of trouble, even friends disappear, as Thy holy apostle Paul saw, for whom Luke alone was of comfort in his imprisonment (2 Tim. 4:10). O Lord, grant that I may never forsake Thee, but remain steadfast to the end, though it should cost me life and limb, blood and belongings, and the whole world! O Lord Jesus, forsake me not, that I may never forsake Thee! Amen.

Mel.: Von Gott will ich nicht lassen

A curse wast Thou made for us,
  Thy life Thou gavest o'er,
Thy zeal sought man inglorious,
  Corrupted to the core.
Yea, name and deed make plain
  That we may all acclaim Thee
  The Bread of Life, nor name Thee
The sinner's Hope in vain.

(continued)

Let me believe this surely,
  Yet give Thou me the pow'r,
To hold the hope securely
  Wrought by Thy dying hour,
And that with faith I may
  Draw from Thy fount o'erflowing
  The grace of Thy bestowing,
Forever, night and day!

Yet if anew I wander,
  Now here, now there, ah, then
Let me, dear Shepherd, ponder
  Thy faithfulness to men!
Yea, wake and stir Thou me,
  That I may not be turning,
  But for Thee may be yearning,
My Shepherd, ceaselessly!

DEVOTION 25

Christ Is Taken Captive and Bound

Mel.: Freu dich sehr, o meine Seele

Bonds of Jesus, I embrace you!
  Bind me also to my Lord.
Bonds of heaven! Those who trace you
  Find a wise and guiding cord;
Here's my Bridegroom's nuptial chain,
Cords that bind the Lamb once slain,
  Ropes to cordon off all error,
  Ribbons of the Trophy-bearer!

I should have been bound forever,
  But by you I am set free
From the tyrant and enslaver,
  Who would fain imprison me.
Praises to the King, who hath
For my sake been bound in wrath,
  Thereby me acquitted sending
  Into freedom never ending.

O ye bonds of Jesus, tie me
  To my Lord upon the Tree;
Let the world no joy supply me
  But be crucified to me.
O ye bonds, give strength to fight,
Brace me in life's little night
  Till, release from bonds receiving,
  I shall reign with all the living.

Thou hast put away my friends far from me; Thou hast made me an abomination unto them: I lie captive, and I cannot come forth.

Psalm 88:8

Then the band and the captain and officers of the Jews took Jesus, and bound Him, and led Him away to Annas first; for he was father-in-law to Caiaphas, which was the high priest that same year. Now Caiaphas was he which gave counsel to the Jews that it was expedient that one man should die for the people. And they led Him away to Caiaphas the high priest (that is, the prince of the priests), where all the chief priests and scribes and elders were assembled.

Matthew 26:57; Mark 14:53; Luke 22:54; John 18:12-14

Here begins the external suffering of the Lord Christ in His most holy body, and here is fulfilled what the patriarch Jacob prophesied, "Simeon and Levi—their swords are murderous weapons. O my soul, come not thou into their counsel; mine honor, be not thou in their assembly; for in their anger they slew a man" (Gen. 49:5-6).

First, we learn here the *patience* of the Lord Jesus, in that He, who never did wrong nor injured any man, but showed all good to every man, let Himself be taken captive and bound as an evildoer; so that one may justly be amazed that He could suffer these things, since He might easily have altered the circumstances, as He demonstrated His power before with a word. For it is the wicked and those who have deserved it that are customarily bound, not the honest (2 Sam. 3:34). The chief priests themselves should have been taken captive and bound, since they distorted the teaching of the divine Word, made the Temple a den of dealing, devoured widows' houses under the pretense of religion, and, insofar as they were able, even slew souls with their poisonous statutes. Publicans and usurers should have been taken captive and bound, who were a cause of all oppression and poverty in the people of God. Rogues and scoundrels should have been taken and bound, who at that time openly committed all manner of willful sins in the city of Jerusalem, such as unchastity, adultery, and murder, as Josephus writes of them. But as Shadrach, Meshach, and Abednego were innocently bound and cast into the fiery furnace (Dan. 3:20ff.) while the wicked went free throughout the kingdom, so was it also with the innocent Son of God. He was taken prisoner in the fiery wrath of God on account of our sin, that we might not be bound with chains of darkness and cast out into everlasting darkness.

Second, we are to ask ourselves here what *our own prison and bonds* were. This the church answers in her song:

> I captive to the devil lay,
>   By death of hope bereavèd;
> My sins distressed me night and day,
>   In which I was conceivèd;
> In them I ever deeper fell:
> Not one thing in my life was well,
>   For sin possessed me wholly.

Third, we see here that Christ, as the Lamb of God that bears the sin of the world, *was led bound to His killers* from the Mount of Olives down through the deep valley of Jehoshaphat and by the Sheep Gate into the city of Jerusalem, and was brought first to *Annas*, the father-in-law of Caiaphas. These things happened for the sake of honor, that He might merit thanks. For they all rejoiced at the fact that they had now caught the Nazarene, as the Philistines long before did to Samson and the Ark of God (Judges 16:23–24; 1 Sam. 5:1–2). Similarly, it happened on account of prejudice, for they desired that He should be recognized not by one only, but by many, as an evildoer deserving of death.

Thence they bring Him to *Caiaphas,* who was elevated to the high priestly office by the previous governor at the abdication of his predecessor, but afterward was removed by another, and Jonathan was appointed in his place. For at that time too, the ungodly turned *Gott* into *Gold* (God into gold) and *Geist* into *Geiz* (Spirit into greed). But St. John writes even more distinctly of the chief priest "that same year," Caiaphas, that it might be known what good Christ was to expect from him. For he had briefly counseled the Jews (John 11:49–50) that it would be expedient that one man should be slain for the people. "And this spake he not of himself," adds the evangelist, "but being high priest that year, he prophesied.

For Jesus was to die for that nation; and not for that nation only, but that also He should gather together in one the children of God that were scattered abroad." Chrysostom says, "This prophecy shows that these things happened for our sake, and the truth is so plain and clear that even the enemies prophesied concerning it. And this announcement is mentioned so that we may not take offense at the bonds of Christ, for the salvation of the world depends on the death of Christ."

But Theophylact shows that Caiaphas was not a true prophet, even though he said something true here, just as a man is not suddenly a physician or true doctor when he has once cured something or prepared a remedy. For God sometimes performs something even through wicked men, not to their salvation, to be sure, but that afterward they may have no excuse. It is in this way that Balaam's ass was made to speak (Num. 22:28).

Therefore the words of Caiaphas have two meanings. First, they mean that the high priest was himself opposed to the Lord Christ out of bitter hatred and envy, that is, that it would be conducive to them all if the Nazarene who caused so much unrest might be put to death once and for all, even though He is innocent. But second, the evangelist adds to this that God had another thing in view in the counsel of His eternal, divine Majesty, namely, that it was not only expedient, but also necessary that the Righteous should die for the unrighteous, that "He should gather together in one the children of God that were scattered abroad," and by this means bring them to God and enable them to enter into life everlasting. Thus is God able to turn to good the endeavors of the unbelieving, and here in particular that word holds true which Joseph spoke to his brothers: "Ye meant to do evil with me, but God meant to do good, that He might save much people alive, as it is this day" (Gen. 50:20). In this way, by the miraculous governance of God, even the counsel of wicked Caiaphas so served to advance the salutary sufferings of Christ and thus the salvation of mankind.

Prayer

O dearest Lord Jesus, I give Thee praise and thanks for Thy cords and bonds, for Thy chains and fetters, with which Thou didst suffer Thyself to be taken captive and bound! When I contemplate Thee in Thy bonds, O Lord Jesus, when I consider how unmercifully the bloodthirsty soldiers treated Thee, how one seized Thy holy arms, the other Thy holy feet, how one cast an iron chain about Thy throat, another constrained Thine innocent hands with cords, and how they led Thee cruelly out of the Garden up and down, over rocks and stones, till they brought Thee to Jerusalem through the Sheep Gate to Annas, and from Annas to Caiaphas—O my Lord Jesus, when I consider all these things, I am distraught, I am sorrowful, and mine eyes are filled with tears! Yet when I again call to mind the fact that Thy bonds are my comfort, Thy cords my redemption, Thy fetters my freedom, then my heart is cheered, my soul lives, and my mouth praises Thee. For Thou, Lord Jesus, art bound, and hast unbound me from the punishment of everlasting death. Thou art bound, and my soul is bound up in the bundle of the living. O blessed unbinding! O blessed binding up! As long as I am encompassed round about with the bonds of this mortal life, O Lord Jesus, grant me a free heart and a free tongue, that I may extol Thee with great boldness and take refuge in Thee in all anguish and adversity. Let me be bound to Thee, Lord Jesus, in upright godliness. Let me flee the sinful cords of wickedness and shun the works of darkness. O Lord Jesus, Thou hast set me free: preserve me, I pray, in Thy freedom, and bring me to everlasting glory! Amen, Lord Jesus! Amen.

Mel.: Jesu, der du meine Seele

By the bonds that once restrained Thee,
  From the devil set me free;
Let the ridicule that pained Thee
  Be my crown and majesty.
Balm of souls, and earth's Salvation!
Save me from humiliation.
  Let Thy Passion's agony
  Not have been in vain for me.

DEVOTION 26

Peter Denies the Lord for the First Time

Mel.: Jesu, du Gottes Lämmelein

O Jesus, dearest Lamb of God,
  How deep the wounds that fill us!
Pour by Thy Word Thy precious blood
  Into us now and heal us!

So we, Thy bitter agony
  In true faith having claimèd,
In cross and woe may follow Thee,
  Of Thy cross unashamèd.

For this our hearts we ready yield
  To hear Thy holy Passion;
Therein be by Thy Spirit sealed
  These words for our salvation!

For Thy sake do I bear reproach. My face is filled with shame. I am become a stranger unto my brethren, and unknown to my mother's children.
Psalm 69:7–8

And Simon Peter followed Jesus afar off, and so did another disciple: that disciple was known unto the high priest, and went in with Jesus into the palace of the high priest. But Peter stood at the door without. Then went out that other disciple, which was known unto the high priest, and spake unto her that kept the door, and brought in Peter. And the servants and officers stood there, who had made a fire of coals beneath in the midst of the palace; for it was cold: and they warmed themselves: and Peter stood with them, and warmed himself, to see the end. But the maid of the high priest, the damsel that kept the door, saw Peter by the light, that he was warming himself, and earnestly looked upon him, and said, And thou also wast with Jesus of Galilee; art not thou also one of this Man's disciples? But he denied before them all, saying, Woman, I am not, I know Him not, neither understand I what thou sayest.

Matthew 26:58, 69–70; Mark 14:54, 66–68;
Luke 22:54–57; John 18:15–18, 25

Peter heartily loved Christ, as he himself says, "Lord, Thou knowest all things, Thou knowest that I love Thee heartily." Therefore he follows Him from afar into the palace of the high priest, accompanying another disciple, who in Theophylact's opinion was St. John. There he stands by the charcoal fire to warm himself, since it was somewhat brisk and chilly at night, and desires to see how this curious business will turn out. Now, before he is properly warmed, the high priest's damsel keeping the door comes up to him, looks closely at his face, and says, "And thou also wast with Jesus of Galilee; art not thou also one of this Man's disciples?" From that hour Peter loses all courage and openly denies it, saying, "Woman, I am not, I know Him not, neither understand I what thou sayest."

Here begins the fall of Peter, which all the evangelists describe carefully, not in order to censure their fellow apostle, but to remind us what an evil it is not to cling wholly and utterly to God, and rather to trust in oneself.

Therefore we see here what miserable creatures and fragile vessels we are. Oh, how quickly the crafty devil with his thousand arts may trip a man and make him fall if God withdraws a little His hand of grace! "A great saint has seldom come into heaven whose feet Satan has not first befouled," says Luther. Did not Adam and Eve reside in a glorious estate? Yet Satan ran up to them and brought them to a fall. Who was a better preacher of repentance than Noah? Yet when he was surprised by a merry drink, he initiated a great offense in his youngest son, Ham. Who was holier than Lot in Sodom? But in what a terrible sin Satan cast him, that he should in drunken manner commit incest with his daughters! Was Aaron not a well-regarded high priest among the people of God? But what an offense he caused in the wilderness with the molten calf! Who was more pleasing to God than the tremendous, wonder-working prophet, Moses, who spoke with Him as one friend with another. Yet Moses committed the sin of unbelief. Was David not a man after God's own heart and will? Yet he blinded himself in unchaste flames of love for the beautiful Bathsheba and allowed himself to be brought into adultery and murder. Who was wiser than Solomon, to whom God appeared several times and in whose heart the Holy Spirit dwelt? Yet he let himself be brought so far by the coaxing words of his idolatrous wives that he wandered after strange gods, built them high places, and opened the floodgates to idolatry for those that came after him. Elijah, the precious man of God, by his prayer shut the heavens and opened them again; he called down fire from above, kindling his sacrifice and giving public testimony to his teaching. And yet afterward in persecution, he despaired of the help of God and preservation of the church, thought no preacher was left in the land, and longed for death. Who was more blameless than Job, to whom the Lord Himself gave testimony that there is none like him in godliness in all the land? Yet he falls into sin and impatience, and even curses the day of his birth. In short: "For (the forgiveness of sins) shall all the saints pray unto Thee, O God, in a seasonable time" (Ps. 32:6). "Men are nothing, the great err also; they weigh less than nothing, as much of them as there is" (Ps. 62:9). "Even the righteous falleth seven times a day" (Prov. 24:16). "What is man, when God withdraws a little His hand of grace? Nothing else than what Peter was when he denied Christ," says Augustine.

Therefore, dear man, do not go too near the devil through self-security, but hate and shun *all occasion to sin. Do not ally yourself with the wicked,* lest in their company you suffer a fall; for "he that toucheth pitch defileth himself," says Sirach (13:1). "If thy neighbor erreth, laugh not, nor rejoice at his misfortune" (Prov. 24:17). Let the fall of the great be the terror of the lesser. "Let a wise man not glory in his wisdom, nor a mighty man in his might, nor a rich man in his riches. But let him that will glory, glory in this, that he understandeth and knoweth God, who exerciseth lovingkindness, judgment, and righteousness in the earth" (Jer. 9:23–24). "Whoever thinketh that he standeth, let him take heed, lest he fall" (1 Cor. 10:12). Do not be presumptuous, do not trust or build upon your own powers! Always remember the words of Christ, "Apart from Me, ye can do nothing" (John 15:5). Whoever sings the song of victory early in the battle is commonly defeated. Live in constant fear of God and humble yourself under the mighty hand of God. Serve the Lord with fear and trembling, sigh and pray daily, "Create in me a clean heart, O God, and give me a new, certain spirit. O LORD God, show me Thy ways, and teach me Thy paths. Lead me in Thy truth and teach me, for Thou art the God that savest me. I wait upon Thee daily. O keep my soul, and deliver me; let me not be ashamed, for I put my trust in Thee!" (Ps. 51:10; 25:4–5, 20).

Prayer

O Lord Jesus, to what end Peter's presumption brings him! Into what straits his impudence casts him! He could have remained outside the court of the high priest; he had no business within. But he thinks he must go in, and goes in, and falls into terrible sin. O Lord Jesus, guard me from these two trespasses—presumption and impudence—for they are commonly the first cause of greater trespasses. Let me also flee with all diligence the wicked company of the ungodly, that I may not be led astray by them, as happened to Thy disciple Peter when he mingled among the wicked servants, ministers, and attendants of Thine enemies! O my Lord Jesus, Peter warmed himself at the charcoal fire, and it proved to his greater harm! His hands and feet were warmed, but his heart was chilled and his light of faith was extinguished. So when the world shows me an alluring sight, when it wishes to lead me away from Thee and the acknowledged truth by the hope of great honor and dignity, by promises of great goods and riches, then keep me with Thee, I pray, and grant that I may firmly and stoutly resist them! Let me far rather follow Thy faithful servant Moses, who, although he could have been rich and respected at the Egyptian court, regarded Thy disgrace as greater riches than the treasures of Egypt, for he looked to the reward which Thou didst promise to those who persevere with Thee to the end! O my Lord Jesus, grant that I too may likewise persevere inseparably with Thee, that I may not suffer any harm to my soul, but may keep it safe from the flames of hell by Thy strength and assistance. Amen, Lord Jesus! Amen.

Mel.: Werde Licht, du Stadt der Heiden
Or: Herr, ich habe mißgehandelt

Oh, what are we without Jesus?
  Needy, mis'rable, and poor!
What are we, but wholly wretched?
  Lord, have mercy, we implore!
As in trouble we are lying,
Kindly hear our pray'r and sighing!

Without Thee, most precious Jesus,
  From this world none may escape.
Every path is pure temptation,
  Every step, a tangling trap;
How it boasts of all its treasures
And ensnares us in its pleasures!

Therefore help us, dearest Jesus,
  In our darkness be our light;
Make our spirit's eyes unblinded,
  Bring Thy kindly face to sight;
Gleam, O Sun, where sin hath stricken,
Send Thy beams, our hearts to quicken!

DEVOTION 27

Jesus Defends His Innocence and Receives a Blow on the Cheek

Mel.: Freu dich sehr, o meine Seele

Jesus stands while cruel fetter
   Binds the hand that framed the world,
Now around Him mockings bitter,
   Laughter, and contempt are hurled.
Heathen rage and Jewish scorn,
Meekly for our sins are borne.
   Precious drops of blood He sheddeth,
   Jesus now the winepress treadeth.

Can we view the Savior given
   To the smiters' hands for us?
Who can stand, unmoving even,
   And behold Him slighted thus?
Jesus standeth in our stead,
All that man hath merited
   Jesus payeth, and endureth
   What the sinner's sin procureth.

They thrust sore at me that I might fall, but the LORD *helpeth me. — For Thy sake do I bear reproach. My face is filled with shame. I set my face like a flint, for I know that I shall not be ashamed.*

Psalm 118:13; 69:7; Isaiah 50:7

The high priest then asked Jesus of His disciples and of His doctrine. Jesus answered him, I spake openly to the world; I ever taught in the synagogue and in the Temple, whither the Jews always resort; and in secret have I said nothing. Why askest thou Me? Ask them which heard Me, what I have said unto them; behold, they know what I said. And when He had thus spoken, one of the officers which stood by gave Jesus a blow on the cheek, saying, Shouldest Thou answer the high priest so? Jesus answered him, If I have spoken evil, bear witness of the evil: but if well, why smitest thou Me? Now Annas had sent Him bound unto Caiaphas the high priest.

John 18:19–24

Caiaphas the high priest asks Jesus about His disciples and His doctrine not only to blame Him for disrupting and undermining their church order, but also in this manner more quickly to find a cause of death, since a false prophet had to be punished with death. For we know that no one is to presume to take up the preaching office unless he be regularly called thereto (Heb. 5:4). Therefore God also terribly punished Korah and his faction because they arrogated to themselves the office to which Aaron and his sons had been elevated (Num. 16). Yet Caiaphas and his clergy had come to sit in Moses' seat by means of bribes and gifts, as Joseph explicitly reports. Thus he holds an utterly evil trial with Christ, the likes of which are not found among any reasonable pagans. For as a religious leader he ought to have known that Christ did not put Himself into honor, but that God the heavenly Father said to Him, "Thou art My Son; this day have I begotten Thee" (Ps. 2:7). Again: "Thou art a Priest forever after the order of Melchizedek" (Ps. 110:4). He should have first come himself to the preaching of the Lord Christ before he undertook to overrule the eternal Wisdom of God. He already had Jesus taken captive and bound as an evildoer; only now does he inquire into what He has done or whether He is the Lamb that muddied the wolf's water—to say nothing of his playing accuser, judge, and all things on behalf of his party. Yet Christ endured this for our sake. For our first parents had risen up against God and had departed from His Word. Therefore, that Christ may make satisfaction for this sin, which was passed down to all their offspring by carnal birth, He lets himself be accused of sedition and of falling away from the Word.

But because Christ answers the question of the high priest by saying that He has neither taught false doctrine nor caused rebellion with His disciples, we learn from His example that we are to be ready to give an answer to every man that asks the reason for the hope that is in us, even if we should come into extreme danger as a result (1 Peter 3:15–16). For first, Christ desires to be known openly before the world, most of all where confession is demanded in the time of persecution. As He teaches us in Matthew 10:32–33: "Whosoever confesseth Me before men, him will I confess also before My heavenly Father. But whosoever denieth Me before men, him will I also deny before My heavenly Father." Thus it is also certainly worthwhile for us to give up all things for His sake, and willingly and in all patience to bear all things, in view of the rich reward that shall come in heaven to all who have endured scorn and persecution for Christ's name (Matt. 5:11–12). It does no good, then, for a Christian to think to himself, "I will believe in my heart whatever I can, but I will not let it be known." Rather, our motto is to be: "I believe, therefore do I speak" (Ps. 116:10), and: "If a man believeth from the heart, he is justified, and if a man confesseth with the mouth, he is saved" (Rom. 10:10). The idea is not that oral confession is the cause or merit of salvation, but that by it one can discern as with an indubitable sign what is living faith. For when a Christian is so fearless that he can confess his Savior before the world even in time of persecution, it follows irrefutably from this that true faith must be present, which justifies here and saves in heaven. In the gospel lesson of the four different kinds of seed, it is said that some believe for a while, but in time of tribulation they fall away, because they were not rooted in faith. A man's faith may be weak under persecution, yet he is to be so rooted that he confesses with his mouth in the daylight what his heart believes in secret; to this then is added prayer and sighing, as we sing with the church:

> Lord, by Thy pow'r prepare our heart,
> To flesh's weakness strength impart
>   That here we may fight valiantly,
>   And press through death and life to Thee.

Now therefore, although Christ answers the high priest's questions with all meekness, nevertheless one of the servants standing there gives Him a blow to the cheek, saying, "Shouldest Thou answer the high priest so?" And this was a quite exceptional disgrace and piteous act of wickedness which was done to the Lord here; for not only does the servant strike Jesus without the judge's command, and an innocent and bound Man at that, but here the Most High is struck by the lowest, God by the sinner, the Creator by the creature, the faithful Savior by him whom He would redeem! Therefore Chrysostom cries out here, "Heaven and earth shake and tremble at the patience of Christ and the shamelessness of the servant." And Augustine says, "If we consider who He is who received the blow, would we not desire that he who struck Him were either consumed with fire from heaven or swallowed up by the earth or possessed by the evil one and cast about hither and thither, or visited with some other and indeed heavier punishment? For the Lord could have certainly done all these things by His power and might, through which the world was made, if He had not much more desired to model and teach us that patience through which the world is overcome." Through this great reproach, when He is struck on the cheek as if an ungodly and dishonorable man, the Lord Christ gained us the power to be forever unashamed. As He Himself says, "Let not them that wait on Thee, O Lord, the LORD of Sabaoth, be ashamed for My sake; let not those that seek Thee be confounded for My sake, O God of Israel. For Thy sake do I bear reproach; My face is filled with shame" (Ps. 69:6–7).

But although Christ bears this reproach in the most patient manner, He nevertheless holds up before the servant his ungodly act, saying, "If I have spoken evil, bear witness of the evil; but if well, why smitest thou Me?" From this we learn that while we are *to suffer* evil, we are *not to endorse* it, lest the wicked be confirmed in their wickedness. Therefore those who suffer wrong are free to demonstrate their innocence and, where necessary and possible, to call on the authorities. Luther says, "The tongue must be distinguished from the hand." The hand is to be bound and not to take up personal revenge, but the tongue is to be free to make a defense. Yet this defense must be done with gentleness according to the example of Christ, "who, when He was reviled, reviled not again; when He suffered, He threatened not; but committed Himself to Him that judgeth righteously" (1 Peter 2:23).

Prayer

Most gracious Lord Jesus, Thou smitten Rock out of whom waters flowed for My consolation, Thou holy Man of Sorrows, who wast tormented and beaten for My sake, that in great mercy the scattered flock might be gathered together again: Thou didst suffer Thy most holy cheek to be smitten, that I might go unsmitten for my sin. Now I know that, because of the harsh blow given Thee, Thy heavenly Father will deny me no request. Yea, I know in faith that I will not be sent to hell because of the wrath of my Judge, since Thou hast borne my guilt and abundantly atoned for my punishment and shame. But if the messenger of Satan must buffet me, I will not waver, but will suffer the blows with patience; for those which Thou didst suffer for me were far more painful. Thou didst suffer innocently, and I am only paying what is owed by my guilt, and am beaten and whipped because of my own great sin. Yet shouldst Thou smite me, my Savior, smite me with kindness; it shall benefit me, as balm upon my head (Ps. 141:5). Thy blows are blows of love and serve for my good. Only grant me a contrite heart on account of my sins, and let me gladly suffer and endure all reproach with Thee, if necessary, that I may one day also enjoy that glory in heaven which Thou hast won for me through all Thy disgrace. Amen.

Mel.: Herzliebster Jesu, was hast du verbrochen

Praise be to Thee, Lord Jesus, dearest Savior!
Thou hast displayed to me true love and favor,
   In love Thou lett'st Thyself of life be drainèd,
     And deeply painèd.

Willing all bonds and bitter scorn to suffer,
Thou dost Thy face to blows and spitting offer,
   Turning my shame to highest celebration,
     And consolation.

Fitting return of thanks in heav'n I'll sing Thee;
Poor is the best that I today can bring Thee!
   There for Thy proofs of love I will endeavor
     To praise Thee ever.

DEVOTION 28

Peter Denies Again, but Repents

Mel.: Herr, ich habe mißgehandelt

Lord, to Thee I make confession,
  I have sinned and gone astray,
I have multiplied transgression,
  Chosen for myself my way.
Led by Thee to see my errors,
I would hide me from Thy terrors.

But from Thee how can I hide me?
  Thou, O God, art everywhere.
Refuge from Thee is denied me,
  Both by land and sea and air;
Nor could shades of death enfold me
So that Thou shouldst not behold me.

Yet, though conscience' voice appall me,
  Father, I will seek Thy face;
Though Thy child I dare not call me,
  Yet receive me to Thy grace;
Do not for my sins forsake me;
Let not yet Thy wrath o'ertake me.

Weep, oh, weep at God's displeasure,
  Ye mine eyes, a river broad!
Oh, that I had tears in measure
  To bemoan my shameful load;
Oh, that from these wells unwilling
I might stronger streams be spilling!

DEVOTION 28

I will seek that which was lost, and bring again that which went astray, and will bind up that which was wounded, and will attend to that which was weak: and what is fat and strong I will protect, and will care for them, as is just.

Ezekiel 34:16

And Simon Peter stood and warmed himself. And a little after the first denial, when he was gone out into the porch, the cock crew. And another maid saw him, and began to say to them that stood by, This one also was with Jesus of Nazareth. They said therefore unto him, Art not thou also one of His disciples? And another said, Thou art one of them. And again he denied with an oath, saying, Man, I am not, nor do I know the Man. And about the space of one hour after another confidently affirmed with them that stood by, and said, Surely thou also art one of them; for thou art a Galilaean, and thy speech bewrayeth thee. One of the servants of the high priest, being his kinsman whose ear Peter cut off, saith, Did not I see thee in the Garden with Him? Then began he to curse and to swear, saying, I know not the Man of whom ye speak. And immediately, while he yet spake, the cock crew the second time. And the Lord turned, and looked upon Peter. And Peter remembered the word of the Lord, how He had said unto him, Before the cock crow twice, thou shalt deny me thrice. And he went out, and wept bitterly.

Matthew 26:71–75; Mark 14:69–72; Luke 22:58–62; John 18:18–27

It was not a simple and insignificant fall, but a great and serious one, which Peter suffered not only once but thrice. And he denied Christ, with whom he had been ready to go into death, not with simple words, but invoking the name of God and cursing himself. Yet since the Lord looks not with unkind expression, but with the eyes of His mercy, Peter is consoled, knowing that the good and faithful Savior will not cast him away (as He also causes him to be told immediately after His joyous resurrection, and then Himself appears and comforts him). And although Peter knows that Christ said, "Whosoever denieth Me before men, him will I also deny before My heavenly Father" (Matt. 10:33), yet he takes comfort in the fact that this thundering word is directed only against those who do not repent before they leave this world. Bishop Marcellinus of Rome, through the threat of the Emperor Diocletian, also allowed himself to be persuaded to burn incense to the pagan idols; but he immediately examined himself again and became a public penitent and holy martyr. "I look upon the needy, and him that is broken in spirit, and that feareth My Word," says God (Isa. 66:20). Therefore no Christian who has suffered a fall should despair as though, after he has been taken up into the covenant of God but has fallen out of grace again, he cannot come back into God's grace after that fall, as the Novatians and Cathars claimed, for which reason Novatus* was not unjustly called "an enemy of mercy, a murderer of penitence, a corrupter of the truth, and a betrayer of love." Emperor Constantine, however, speaking to someone of the same mind as Novatus at the Council of Nicaea, said very courteously, "Pray, lean a ladder on heaven and climb up by thyself." In Ezekiel 33, God makes a lofty affirmation and swears by His own holiness that He does not desire the death of the ungodly, but that the ungodly should turn from his ways and live; and Peter writes, "God hath patience with us and will not that any man should be lost, but that every man should turn to repentance" (2 Peter 3:9).

But because Peter first turns to repentance when the Lord turns and looks at him, we see from this that true repentance and conversion are a work solely of God, and specifically a work of His goodness and mercy. Hence Augustine also says very admirably, "We need mercy not only *when* we repent, but also *that we may be able* to repent." The cockcrow was a reminder to Peter of his fall and an exhortation to repentance. But by it he would not have come to repentance if Christ had not looked at him. "Turn Thou me, and I shall be turned; for Thou art the LORD my God. Surely after that I was turned, I repented" (Jer. 31:18–19). "Him hath God exalted with His right hand to be a Prince and a Savior, for to give repentance to Israel, and forgiveness of sins" (Acts 5:31). Therefore we have from Christ not only forgiveness of sins, but also repentance and conversion, in which we can go—as He also commands us—to preach in His name "repentance and forgiveness of sins among all nations" (Luke 24:47). Therefore we are to pray from our heart with the blessed saints of old, "Lord Jesus Christ, look upon me, a

---

* Novatus or Novatianus, a minister of the church in Rome about the middle of the third century, refused to admit to the fellowship of the church any longer those who had fallen away. His adherents called themselves Cathars, that is, the pure.

poor sinner, with the eyes of Thy mercy, with which Thou didst look upon Peter in the palace, upon Mary Magdalene at the banquet, and upon the thief on the cross. Grant me also, O God Almighty, with Peter to weep heartily, with Mary Magdalene to love Thee truly, and with the penitent thief to see Thee eternally."

Neither should any man think that because conversion is a work of God, he must therefore drop his hands and feet and despise the means ordained by God. Far be it! For God has directed us, one and all, to the regular preaching office, where we are to hear what God's ordained ministers proclaim from His Word, and not perilously to put off repentance at their cry and preaching of repentance, lest Christ turn His face from us, withdraw His hand from us, and leave us to sink into destruction. "Today if ye will hear His voice, harden not your heart" (Ps. 95:7–8). "Repent, and believe the Gospel" (Mark 1:15). We are to weep bitterly with Peter; there are to be no hypocritical tears of Esau, nor the slippery appearance of Ahaz, but they are all to flow from a contrite heart (Ps. 6:6–8). This is that godly sorrow that "worketh repentance to salvation not to be repented of" (2 Cor. 7:10). The tears of sinners are the wine and gladness of the angels.

However, we are not to be content simply with weeping and lamenting, but with Peter to remember the words of Jesus, which He speaks to all: "Come unto Me, all ye that are weary and heavy-laden; I will refresh you. Whosoever cometh to Me, him will I not cast out." Surely from the comforting words of the Lord Christ, and particularly the words: "I have prayed for thee, that thy faith fail not," which now fall on his heart anew, and in addition from His gracious face and expression, the dear apostle is given firm and certain confidence that he will find forgiveness for the sake of Christ's suffering. This is to look back at Christ in Word and Sacrament by true faith in the power of the Holy Ghost, who is active through such means, and with believing confidence to say within oneself, "I believe in the forgiveness of sins."

After this there belongs the fruit of repentance, namely, a new, godly life; for Peter does not remain in the palace of Caiaphas, but flees the courtyard in which he denied Christ. He flees the servants and the damsel that kept the door, which gave him occasion to sin. He can no longer stay in the darkness while the light of divine grace gazes upon him and the light of faith has been kindled in him. "To shun sin is to shun the occasion for sin."

Prayer

O my Lord Jesus, though I have turned away from Thee, yet turn, I beseech Thee, Thy countenance of grace to me! Though I have often and sorely forgotten Thee, yet remember me for good before Thy heavenly Father! Oh, that my eyes were fountains of tears to mourn my sins which I have committed with great delight and desire! Oh, that my feet, that have stood in the way of sinners, might speedily turn back! Oh, that my mouth, that has often and sorely denied and spoken against Thee, might confess Thee steadfastly unto the shedding of my blood! Now, Lord Jesus, there is nothing else to say but this: Though I have, alas, been like Peter in his sin, I will also seek to become like him in his repentance. The strength and means for this Thou alone must bestow by Thy grace, and that wilt Thou certainly do. Amen. Amen.

Mel.: Mein Heiland nimmt die Sünder an

How love-filled was His tender look
  When Peter's deep-dyed sin He pondered!
Ah, not alone this course He took
  When in this vale of tears He wandered;
Eternal love is still the same,
The Friend of sinners is His name.
  As on the cross His love was given,
  Thus from His glorious throne in heaven
He gives to sinners kind reprieve:
My Savior sinners doth receive:
My Savior sinners doth receive.

DEVOTION 28

O come, then, child of sinful men,
  Come well thy griefs and sorrows knowing;
Approach the One who knew no sin,
  And stoops to sinners, lowly bowing!
What, wilt thou stand in judgment's light
And perish without heart contrite?
  Wilt thou let sin and hell enslave thee
  When Christ is manifest to save thee?
Oh nay, sin's erring byways leave!—
My Savior sinners doth receive:
My Savior sinners doth receive.

DEVOTION 29

Jesus Is Silent at the False Testimony against Him

Mel.: Jesu, der du meine Seele

Do Thy silence not refuse me:
  Jesus, let it plead my cause,
When my sin and guilt accuse me,
  Ever pointing to Thy laws—
When my conscience, full of evil,
Cries and threatens hell and devil.
  Let Thy Passion's agony
  Not have been in vain for me!

O God, my Praise, hold not Thy peace; for they have opened their wicked mouth and deceitful lips against me, and they speak against me with a lying tongue; and they speak poisonously against me on every side, and fight against me without a cause. For my love to them they are my adversaries; but I make supplication. — Make their tongues divided, O Lord, *and let them be destroyed. — And as for me, Thou upholdest me because of mine integrity, and settest me before Thy face forever.*

Psalm 109:1–4; 55:9; 41:12

Now the chief priests, and elders, and all the council, sought for false witness against Jesus, to put Him to death, and found none; yea, though many false witnesses came, yet their witness agreed not together. At the last there arose and came two false witnesses, and bare false witness against Him, saying, We heard Him say, I am able to, and will, destroy the Temple of God that is made with hands, and within three days I will build another made without hands. But neither so did their witness agree together. And the high priest stood up in the midst, and asked Jesus, saying, Answerest

DEVOTION 29

Thou nothing to that which these witness against Thee? But Jesus held His peace, and answered nothing.

Matthew 26:59–63; Mark 14:55–61

The leaders of the Jews had long decided to put the Lord Christ to death. But because they knew that in the Law, God had commanded matters in court to be handled with *witnesses* (Num. 35:30; Deut. 17:6; 19:15), and because the Word of Christ to the servant, "Bear witness of the evil," had struck their heart, and because they feared that they and their suit would be referred before Pilate if they could not prove it by means of witnesses, therefore they *sought* witnesses. But being unable to find any *true* witnesses against Christ, they take *false* witnesses, which of course was an abominable transgression that God had commanded the priests and judges to punish severely (Deut. 19:16–20). But although various witnesses are brought forward, they disagree one with another, and it will by no means hold water, and they have no chance to succeed with them. The more the adversaries toil to lay blame on Christ by false witnesses, the clearer His innocence shines, since the witnesses do not agree.

Finally, the wicked villains suppose they will find support from His own sermon which He preached on the first feast of the Passover concerning the tearing down of the Temple (John 2:19), by *twisting* His words, since He neither said that *He* would tear it down, nor that this temple which they would tear down but He would build up was made *with hands*." Likewise, they misconstrue His words as though He were speaking against the house and sanctuary of God, and was to die on account of it, despite the fact that He had thereby referred to the temple of His own body (John 2:21), in which the whole fullness of the Godhead dwelleth bodily (Col. 2:9). Therefore it was open slander and palpable falsehood. For the words of Christ are clear: "Tear down this temple, and on the third day I will raise it up." This the high priests and Pharisees themselves understood of His resurrection, for afterward they mocked Him while He hung on the cross with the words: "Aha, how well Thou destroyest the Temple and buildest it up in three days! Save Thyself, if Thou art the Son of God!" and finally when they said to Pilate after His death, "Lord, we remember that this deceiver said while He yet lived, I will rise after three days," etc. In such manner also the Jews twisted and misconstrued the words of the prophet Jeremiah long before, when they said, "This man is worthy of death, for he hath prophesied against this city, as ye have heard with your own ears," whereas the prophet had only threatened the city and temple with God's judgment if they would not repent (Jer. 26:4ff.). Likewise, they did the same with Stephen later in the New Testament, when they accused him falsely with the words, "This man ceaseth not to speak blasphemous words against this holy place, and the Law; for we have heard him say that this Jesus of Nazareth shall destroy this place and shall change the customs which Moses gave us." (Acts 6:13–14).

Therefore we are to flee and shun all manner of lies and false witness. For sometimes (to thwart the bloodthirsty assaults of the ungodly against the godly) someone may well withhold the truth and remain silent toward those who misuse it to put down the innocent, as may be seen in the midwives in Egypt, Rahab, Jonathan, Saul's son, David's friend Hushai, and others. Yet concerning other lies, we are to keep ourselves from them as from the devil himself. For a lie does not spring from God, who is the eternal, unchangeable truth, but from the devil, who is a liar from the beginning, and the father of lies (John 8:44). Rather, God's judgment is clear: "Thou destroyest him that speaketh leasing; the Lord abhorreth the bloody and deceitful man" (Ps. 5:6). Again: "A false witness shall not be unpunished, and he that speaketh lies shall not escape" (Prov. 19:5).

Our dear Lord Christ willed to endure for us this injustice of false accusations. It was not one of the least parts of His suffering that He had to hear these lies and false accusations against Him, which He also laments in Psalm 27:12; 35:11; 69:12. Yet He willed to burden Himself with false accusations for our sake, to free us from the true and well-founded accusations which the Law (John 5:45), the testimony of our own conscience (Col. 2:14; 1 John 3:20; Rom. 2:15), Satan (Rev. 10:12; Luke 22:31), and all creation (Rom. 8:22; Heb. 2:11; James 5:3–4) bring against us. Now therefore, because Christ endured those false accusations against Him to free us from the true accusations, we also ought to shout joyfully with St. Paul, "Who will charge God's elect? God is here, who justifieth. Who will condemn? Christ is here, who died, yea rather, who is risen again, who is at the right hand of God and maketh intercession for us" (Rom. 8:33–34).

DEVOTION 29

What then does Christ do after such lies and false accusations? He holds His peace, yet not only because they are not worthy of His response, but also because He wished by His silence *to atone for the babbling and chattering of our mouth.* Our first parents not only failed to keep silent when they were rightly accused by God on account of their sins, but even laid the blame on others and portrayed themselves as innocent, yea, finally put it on God Himself, as if He were the cause. Therefore Christ must here be as a deaf man and not hear, and as a dumb man that openeth not his mouth, and must be as a man that heareth not, and in whose mouth are no reproofs (Ps. 38:13–14).

But He also wished to give us an example, that we might follow in His steps. Therefore, even if it is bitter when all manner of lies are spoken against us, and especially when our right and well-meaning words are wickedly perverted and distorted, yet after Christ's example we are to hold our peace and, by letting hearing pass for speaking, to cut off the blasphemers' occasion to slander or blaspheme further; and in the process, we are to take comfort in the example of Christ and the testimony of a good conscience. But when we note that our answer may redound to the glory of God and the confirmation of the truth and the edification of our neighbor, above all when our confession is demanded of us, we ought boldly to open our mouth, as we shall soon see in Christ.

Prayer

Yes, my Lord Jesus, so it must be! The testimonies of the false witnesses which stood up against Thee and perverted the sense of Thy holy words could not agree; for otherwise Thine innocence would not have been made so well known, nor Thy righteousness so manifest. O Lord Jesus, I thank Thee that, although Thou wast innocent, yet Thou didst present Thyself as one guilty, and as a sinner, before an unjust court. Oh, purge my guilt by Thy guiltlessness, purge my unrighteousness by Thy righteousness, purge my manifold sins and transgressions by Thy holiness, and let me one day be found holy, righteous, and innocent before Thy just tribunal! Yet I also thank Thee for Thy holy silence, by which Thou hast atoned for my sinful utterance, and by which Thou hast obtained for me the ability to cry, "Abba, dear Father!" here, and to have joyful converse with Thee and all the elect hereafter. O Lord Jesus, teach me with Thy silence to be patient, and under cross and trial, disgrace and mockery, blasphemy and lies of wicked lips, not to murmur against Thee, but to be strong through silence and hope! I will hold my peace in all that speech by which I might sin against Thee or my neighbor, and will vow to Thee with David, "I have resolved that I may not sin with my tongue; I will bridle my mouth" (Ps. 39:1). Yet grant, O Lord Jesus, that I may not be silent in the defense of heavenly truth! When it concerns my own honor, I will gladly hold my peace, but when others will attack Thine honor, then will I speak with a hundred tongues, and pray the Holy Spirit to grant me a golden mouth, an angel's tongue, and fiery lips like Isaiah. Oh, Lord Jesus, for now I must frequently hold my peace and swallow my grief; but hereafter in eternity I will open my mouth all the more, glorify Thy name, and give thanks to Thee with a new song forever and ever! Amen.

Mel.: Schwing dich auf zu deinem Gott

In Christ's innocence I boast,
  His right is my glory,
Mine His merit, there I trust
  As in stronghold hoary,
That the rage of every foe
  Evermore resisteth,
Though the might of hell below
  It to storm assisteth.

Now upon this holy ground
  Build I most securely,
See how hell's malicious hound,
  Spends 'gainst me his fury.
He can never overthrow
  What God hath upraisèd,
But what Satan's hand doth do
  That shall be abasèd.

DEVOTION 30

Christ Is Condemned to Death as a Blasphemer

Mel.: Wie schön leucht uns der Morgenstern

God's Son from all eternity!
How blessèd for humanity
  The time when men could view Thee!
Their eyes were filled with glory's sight,
Their ears were filled with love's true light;
  How glad they were who knew Thee!
Many, many,
  Pow'rs majestic,
  Seers prophetic
Sight desirèd,
Which the Twelve with hope inspirèd.

Yet, oh, how brief that moment here
When that great Light was shining near
  In flesh, with gaze astounding!
Soon, said the Lord, soon shall it be
When ye no more this face shall see,
  With light and love abounding;
Soon I must die,
  Pain must suffer,
  Self must offer,
Deathward going,
For your sins chastisement knowing.

(continued)

Be praised, O Jesus, Lamb of God,
  Who first upon the wrathful rod
The serpent's head hast broken;
  Thy wounds spring up a heav'nly flow'r,
Thy resurrection is the pow'r
On which my pray'r is spoken.
With Thee in me,
  Warfare waging,
  Satan's raging,
Sin, damnation—
Conquered lie in ruination.

Mine enemies speak evil of me: When shall he die, and his name perish? . . . They have devised mischief for me: When he lieth, he shall rise up no more.— The Stone which the builders refused is become the cornerstone. This is done by the LORD, *and is a marvelous thing in our eyes.*

Psalm 41:5, 7–8; 118:22–23

Again the high priest asked, and said unto Him, Art Thou the Christ, the Son of the Most Blessed? I adjure Thee by the living God, that Thou tell us whether Thou be the Christ, the Son of God. Jesus said, Thou sayest it, I am. Nevertheless I say unto you, Hereafter shall ye see the Son of Man sitting on the right hand of power, and coming in the clouds of heaven. Then the high priest rent his clothes, saying, He hath blasphemed; what further need have we of witnesses? Behold, now ye have heard His blasphemy, what think ye? And they all condemned Him and said, He is guilty of death!

Matthew 26:63–66; Mark 14:61–64

Here we see how Christ is condemned to death before and by the Sanhedrin. When Caiaphas, the hopeless scoundrel, perceives that the false witnesses are not holding up, and the Lord declines to answer for Himself, behold, he rises himself, acts as though the glory of God were most important to him, and says, "Art Thou the Christ, the Son of the Most Blessed?" Yea, he immediately adds the most solemn oath, "I abjure Thee by the living God, that Thou tell us whether Thou be the Christ, the Son of God." The words have a great appearance, but the heart is deceitful. Caiaphas thinks, "If He says Yea, I will condemn Him to death, for there is only one God. If He says Nay, He must die all the same, for He hath given out before that He is the Son of God. Even if He holds His peace, He is guilty of death, for He despiseth God and the high priest which abjureth Him in the name of the divine and blessed Majesty to tell the truth."

What then does Christ do? Because He is so gravely exhorted by the glory of His heavenly Father, and "to this end He was born, and for this cause came He into the world, that He should bear witness unto the truth" (John 18:37), He can no longer refrain, and makes a beautiful confession, though His life is at stake. "Yea," He says, "Thou sayest it: I am He after whom Thou inquirest. Though I now stand before your eyes in this poor form, and must live by your grace, yet know this: Ye shall certainly see Me sitting on the right hand of the power of God and coming in the clouds of heaven, as the appointed Judge of the quick and the dead. Look well with whom ye have to deal, be warned of temporal and eternal harm." But when did the Pharisees and chief priests see Christ seated on the right hand of the power of God? When He says they shall see Him "hereafter," this refers to the whole state of Christ's exaltation, which began immediately after His resurrection, in which Christ "was demonstrated mightily as the Son of God" (Rom. 1:4). And after the glorious ascension into heaven, when the Holy Ghost was poured out abundantly upon the apostles, Christ showed before the eyes of all that He was exalted to the right hand of God, wherefore Peter says in his Pentecost sermon, "Therefore being by the right hand of God exalted, and having received of the Father the promise of the Holy Ghost, He hath shed forth this, which ye now see and hear" (Acts 2:33). Certainly, the chief priests shall most powerfully see Christ "sitting on the right hand of power, and coming in the clouds of heaven" on the Last Day.

This earnest preaching of Christ ought justly to have moved the inmost soul and heart of the whole Sanhedrin present to withdraw from their wicked and murderous enterprise. But Caiaphas acted as one mad, rent his garment, and cried, "He hath blasphemed; what further need have we of witnesses? Behold, now ye have heard His blasphemy, what think ye?" — At once the bell was cast. They all blew the same horn and said, "He is guilty of death!"

Thus the eternal Prince of Life is innocently condemned and judged to contemptible death. This happened for our sake. Our first parents made us guilty of blasphemy, for they wished to be as God, withheld from God His glory and due obedience, and laid the blame for their fall on God Himself. But what do we, their descendants, do with our sin other than actually withhold from God the glory of His omnipotence, truth, and righteousness, as if He did not see our iniquities, let them go unpunished, and was not serious with His threats? To atone for our debts and to free us from the most just judgment of condemnation, which we all merited before God's judgment seat, Christ let Himself be unjustly condemned as a blasphemer, and this His suffering and death is efficacious to redeem and reconcile the whole world, because He is Christ, the Son of the Most Blessed. The Stone which the builders refused is therefore become the Cornerstone (Ps. 118:22). Accordingly, whoever believes "cometh not into judgment, but is passed from death unto life" (John 5:24), and is given "power to become children of God" (John 1:12), and is made a partaker of the divine nature (2 Peter 1:4).

But we are also to follow the beautiful example of Christ here, and freely and steadfastly to confess before men by the Holy Ghost the eternal, divine truth, even if we must suffer death because of it. Especially, however, we are to confess Christ, the Son of the living God, with sure and bold words, the more He is slandered and denied in the world, and to say, "I believe that Jesus Christ, true God, begotten of the Father in eternity, and also true Man, born of the Virgin Mary, is my Lord, who hath redeemed me, a lost and condemned man, purchased and won me from all sins, from death, and from the power of the devil, not with gold or silver, but with His holy and precious blood and with His innocent suffering and death, that I may be His own, and live under Him in His kingdom, and serve Him in everlasting righteousness, innocence, and blessedness, even as He is risen from the dead, and liveth and reigneth in eternity. *This is certainly true!*"

Prayer

Lord Jesus, Son of the Most High, Thou couldst have had joy, but chosest reproach and persecution, that we might be saved. Thou madest a good confession before the Sanhedrin, and for this wast sentenced to death as a blasphemer. No, Lord Jesus, Thou wast not guilty of death, but I am, who have robbed God of

His glory and have so often profaned and blasphemed His name. But Thou didst suffer Thyself to be condemned to death, that through Thee I might live and become a child of God and a fellow-heir with Thee. Oh, then be of good cheer, my soul! Let go of all terror; for whoever believes in the Son of God "cometh not into judgment, but is passed from death unto life"! O my Lord Jesus, how glad I am when I think of this life which Thou hast won for me by Thy death! Oh, when shall the blessed hour come when Thou wilt break in with Thy Last Day and bring my body and soul to the joy of heavenly life, when I shall see Thee coming in the clouds of heaven and sitting on the right hand of power, casting down the pope and Turk and all the vile ungodly from their thrones? O Lord Jesus, when the Jewish clergy heard of Thy coming again, they counted it blasphemy. But when I hear of it, I regard it as the highest comfort of my heart; for I know that the day of Thy last appearing shall be the day of my deliverance, my quickening, and my complete redemption. Therefore, O Lord Jesus, come soon with Thy blessed Day! Yea, come, Lord Jesus, deliver me and confess me then before Thy heavenly Father, for I believe in Thee, I love Thee, and I confess Thee! Amen, Lord Jesus! Amen.

Mel.: Wie schön leucht uns der Morgenstern

God's Son from all eternity,
We wait, Thy gracious face to see,
   When days at last are ended!
Then eyes are filled with glory's sight,
Then ears are filled with love's true light;
   By Thine appearing splendid;
Clearly, clearly
   Pow'rs majestic,
   Seers prophetic
Shall be given
To behold Thee, Lamb of heaven!

DEVOTION 31

Christ, the Son of God, Is Mocked and Mistreated

Mel.: Jesu, meines Lebens Leben

Christ, the Life of all the living,
  Christ, the Death of death, our foe,
Who Thyself for me once giving
  To the darkest depths of woe,
Madest reconciliation,
And hast saved me from damnation:
  Thousand, thousand thanks shall be,
  Dearest Jesus, unto Thee.

I gave my back to them that smote me, and my cheeks to them that plucked out my hair. I hid not my face from reproach and spitting. For the Lord, the LORD, helpeth me; therefore am I not confounded. Therefore have I set my face like a flint; for I know that I am not confounded. — The Son of Man shall be mocked and reproached and spitted on.

Isaiah 50:6–7; Luke 18:32

And the men that held Jesus mocked Him, and did spit in His face, and buffeted Him. But some covered Him, and struck Him on the face, especially the servants, and said, Prophesy unto us, Thou Christ, Who is he that smote Thee? And many other blasphemies spake they against Him.

Matthew 26:67–68; Mark 14:65; Luke 22:63–35

Now, after the judgment is passed by the high council, and the Lord Jesus has been denied His life, the assembly dissolves. The consistorial lords lie down in peace and snore a little, that they may supervise the business and discuss the matter all

DEVOTION 31

the more diligently the next morning, and meanwhile commit Jesus, bound, to their servants and henchmen, who now perpetrate all manner of malicious acts and put on a veritable Shrovetide play with Jesus the whole night through. Prisons otherwise are simply to be places of holding, to keep a person so that he may be brought out again at the proper time, but they turn it into an agonizing torture and villainous torment.

Here then let every man take to heart and consider what was done to Christ. He was sentenced to death by the Sanhedrin, but where are the counselors normally committed to those condemned to death and to the worst evildoers? These wicked villains allowed Him neither peace nor rest, and did to Him all that was grievous. Soon they cleared their throats and spewed their stinking filth and spit on His sacred face, at which even the angels longed to look. The waves of the sea were moved with horror at His face, the bright-shining sun hid her beams, and here the wicked villains spit on it, now buffeting it, now covering it, and treated Christ as a fool, who was that Prophet who was to come into the world (Deut. 18:15ff.), which reproach must especially have broken Christ's heart (Ps. 69:20), seeing they covered that face which their fathers desired with great longing, groaning, and sighs to see. Yea, there is so much grief that even the evangelists' pens fail them, and they can count more for sheer sorrow, but the evangelist Luke says, "And many other blasphemies spake they against Him."

First, then, this is all a true picture of infernal damnation, in which we ought to dwell in the darkness, and all spirits of hell ought to work their horrible malice and wickedness upon us, and mock and spit on us, and beat and drag and strike us back and forth—all of which Christ suffered in accordance with the prophecy of the prophet Isaiah (50:7) and according to His own prophecy (Luke 18:32), that He might deliver us from the horror of all devils, and bring us out of the darkness into the light, where we shall see God with face uncovered, and through His great sufferings in the night come to the joyous day of the eternal life of gladness in heaven. Second, it is also a foretaste of how the world will treat believers, and has done such things before and since. Elisha had to be mocked by wicked boys, "Go up, thou bald head!" (2 Kings 2:25). Isaiah laments how they sported themselves against Him, made a wide mouth, and drew out their tongue against Him (Isa. 57:4). Ezekiel was whistled at by his hearers during his sermon (Ezek. 33:31). The apostles were all beaten (Acts 5:40). "The high priest Ananias commanded them that stood by him to smite Paul on the mouth" (Acts 22:2). And still today it is a common occurrence that faithful preachers are scornfully mocked, their office disgraced and despised, their doctrine distorted, and even their own person and office violently trampled in derisive ditties and disgraceful writings, and those who do such things are even applauded and assisted, and they laugh behind the preachers' back. Is this not to mock and spit upon Christ as ever, and to cover His face and buffet Him? Now therefore, whoever must bear such reproach of the world, let him look to Christ, who in this passage is made to endure mockery and mistreatment by wicked villains. We are to join Him here and endure a little discomfort from time to time. Are we better than our Lord and Master? What use to complain much if the world should deal with us in such a manner? Such sufferings have certainly come upon our brethren more, and we shall hardly be the last. It is surely better to suffer discomfort a little while with Christ here than to have the honor and glory of the world, which is finally put to shame, and its end is damnation. Those therefore who suffer with Christ here will also be exalted with Him to glory hereafter.

It would not have been surprising if the earth had opened and those who thus dealt with Christ had been swallowed up or fire and brimstone had rained upon them. Although Christ here suffers these things with great patience for the good of the world, and at the same time as an example for us, the wickedness of the Jews was readily given them to drink and was poured out upon their own heads, since they did not repent, and God brought the just wrath of the Romans upon them. Then God avenged well the reproach and mistreatment of His Son, when they were horribly mocked, spit on, tormented, and slain by the Romans, and after that hid His own face from them and smote them with blindness, so that "when Moses is read, a veil hangeth before their heart" (2 Cor. 3:13–15), and they do not understand Scripture, though they read it in their own mother tongue—to say nothing of the eternal punishment, where they, who so horribly and devilishly scorned and mocked Christ here, shall have mockery and scorn from all devils and spirits of hell.

DEVOTION 31

Prayer

O Lord Jesus, what more terrifying thing can be heard than the many mocking words from the mouths of the torturer's ungodly servants which Thy holy ears were made to bear? What more terrible and wicked thing can be felt than Thou didst feel when Thou wast mocked, spit on, and smitten thus, and Thine adorable face was so disgracefully covered? O most blessed Jesus, what an evil night was spent by Thee! I am left speechless, and all my blood freezes in my veins, when I consider how Thou wast mocked and spit on, bound and smitten, scorned and despised, and when I ponder how Thou didst endure all these things for my sake. O dear Lord Jesus, direct me by Thy Holy Spirit, that as I brought this all upon Thee by my sins, so I may never by intentional and malicious transgressions mock Thee anew, nor spit on, smite, and besmirch any more Thy majestic face that shines like the sun! Rather grant me Thy Holy Spirit, that for Thy name's sake I may willingly and patiently bear mockery, spitting, mistreatment, and all manner of slanderous words, and let Thy Holy Spirit comfort me mightily in the midst of it all. Have mercy on my fellow brothers and sisters, who encounter such sufferings in the world, who lie captive in darkness, and who are also afflicted and disquieted by the ungodly, or whom the devil, that spirit of darkness, instills with fear and terror by his apparitions and illusions so as to make them despondent and fainthearted. Help them to recognize and despise the foe's cunning and malice, and to defend themselves with the sword of the Spirit, so that he must depart and have no power over them. Amen, Lord Jesus! Amen.

Mel.: Jesu, meines Lebens Leben

Thou, ah! Thou, hast taken on Thee
   Bonds and stripes, a cruel rod;
Pain and scorn were heaped upon Thee,
   O Thou sinless Son of God!
Thus didst Thou my soul deliver
From the bonds of sin forever.
   Thousand, thousand thanks shall be,
   Dearest Jesus, unto Thee.

Thou hast borne the smiting only
   That my wounds might all be whole;
Thou hast suffered, sad and lonely,
   Rest to give my weary soul;
Yea, the curse of God enduring,
Blessing unto me securing.
   Thousand, thousand thanks shall be,
   Dearest Jesus, unto Thee.

DEVOTION 32

Christ Is Again Judged by the Sanhedrin

Mel.: Singen wir aus Herzensgrund (p. 324)

Jesus Christ, Thou great High Priest,
  Who hast founded Thee a feast,
Entered in the Holy Place
  By Thy bitter death and cross,
Reconciled us with Thy blood,
Snuffed hell's flame and fiery brood,
And restored the highest good:

Seated at the Father's right
  One with Him in glory and might,
Mediator, Advocate,
  Crown and Joy of high estate,
Carried in the Father's breast—
As He loves Himself the best,
Never spurning Thy request:

Show to Him Thy wounds so red,
  Show Thy cross, how Thou wast dead,
And all else which Thou hast done
  For our sake let Him be shown!
Tell how Thou hast paid our debt,
On the altar-cross wast set,
And salvation there didst get.

(continued)

DEVOTION 32

> Others in their strength confide,
>   In their luck or skill or pride.
> But Thy Christians trust in Thee—
>   Yea, in Thee unswervingly!
> Let them not be put to shame,
> Help and guard those who Thee claim,
> For Thou know'st them all by name.

After threescore and two weeks shall Christ be cut off and be no more. — What have I done unto thee, O My people? and wherein have I wearied thee? Tell Me!

Daniel 9:26; Micah 6:3

And in the morning, all the chief priests and scribes and elders of the people came together and the whole council, came together, and took counsel against Jesus, to put Him to death, and led Him into their council, saying, Art Thou Christ? Tell us. And He said unto them, If I tell you, ye will not believe; and if I ask you, ye will not answer, and yet will not let Me go. Therefore, from henceforth shall the Son of Man sit on the right hand of the power of God. Then said they all, Art Thou then the Son of God? And He said unto them, Ye say it, for I am. And they said, What need we any further witness? We ourselves have heard it of His own mouth.

Matthew 27:1; Mark 15:1; Luke 22:66–71

Here, Christ's death-sentence is repeated early the next day, and He is condemned by the *whole* high council; for since the trial was begun in great haste at night, they wish to give the case the appearance of due process, as if they had considered and investigated everything properly and had pronounced the sentence of death without excessive haste. Therefore not only do they assemble early in the morning for this business, but so do the elders of the people, and with them the whole council, as the evangelists report, that they may complete with all the more voices the death-song which they began, and in this second session mightily complete the judgment of blood, and all the better hand Him over to the governor. They therefore ask Jesus whether He still insists that He is Christ and the Son of God.

Hereupon He gives them another repentance sermon, and says, "Ye are hardened people. If I tell you, ye will not believe. Watch out, lest faith fall into your hands some day! For the present I must live at your mercy, stand in your sight and judgment, and be sentenced to death by you; but know ye this, that by My suffering I will soon come into My glory, and sit on the right hand of the power of God, as it is written: 'The LORD said unto My Lord, Sit Thou at My right hand, until I make Thine enemies Thy footstool' (Ps. 110:1)." Hereupon they unanimously decide that because Jesus is claiming to be the Messiah, yea, the Son of God, they have no need of further witness. They accordingly remain with the previous capital decree: He shall and must surely die.

In this decision in the early morning hour, that word is fulfilled which the Holy Ghost spoke by the mouth of David when he sings "of the hind that is hunted at morning" (Ps. 22). From this, however, we learn how great the hatred of these people for Christ was, and how the adversaries of Christ and the children of this world are so awake and alert toward evil. The disciples of Christ are slow and lethargic toward good, but the soldiers and servants wake all night, and although the lords of the Sanhedrin sat long and were somewhat vehemently occupied with the captive Jesus, they are already up at break of day to finish their wicked enterprise, and allow no toil or care to annoy them. It is the same way today. "The children of this world are shrewder," that is, more alert, more zealous in evil, "than the children of the light in their generation," that is, toward good (Luke 16:8). How alert Absalom was to persecute his father! How diligently Ahithophel gave counsel and action in support of this! How cunning King David was, after he fell, to become a partaker with Bathsheba! How easily we can rub the sleep from our eyes at the promise of worldly delight and luxury; but how sluggish and dull we are to hear the divine word, and we soon grow sleepy! Therefore this vigilance and this zeal of the worldlings ought to make us blush for shame, so that with David we too may rise at midnight to give thanks to the Lord for the statutes of His righteousness (Ps. 119:62), attend early unto His cry, early commit ourselves unto Him (Ps. 5:3), pondering day and night how we may not miss the Bridegroom, Jesus Christ, as did the foolish virgins.

Likewise, we also see here the great, terrible blindness of the Jews. They know that the Christ was to come and save them, and had long waited for Him with their fathers. But now that He is here, they do not believe Him, but even condemn Him to death because He confesses that He is the Christ. Yet so was it prophesied that Christ would be cut off and be no more (Dan. 9:26). Yea, so was it written that He would give His life as a guilt offering, be cut off from the land of the living, and be stricken for the transgressions of His people (Isa. 53:8–10).

But because His own people rejected Him, He was set as the light for us Gentiles, that He might be our only salvation to the end of the earth. Therefore He is to be our only consolation, our firm hope, and our sole refuge; for there is surely no other salvation, nor is there any other name given to men wherein we are to be saved (Acts 4:12). And because He freely testifies here that He shall sit on the right hand of God, we also have the consolation that He represents us there with unspeakable groanings, and that the very Lord who is now our Advocate and, as the Son of Man, our Brother, shall at the Last Day also be our gracious Judge. When we see Him, we will rejoice far more than the children of Jacob did when they saw how their brother Joseph was a lord and prince in Egypt.

Prayer

O Lord Jesus, who early in the morning of Holy Good Friday wast again set before the Sanhedrin as the hind that is hunted at morning, and wast once more sentenced to death because of Thy person and Thy glory to come: I give thanks to Thee not only for Thy repeated confession, but also for the salutary fruit thereof, for because of Thee I shall be able to stand in the Last Judgment and to partake of Thy glory. Help me also that, believing in Thee, I may live and die on this confession, and thereby be saved. But as by contemplating Thine exaltation to come Thou didst lessen Thy humiliation then being suffered, and didst soften Thy grievous mockery and sweeten all Thy bitter suffering, so grant that, following Thee, I may find that my chiefest comfort in my affliction, my joy in my sorrow, and my refreshment in my tribulation is the assurance that this time of suffering is not worthy to be compared with the glory which shall be revealed in me! Amen, O Lord Jesus! Amen.

Mel.: Ach, wir armen Sünder (p. 322)

Christ, to Thee be glory
　For Thy bitter pain,
On the cross of suff'ring
　Dying for our gain,
Now with God the Father
　Reigning without end:
Help us wretched sinners,
　And salvation send!
　　　Kyrie eleison,
　　　Christe Eleison,
　　　Kyrie eleison.

DEVOTION 33

Christ Is Delivered to the Gentiles

Mel.: Ach, wir armen Sünder (p. 322)

Oh, what wretched sinners
  Are we here on earth!
Sinners from conception,
  Sinners from our birth!
Brought by our transgression
  Into such distress,
We deserve damnation
  For our sinfulness.
    Kyrie eleison,
    Christe Eleison,
    Kyrie eleison.

Our escape could never
  Out of death be gained
By our own endeavor—
  Sin too strongly reigned;
For to gain redemption
  Nothing else could be
But God's Son must suffer
  Death and agony.
    Kyrie eleison,
    Christe Eleison,
    Kyrie eleison.

PASSION-BOOK

They said unto him, We are come down to bind thee, that we may deliver thee into the hand of the Philistines. . . . And they bound him with two new cords, and brought him up from the rock. — And they shall deliver the Son of Man to the Gentiles to mock and to scourge and to crucify Him.

Judges 15:12–13; Matthew 20:19

And the whole multitude arose and bound Jesus and led Him from Caiaphas unto the hall of judgment, and delivered Him to Pontius Pilate the governor; and it was early.

Matthew 27:2; Mark 15:1; Luke 23:1; John 18:28

The supposed spiritual leaders with their retinue can have no rest or peace until the decision and judgment of the council against Jesus, now bound a second time, has been fulfilled by Pilate. For with the wicked, the rule is, The longer, the lowlier (2 Tim. 3:13). Every apostate is a hater and persecutor of his own order, as the saying goes. And if the murderous pope will see in the long run that Lutherans are rather too firm and steadfast for him, he will look around for a Pilate.

But we are to learn here the reasons *why the Lord Christ is delivered to the Gentiles,* for this consideration is necessary for us all.

The first reason is that the prophecies of the prophets had to be fulfilled. For the patriarch Jacob announced that the royal scepter and Jewish government was to remain in the tribe of Judah and his descendants until the Messiah should come (Gen. 49), who would then suffer, die, and accomplish the work of redemption. Therefore the Jews had at that time no scepter or king of their own, but were subject to Roman rule, and thus to the Gentiles. This is referred to also by the seventy weeks of years in Daniel, which match precisely when Christ was to be cut off, that is, to be killed under the Roman governor (Dan. 9:26).

The second reason is that the Jews had lost the right to put criminals to death, which right was reserved strictly to the Roman governor.

The third reason is that Christ was to suffer in a Gentile manner by the contemptible death of the cross. For David wrote of this in Psalm 22 as clearly and plainly as if he had stood under the cross and watched it, since he introduces the Son of God thus speaking of His death: "For dogs have surrounded Me, and the company of the wicked hath beset Me round; they have pierced My hands and feet; I can number all My bones, but they see their pleasure in Me." What clearer could have been said of the crucifixion of Christ? For by this, not only the death of the Messiah, but also His crucifixion performed according to the manner of the Gentiles, is indicated as if with the fingers. As Christ Himself says, "They shall deliver the Son of Man to the Gentiles, to mock and to scourge and to crucify Him" (Matt. 20:19).

The fourth reason is that the Jews accused Him of being a rebel who had stirred up the people. Now according to Roman law, it was ordained that such evildoers were either to be nailed to the cross or thrown to the wild beasts, or if they were of the nobility, to be exiled to a certain island for the rest of their life.

The fifth reason is that the Jews by these means can take their head out of the noose and afterward put all in the bosom of the Roman governor, for they knew well that Christ was in great esteem among everyone. Therefore they said to the apostles, "'Ye intend to bring this Man's blood upon us' (Acts 5:28) as if we had slain Him. In this ye are mistaken, for not we but his Roman imperial majesty caused Him to be crucified by his steward and governor."

The sixth reason is that the Lord Christ is the Savior of the poor Gentiles; for the Jews here reject the Messiah and send Him away to the Gentiles. Therefore Christ Himself says to them, "The kingdom of God shall be taken from you, and given to a nation bringing forth the fruits thereof" (Matt. 21:43).

From all this we are to find for ourselves two consolations:

First, we are to find consolation in the fact that we are certain of our Christian faith, since we confess, "I believe in Jesus Christ, the Son of God and Mary, who suffered under Pontius Pilate." For because of the circumstances of the time, Pilate is remembered in our Christian Apostles' Creed, to show that the Messiah, our eternal King and High Priest, truly appeared and accomplished the work of our redemption under the Roman governor in Jerusalem.

Second, it is a consolation that whoever believes in Christ, whether Jew or Gentile, shall not be hindered in his salvation by virtue of his descent or anything else. For here in the Passion of the Lord, both Jews and Gentiles come together and help to bring it to pass. "There is no difference between the Jew and the Greek; for there is one Lord of all, rich unto all that call upon Him" (Rom. 10:12). Who was ever ashamed that hoped in Him? (Sir. 2:10).

Prayer

O Lord Jesus, Thou Hind hunted at morning, how Thou wast driven to and fro! From the Garden Thine enemies brought Thee to the high priest and the religious court of the Sanhedrin. Now the Sanhedrin brings Thee to the Roman governor and the secular court. Thou art delivered by Thine own people to a stranger; Thou art handed over by the Jews to Pilate, the Gentile, by whom Thou art condemned to death. O my Lord Jesus, shall the Gentiles also be responsible for Thy painful death? Yea, my own soul! Surely both Gentiles and Jews share the guilt when Jesus the innocent is tortured, when Jesus the Son of God is tormented, when Jesus the Prince of Life is killed and crucified; thus both Jews and Gentiles now can take comfort in Him and in Him be eternally saved. Now therefore, O Lord Jesus, let me, who am a Gentile according to my natural descent, find salvation through Thine agony and torment, through Thy distress and death! Oh, let Thy bloody suffering not be lost on me! Amen, Lord Jesus! Amen. Amen, Lord Jesus! Amen.

Mel.: Der am Kreuz ist meine Liebe (p. 323)
Or: Freu dich sehr, o meine Seele

Now the Lamb of God is given
  Over into sinners' hands
That thy fetters may be riven;
  By the Jews' and Gentiles' bands
Now the Stone away is thrown
Who is yet the Cornerstone;
  Ah, the Righteous is afflicted
  For these slaves by sin constricted!

DEVOTION 34

Judas Comes to a Horrible End

Mel.: Werde munter, mein Gemüthe

Blest is he who never taketh
  Counsel of ungodly men!
Blest, the right who ne'er forsaketh,
  Nor in sinners' paths is seen,
Who the scorners' friendship spurns,
From their seats away who turns,
  Who delight in God's word taketh,
  This his meditation maketh.

But he who in sin's ways goeth
  Is like chaff the wind before,
When it riseth up and bloweth,
  And we find it here no more.
Where the Lord His people guide,
There the godless ne'er abide,
  God the faithful loves and guideth,
  On the wicked wrath abideth.

Let his days be few; and let another take his office. . . . He desired the curse, so shall it also come unto him; he delighted not in the blessing, so shall it also abide far from him. And he put on the curse like as his garment, and it came into his bowels like water, and like oil into his bones.

Psalm 109:8, 17–18

Then Judas, which had betrayed Him, when he saw that he was condemned, repented himself, and brought again the thirty pieces of silver to the chief priests and elders, saying, I have done evil in that I have betrayed the innocent blood. They said, What is that to us? See thou to that. And he cast down the pieces of silver in the Temple, and departed, and went and hanged himself, and [falling headlong, he] burst asunder in the midst, and all his bowels gushed out.

Matthew 27:3–5; Acts 1:18

In the terrifying example of Judas we are first to learn what a detestable thing a wicked conscience is when it awakes. For then it allows a man no rest or peace until it finally brings him to despair (unless God gives him special help). This is what God says to Cain in Genesis 4:7: "Sin resteth at the door," and can quite easily be wakened by the creaking with one's frequent going in and out. Finally, the lurking, slumbering sin wakes with a start like a vicious guard-dog and snaps at everything around, inflicting wounds that none but Christ can heal. On this, Paul speaks in Romans 7:8 how sin in a man is sometimes as though dead for a time, but when it is wakened by the Law, it makes him anxious and afraid, so that he does not know where to go outside of Christ. These are the fiery darts of the evil one. Therefore we are to hold faith and a good conscience (1 Tim. 1:19). "Blessed is he that hath not an evil conscience, and his trust is not fallen from him" (Sir. 14:2).

Second, we learn here the distinction between Peter's true repentance and conversion and the traitor Judah's remorse induced by the gallows. For it is explicitly said of him here that he was a remorseful but not truly converted man, since he "repented himself" of his evil deed of betraying innocent blood, but did not then truly repent. For it is not yet repentance and conversion to God when a man simply regrets something, but with such a man the last state is sometimes worse than the first (Matt. 12:45). For believers, "godly sorrow worketh repentance unto salvation, whereof no man repenteth," but for unbelievers, "the sorrow of the world worketh death," so that they doubt God's grace and fall into despair (2 Cor. 7:10). Therefore, whenever we have sincere remorse and sorrow because of our sin, even as our whole life is to be a constant repentance and conversion to God, we must hold in true faith to the gracious promise of God given and pledged to us in Christ Jesus, from whom repentance comes as well as the forgiveness of sins (Acts 5:31). For a Judas-like repentance is of no help if a man goes his way in unbelief, counting his sin greater than the mercy of God and merit of Christ.

The papists teach and have their Judas-like repentance, of which they count three parts; for first there is *contritio cordis,* that is, perfect remorse; then *confessio oris,* that is, pure confession; and finally, *satisfactio operis,* that is, personal satisfaction and compensation for the sin. If this were an accurate description of true repentance, Judas would not have "repented himself" wrongly. For when remorse stings him hard, he makes a clean confession and proceeds at last to satisfaction by casting the silver coins at the feet of the chief priests. This, however, can help him neither from the temporal gallows nor from the eternal. Augustine therefore writes, "Let no man despair of God's mercy, even if he has committed a hundred sins, yea, a thousand crimes." Again: "Repentance and conversion to God is like the voyage of a ship, where pardon and forgiveness of sins are the port for which we are to direct the bow of the ship, that we may sail to righteousness."

Third, we have in Judas a mirror of the wrath of God, so that no one should willfully and maliciously sin against the grace of God, nor abuse the precious merit of Christ. For while God is patient, yet "He can be as quickly angered as He is merciful, and His indignation upon the ungodly hath no ceasing" (Sir. 5:6). In just anger He permits the devil to have power over the children of unbelief, and to lead them captive with his cords according to his every whim (Eph. 2:2–3; 2 Tim. 2:26). Since the traitor was a despiser of God's Word and of all Christian admonition, he came to a terrible end "and hanged himself, and burst asunder in the midst," as the children of Seir or the Edomites long before (2 Chron. 25) and Arius later all spilled their bowels. Of this Peter says, "(Judas) purchased the field with the unrighteous reward, (and hanged himself) and burst asunder in the midst, and all his bowels gushed out."

The horrible demise of Judas is therefore a sure sign of divine punishment and vengeance for all who do not turn to God in the time of grace. Dathan, Korah, and Abiram with their faction are partly swallowed by the earth, partly consumed by fire. Saul transfixes himself; Absalom is left hanging by his hair in the oak tree and is gored by three spears; the queen Jezebel is cast down from her house and the dogs lick her blood and eat up her flesh. This all happens as a special punishment from God on account of their willful, persistent sins.

Prayer

O pangs of conscience! O pangs of conscience! Alas, such horror sin brings when it wakes, such despair men's pangs of conscience cause when they take the upper hand, that he will even take from his own self both temporal and eternal life! O Lord Jesus, govern me, I pray, that I may never consent to gross, willful, and malicious sin, nor burden my conscience with intentional trespasses. But if I ever slip into them and suffer so heavy a fall, I beseech Thee, lift me up again, my Lord Jesus! Light my way to true and honest repentance, and help me not to lose hope, but in faith to take hold of Thy love which Thou hast for all poor sinners, in faith to cling firmly to Thy promise which Thou hast made so often to penitent sinners, in faith to appropriate Thy perfect merit, which is far greater than the sin of the whole world, in faith to serve Thee, in faith to live a Christian life, and in faith and steadfast trust in Thee at last to die a blessed death! Amen, Lord Jesus! Amen.

Mel.: Mitten wir im Leben sind

In the midst of hell's dismay,
  Chased by sins impelling,
Whither shall we flee away,
  And be safely dwelling?
To Thee, Lord Christ, Thee only!
  For Thy precious blood once shed,
  Satisfaction for us made.
O holy Lord, our God,
O holy, mighty God,
O holy and merciful Savior:
  Thou ever art God!
Let us not abandon
  This the true faith's comfort sure:
Kyrieleison!

DEVOTION 35

The Chief Priests Take Counsel concerning the Price of Blood

Mel.: Ach Gott vom Himmel, sieh darein
Or: Herr, wie du willst, so schicks mit mir

Great value God thy Lord and King
  To human souls hath given,
And prized them over everything,
  Yea, over earth and heaven.
For whose sake else sent He His Son,
His greatest Joy, the Blessed One,
  To crucifixion's torment?

This work to do God did not deign
  To profit earth or heaven,
But 'twas the cherished souls of men
  Who were this wonder given,—
Yea, precious pledge and costly good!
Had not His Son so shed His blood
  No man would have redemption.

Wherefore do not despise, O man,
  That sore and heavy suff'ring
Which for thy sake o'er Jesus ran,
  But thanks to Him be off'ring,
And shun all ill; see how thy Lord
Thy soul in danger so adored,
  Came to thy aid, and saved thee!

And I said unto them, If it please you, render as much as I am worth; and if not, forbear. And they weighed out as much as I was worth, thirty pieces of silver. And the L<small>ORD</small>

said unto me, Cast it unto the potter. Aye, a goodly sum, whereof I was counted worthy of them! And I took the thirty pieces of silver, and cast them into the house of the LORD, *to be given to the potter.*

Zechariah 11:12–13

But the chief priests took the silver pieces, and said, It is not lawful that we should put them into God's treasury, because it is the price of blood. And they took counsel, and bought with the silver pieces, the reward of unrighteousness, the potter's field, for the burying of sojourners. And it was known unto all the dwellers at Jerusalem, insomuch as that field is called in their proper tongue Akeldama, that is, Field of Blood, unto this day. Then was fulfilled that which was spoken by Jeremiah the prophet, saying, They took thirty pieces of silver, wherewith was purchased he that was sold, whom they bought of the children of Israel, and gave them for a potter's field, as the Lord commanded me.

Matthew 27:6–10; Acts 1:18–19

The high priests and elders are so blinded and hardened by the devil that they are moved neither by the horrible demise of Judas nor by his confession of Christ's innocence. For after Judas casts the price of betrayal into the Temple, they take counsel to decide what to do with the money, that they may not sin. "God hateth the thieve's offering," they say, "therefore we may not and will not put this price of blood in God's treasury. Rather, since it is fitting and God-pleasing to assist widows, orphans, and strangers, it were best that a field should be bought for this money and appointed for the burying of strangers and sojourners, when they come to the high feasts but then depart by death."

Here we see the nature and character of deceivers and hypocrites, who strain at gnats and swallow camels (Matt. 23:24). The chief priests are willing to help strangers, but they kill their own countryman, Christ. Before, they took money from God's treasury without misgiving; when they receive it back, they consider it a mortal sin to put it in again. They have scruples of conscience to put the price of blood into God's treasury, but no compunction about shedding innocent blood, yea, even the blood of the Son of God. The papists too think they commit a great sin if they eat flesh on Friday, yet to carry on fornication, unchastity, adultery, and theft, and to offer up the innocent on the chopping block for the true confession of the divine Word, is to them a jest and game and no sin. Now therefore, although the chief priests and elders wish to cover their wickedness with this deception, yet by this their reproach and shame are more clearly manifested and made known to the all the world; for everyone says, "This is the Field of Blood that was bought from the price of blood."

But concerning this price of blood, not only did the prophets prophesy many centuries before, but God also caused the thirty pieces of silver to be included in the New Testament as an eternal memorial thereof, to show how Christ was thought to be worth so little and appraised so worthless by His own people, whereas to pay according to worth, all the goods and gold of the world would not have sufficed. Now as Christ is counted worthless and disprized by His own people, so also His servants and messengers are counted worthless and disprized by their own people. Of the devil's apostles, the world knows well how to make a great deal, as long as they have a little power and importance; but no one cares about the servants of Christ.

But for us, this valuation of the Son of God is very comforting. For thirty pieces of silver were in the Old Testament the very price by which a foreign servant's death had to be compensated. For such a paltry amount of money here Christ is sold, who took on the form of a servant as the ransom for us, who were one and all servants of sin, sold under sin, and captive under death and eternal damnation. From this eternal servanthood and bondage we are free and released because the eternal Son of God, through His willing servanthood, has freed us indeed (John 8:36).

Likewise, we are to draw comfort from this event, where the Lord Christ secured for us Gentiles and strangers too a place of rest. For as Augustine says, "That a place of burial was provided for sojourners with the money for which the Lord Christ was betrayed and sold happened that we might now know that Christ has also brought us near, who before were guests and strangers and outside the citizenship of Israel, and not only shall our flesh rest and sleep safely, but also rise at the Last Day and walk in the land of the living (Ps. 16:9; 116:9).

Prayer

O Lord Jesus, my Savior, Thou wast sold for me, and didst purchase me for Thy own possession. Help me therefore, my dearest Redeemer, that as Thy dearly bought child, I may live and die to Thee alone. For from Thee alone I have my temporal and spiritual life. I trust in Thee alone, I take refuge in Thee alone, and Thou art my All in all. Let me direct all my deeds and movements according to Thy will and to Thy glory, and so serve Thee continually in holiness and righteousness, that it may be pleasing to Thee. I will die to Thee in living faith, in joyful hope of eternal life, in devout prayer, in heartfelt longing for Thee, and in willing obedience to Thee. Then I shall not die when I die, but shall pass through death into life everlasting, where after the pilgrimage and sojourn of this poor life of exile I may rest from all anguish and labor. Oh, how I long for that rest! O Lord Jesus, bring me to it soon! Amen.

Mel.: O Gott, du frommer Gott

Let me depart this life
   Confiding in my Savior;
Do Thou my soul receive,
   That it may live forever;
And let my body have
   A quiet resting place
Beside a Christian's grave;
   And let it sleep in peace.

And on that solemn Day
   When all the dead are waking,
Stretch o'er my grave Thy hand,
   Thyself my slumbers breaking;
Then let me hear Thy voice,
   Change Thou this earthly frame,
And bid me aye rejoice
   With those who love Thy name.

DEVOTION 36

The Jews' Hypocritical Appeal

Mel.: Was mein Gott will, das gscheh allzeit
*Or: Hilf mir, mein Gott, hilf, daß ich dir**

In God alone I put my trust,
  On His rich care depending;
He will ward off each deadly thrust,
  'Gainst Satan's craft defending.
By Thy dear Word uphold me, Lord,
  And let me keep it purely,
Against the devil's wrath and sword
  And wiles preserved securely.

In Christ alone, th' eternal Son,
  True God from everlasting,
One with the Father on the throne,
  My hope and trust are resting;
Him to this world the Father sent,
  To all men here residing,
For all our sins a testament
  And sacrifice providing.

In Christ alone my comfort stands,
  Who died for me, to save me;
From death by His own bloodied hands,
  Salvation thus He gave me.
My sins He bore, redemption won,
  That so I might receive it;
The Father sees what He hath done;
  God, help me to believe it!

* No. 17 in the appendix of the *St. Louiser Choralbuch*.

And the Lord *saith, Forasmuch as this people draw near Me with their mouth, and with their lips do honor Me, but their heart is far from Me, and they fear Me according to the precepts of men, therefore, behold, I will also deal marvelously with this people, even in the most marvelous and wonderful way, so that the wisdom of their wise men may perish, and the understanding of their prudent men may be hid.*

Isaiah 29:13–14

And the Jews themselves went not into the judgment hall, lest they should be defiled, but that they might eat the Passover. Pilate then went out unto them, and said, What accusation bring ye against this Man? They answered and said unto him, If He were not an evildoer, we would not have delivered Him up unto thee. Then said Pilate unto them, Take ye Him, and judge Him according to your law. The Jews therefore said unto him, It is not lawful for us to put any man to death (that the word of Jesus might be fulfilled, which He spake, signifying by what death He should die).

John 18:28–32

That the Jews take thought for the Passover is right and well, for God had so ordained that no unclean man should eat of the Passover lamb. Now, we are one and all unclean (Isa. 64:6), for "what is a man, that he should be clean? and he which is born of a woman, that he should be righteous" (Job 15:14). Yet the Jews do not regard this inherited uncleanness, but cultivate a hypocritical appearance to enter the court. Here again is aptly seen the true character and image of hypocrites. They have scruples of conscience about entering the court, but they have no compunction about helping to sacrifice the innocent Man contrary to God's Law. Augustine says, "They suppose they may defile another's house, but do not think once that their own wickedness pollutes them. They fear a foreign ruler's court, but are not at all afraid of shedding the innocent blood of Christ (their Brother according to the flesh)." And Theophylact says, "O great folly! They consider it no sin to kill a man unjustly, but to enter the court they regard as an utter crime!" So also, many a man is involved in no public idolatry nor commits any gross, outward sin, but in his heart dwell the idols of mammon, murder, adultery, fornication, unchastity, etc., and wicked lust as a root of all evil.

This outward holiness is very common, and the children of the world know exceedingly well how to act godly and holy on the outside, even though their heart is filled with wickedness—yea, as angels incarnate, though inwardly they are full of devils. Such hypocrisy shall be laid bare by God on that great Day, and rewarded with hellfire for an eternal punishment. And they, the "spiritual," are themselves the worst, and are polluted and afflicted with many filthy sins in their heart, and yet think themselves clean—even as those filthy men, the chief priests, who have in their heart the unjust judgment of blood, and yet are of a mind to keep the Passover. "There is a generation that are pure in their own eyes," says Solomon, "and yet is not washed from their filthiness" (Prov. 30:12). And Jeremiah says, "Though thou wash thee with niter, and take thee much soap, yet thine iniquity shineth before Me" (Jer. 2:22). And Christ says to the scribes and Pharisees, "Ye hypocrites, well did Isaiah prophesy of you, saying, This people draweth nigh unto Me with their mouth, and honoreth Me with their lips; but their heart is far from Me. But in vain they do serve Me, teaching such doctrines as are nothing but the commandments of men" (Matt. 15:7–9).

Now therefore, because the Jews decline to enter the court, Pilate comes out to them. But here see what defiance toward Pilate and what malice toward Christ they show in addition to their hypocrisy; for as Lyra says, they do not ask Pilate to uphold their just cause, but simply to perform their bloody counsel without a hearing. "If He were not an evildoer," they say, "we would not have delivered Him up unto thee." The wicked are selfish-minded and become irritated if men do not do what they wish, for they wish to live according to their mind and without ordinance to be above all, yea, greater than all laws, and "have no heed unto judgment" (Prov. 28:5). They treat their own will as justice, and thus force precedes justice and acts quite otherwise than justice. It annoys their worthy lordships when the judge asks so straitly concerning the charges, and they think he ought to trust them, who held such high, prestigious offices, over against such a Man.

O shameless liars! The Angel of the Lord will find you and destroy you, for with this lie you forfeit your life. What evil did He do you? Ask the blind, whom He made to see, the deaf whom He made to hear, and the dumb whom He made to speak, and the lepers whom He cleansed, and the needy and poor whom He comforted, and the dead whom He raised again. In short, the Fount of grace runs over with utter goodness and benefaction. Are these evil deeds deserving of death? For which work do you wish to kill Him? Perhaps because He conversed with publicans and sinners? Yet He did so as the heavenly Physician to heal poor souls. And so it was prophesied, so must the Christ be numbered among the transgressors and evildoers, all for our good, that we, as poor sinners and evildoers, might not one day have to depart from Him with the evildoers. Therefore Christ is here presented as an evildoer, and hereby atones for our evil deeds, and gives us evildoers His righteousness and holiness, by which we are justified before God and saved. Thus even if we are shamed, slandered, persecuted, excommunicated, tormented, and put to death, we are still to be consoled and willingly to bear all things, for in heaven we will all be repaid and richly rewarded. They know not what they do; yea, they think that they do God service herein. Therefore, we are to approve ourselves "as the ministers of God: in much patience, in afflictions, in necessities, in distresses, in stripes, in imprisonments, in tumults, in labors, in watchings, in fastings; by pureness, by knowledge, by longsuffering, by kindness, by the Holy Ghost, by love unfeigned, by the Word of truth, by the power of God, by the armor of righteousness on the right hand and on the left, by honor and dishonor, by evil report and good report: as deceivers, and yet true; as unknown, and yet well known; as dying, and, behold, we live; as chastened, and not killed; as sorrowful, yet alway rejoicing; as poor, yet making many rich; as having nothing, and yet possessing all things" (2 Cor. 6:4–10).

Prayer

O Jesus, righteous and holy Lord, who for my sake didst suffer Thyself to be accused as an evildoer: grant me Thy righteousness, and number me among those whom Thou hast made free from sins and all evil, from all guilt and all condemnation. Yet help me, Lord Jesus, that my fear of God may not be hypocrisy, nor I serve Thee with a false heart. Grant that I may not be one of those who draw near Thee with their mouth, but their heart is far from Thee. Keep my soul, O my God, from the wicked generation, that are pure in their own eyes, and yet is not washed

DEVOTION 36

from their filthiness. Let me serve Thee all the days of my life in holiness and righteousness, which is pleasing to Thee, so that even though for Thy sake I am reviled as an evildoer by the world, yet by Thee I may be known as Thy servant and exalted to Thy glory. Amen.

Mel.: Nun sich der Tag geendet hat

Christ, in Thy love, salvation free
   And righteousness bestow,
And take my sinful debt on Thee,
   The portion that I owe.

Help me to be upright and true,
   Free from deceit and guile,
That none may fault the works I do,
   Nor lies my lips defile.

Help me to have true godliness
   Without hypocrisy,
That all my life Thy name may bless
   And pleasing be to Thee.

DEVOTION 37

The Jews' Threefold Accusation and Christ's Good Confession

Mel.: Wer nur den lieben Gott läßt walten

My Jesus makes bold declaration:
  Who can accuse Me of one sin?
The foes may try their accusation,
  And throw a thousand slanders in,
Yet Innocence doth freely show
That He is Truth, which all must know.

False witnesses the truth would alter,
  O righteous Jesus! Thee to slay;
Their voice to silence soon must falter.
  Their lies must quickly pass away.
What Thou hast said is verified:
Thy Word must "Yea, Amen," abide.

Though Pilate go on asking ever,
  What in the world the truth may be;
And though they smite Thy cheek, O Savior,
  Truth has no witness more than Thee.
The sun doth e'er its light retain:
Whate'er is true doth true remain.

Thy Word forever true abideth,
  This truth upon me seal and press
Until my hour of death betideth!
  If Thee before men I confess,
Thou wilt confess me, God the Son,
Also before Thy Father's throne.

DEVOTION 37

They that seek after my soul lay snares for me; and they that seek my hurt speak how they will do harm, and are busy with utter deceits. But I must be as a deaf man and hear not, and as a dumb man that openeth not his mouth; and must be as a man that heareth not, and that hath no reproofs in his mouth. — He opened not his mouth, as a lamb that is led to the slaughter, and as a sheep that before his shearers is dumb and openeth not his mouth.

Psalm 38:12–14; Isaiah 53:7

Then began the chief priests and the elders to accuse Him sternly, saying, This One we find perverting the nation and forbidding to give tribute to Caesar, and saying that He is Christ, a King. Then entered Pilate into the judgment hall again and called Jesus and asked Him, saying, Art Thou the King of the Jews? Jesus stood before him and answered, Sayest thou this thing of thyself, or did others tell it thee of Me? Pilate answered, Am I a Jew? Thine own nation and the chief priests have delivered Thee unto me; what hast Thou done? Jesus answered, My kingdom is not of this world; if My kingdom were of this world, then would My servants fight, that I should not be delivered to the Jews. But now is My kingdom not from hence. Then said Pilate unto Him, Thou art a King then? Jesus answered, Thou sayest it; I am certainly a King. For to this end was I born, and for this cause came I into the world, that I should bear witness unto the truth. He that is of the truth heareth My voice. Pilate saith unto Him, What is truth? And when he had said this, he went out again unto the Jews, and said unto them, I find no fault in Him. And when He was accused of the chief priests and elders, He answered nothing. But Pilate asked Him again and said, Answerest Thou nothing? Behold, how sternly they accuse Thee. Hearest Thou not? And He answered him to never a word, insomuch that the governor marveled greatly.

Matthew 27:11–14; Mark 15:2–5; Luke 23:1–4; John 18:33–38

Because the chief priests see that Pilate will not condemn Christ without a demonstrable reason and cause, they bring their accusation against Christ and insist that Christ is a stirrer up and agitator of the people, so the governor ought to punish

Him as such according to the office that he bears. And they base their argument on three points: (1) that He perverted the nation, (2) forbade to give tribute to Caesar, and (3) claimed to be a king. These were serious charges, yet a worthless argument. For the chief priests themselves were deceivers of the nation with their false doctrine of human statutes. And that Christ warned His disciples and hearers against the leaven of the Pharisees and scribes (Matt. 16:6) was far from a perversion of the nation, but rather a right instruction. Neither did He forbid to give tribute to Caesar, but rather commanded it and reaffirmed it (Matt. 22:21), as they well knew; to say nothing of the fact that He willed to be born during the census (Luke 2:5), and gave the Temple coin for Himself and Peter (Matt. 17:24–27). He was so far from thinking of a physical or temporal kingdom that He even fled from the crown and scepter (John 6:15), and admonished His disciples, who always had delusions of a temporal kingdom, to be humble and patient in cross and trial in this valley of sorrow (Matt. 19:29; 20:23; Luke 22:25–30).

But we are given a constant comfort here by the fact that the Man from whom all emperors, kings, princes, and lords receive their fief and have their dominion is accused of being a rabble-rouser and agitator for us. For we were true rabble-rousers against God and the high Majesty, and sought after His crown (Gen. 3:5). The eternal Son of God atones for this, so that there is now to be "no condemnation to all them which are in Christ Jesus" (Rom. 8:1). "Hereby we know that we are of the truth, and can assure our hearts before Him, that if our heart condemn us, God is greater than our heart, and knoweth all things" (1 John 3:19–20).

Accordingly, because the accusation that Jesus calls Himself a King especially aims at rebellion, and the Jews were waiting for such a king to free them from Roman rule and to restore them to their former kingdom, Pilate therefore addresses this accusation alone, and asks Christ whether He is a king, at which Christ makes a confession of His office and His kingdom, which is certainly good, as St. Paul says. Christ was of course to be a King and is a King, as David long before sang in a beautiful wedding hymn (Ps. 72). For He was of the royal line of *Judah* (Gen. 49:10), and not an everyday king, but one who would have increase of government (Isa. 9:7), a King who would govern well and bring judgment and justice on earth. All this can surely refer to no temporal king. Further, Ezekiel 37:25 says that this King will be a King *of David;* but David did not rise again, so this King must have a different kingdom, and one within which David also is found after death. This, then, is Christ, the King of all kings.

From such glorious prophecies all the Jews turned their eyes, wherefore they do not know their own King either, but despise Him and do not want Him to rule over them. But His kingdom is not of this world, nor will He admit entry to any other king. For His kingdom does not consist of earthly things, but His kingdom is a spiritual kingdom, where He sits on the right hand of His heavenly Father and gathers for Himself a church here on earth both now and at all times through the Word of truth, and distributes righteousness and forgiveness of sins to His faithful, and hereafter eternal life and salvation. Hence Paul also says that the kingdom of God is "righteousness and peace and joy in the Holy Ghost" (Rom. 14:17). This His eternal kingdom He rules not by the force of the physical sword, as do temporal kings, but by His Word and Gospel, which impart nothing but grace. But those who wish to bear the physical sword in the kingdom of God did not learn it from Christ nor from His apostles, for none of them fought with the sword, but they converted the nations with teaching and preaching. Other kingdoms have their fixed boundaries, but not so the kingdom of Christ. Rather, "His kingdom ruleth over all" (Ps. 103:19), and "from the rising to the setting" (Ps. 107:3), and "from one sea to the next, and from the river unto the ends of the earth" (Ps. 72:8). Other kingdoms, however glorious they may be, are perishable; but the kingdom of Christ is an imperishable and everlasting kingdom, and His "dominion endureth from generation to generation" (Ps. 145:13). What then would the Roman emperor have to fear from Christ's kingdom, since it consists of nothing but heavenly matters, and His dominion does not properly commence until His final return, for which all believing Christians wait with painful longing, and for the sake of the heavenly relinquish all that is earthly!

This confession of Christ's before Pilate is especially comforting. For Paul with all diligence refers us to this with very comforting words when he writes, "I give thee charge in the sight of God, who quickeneth all things, and before Christ Jesus, who before Pontius Pilate witnessed a good confession, that thou keep this commandment without spot, unrebukable, until the appearing of our Lord Jesus Christ" (1 Tim. 6:13–14). Christ confesses before Pilate that His kingdom is of truth, even as through Him a man is truly to obtain grace with God and true righteousness and blessedness, namely, when from His Word he learns to know Him and clings to Him in true faith. That man is of the truth who believes in Christ, who is the Truth (John 14:6), and in His Holy Word, which is also called the truth (John 17:17), and who trusts therein in life and in death. That man can stand at the time of the appearing of Jesus Christ and enter with Him into the kingdom of glory.

Prayer

O Lord Jesus, spotless Lamb of God, my God and my Lord, who for our sake wast made to be reviled and accused as a rebel before Pilate: comfort me and all true Christians when even today we are made to bear this name of disgrace, and so are conformed to the likeness of Thine image. Yet thanks be to Thee, dearest Lord Jesus! Thanks be to Thee for Thy glorious and comforting confession which Thou didst make before Pontius Pilate! What can be more comforting to me, a poor, wretched man, than Thou? My King and my God, only let me ever be and abide Thy faithful subject. Maintain for me Thy mighty protection and shelter against the strong, armed prince of darkness, and against all mine enemies bodily and spiritual, seen and unseen. Govern me by the scepter of Thy Word, that I may persevere steadfast in the only saving Truth and pay no heed to the mockery and hatred of the world, but may boldly confess Thy Word and Thy Truth, and for their sake suffer in quietness and forbearance. In all my troubles let me also take refuge in Thee and seek and find grace and counsel, comfort and help in Thee. Then will I heartily thank and highly adore Thee, and say: To God the King of all kings, who alone hath immortality, be glory and majesty, power and dominion, now and for all eternity! Amen.

DEVOTION 37

Mel.: Ich dank dir, lieber Herre

Thou art a mighty Monarch,
   As by the Word we're told,
Yet carest Thou but little
   For earthly goods or gold;
On no proud steed Thou ridest,
   Thou wear'st no jeweled crown,
Nor dwell'st in lordly castle,
   But bearest scoff and frown.

Yet art Thou decked with beauty;
   With rays of glorious light;
Thou ever teem'st with goodness,
   And all Thy ways are right.
Vouchsafe to shield Thy people
   With Thine almighty arm,
That they may dwell in safety
   From those who mean them harm.

Ah, look on me with pity,
   Though I am weak and poor;
Admit me to Thy kingdom,
   To dwell there, blest and sure!
I pray Thee, guide and keep me
   Safe from my bitter foes,
From sin, and death, and Satan;
   Free me from all my woes.

DEVOTION 38

Christ Is Brought to Herod and Ridiculed by Him

Mel.: Alle Menschen müssen sterben

Jesus is the One I ponder,
  Jesus ever fills my mind:
From His side I'll never wander
  While my life on earth I find.
For mine eyes He is a pasture,
For my heart the highest pleasure,
  For my soul the crown most fair,
  Jesus I will love fore'er.

Jesus in my heart is blazing
  Like a star of gold divine,
All my grief and sorrows chasing,
  I am His and He is mine;
Him I'll grasp with jubilation
When I must depart this station;
  Jesus is my life's true light:
  Jesus shall not leave my sight.

Why do the heathen rage, and the people speak so vainly? The kings in the land set themselves, and the lords take counsel together against the Lord, *and against his Anointed. — Elias is come already, and they knew him not, but have done unto him whatsoever they listed. Likewise shall also the Son of Man suffer of them.**

Psalm 2:1–2; Matthew 17:12

---

* It is certain that, under the name Elias, John the Baptist is understood, for so it is explained in the following (13th) verse. Of him Christ says, "They—read: Herod and Herodias and their servants—have done unto him whatsoever they listed." Hence when Christ adds that the Son of Man shall also have to suffer many things *of them,* He explicitly refers to that part of His suffering which He had to endure in the house of Herod for our sake. —J. Gerhard.

DEVOTION 38

And they persisted, saying, He hath stirred up the people, teaching here and there throughout all Jewry, beginning from Galilee to this place.

But when Pilate heard of Galilee, he asked whether He were a Galilaean. And as soon as he knew that He belonged unto Herod's jurisdiction, he sent Him to Herod, who himself also was at Jerusalem at that time. And when Herod saw Jesus, he became exceeding glad, for he had been desirous to see Him of a long season, because he had heard many things of Him; and he hoped he would see a sign of Him. And he questioned with Him in many words; but He answered him nothing. And the chief priests and scribes stood and vehemently accused Him. But Herod with his men of war set Him at naught, and mocked Him, and put on Him a white robe, and sent Him again to Pilate. On that day were Pilate and Herod made friends together, for before they were at enmity between themselves.

And Pilate, when he had called together the chief priests and the rulers and the people, said unto them, Ye have brought this Man unto me, as one that perverteth the people: and behold, I, having examined Him before you, find no fault in this Man touching those things whereof ye accuse Him; no, nor yet Herod, for I sent you to him, and lo, nothing worthy of death was done unto Him. I will therefore chastise and release Him.

Luke 23:5–16

That Pilate may not be forced to condemn the innocent Jesus against the testimony of his conscience nor invite upon himself the enmity of the chief priests, he thinks happily to extricate himself from the business by sending Christ to Herod.

Accordingly, as glad as Pilate is at last to be rid of Christ, so glad is Herod to get a chance to see Him. But this was no gladness of devotion, but of sheer curiosity, for he hoped to see many miracles and amusements from Christ. In a far different way do believers rejoice in the Lord Christ, for they have their greatest delight and joy in the manifold glorious benefits which He bequeathes and makes our own by His suffering, cross, and death, and we are not to forget them all our life long.

The ungodly Herod is not worthy of seeing a sign from Christ, nor of receiving any answer to his curious and mocking questions. So when he and his courtiers here regard the Lord Christ as nothing and despise Him and mock Him, as great lords today also deride and mock the Gospel, and when he puts on Him a white robe according to the Roman manner, as though He were a candidate for government office—when the most high King of Glory and of our salvation and blessedness lets Himself be brought so low to hell and made the most despised and discounted of all, yea, so despised that men hid their face from Him (Isa. 53:3)—it is done for our consolation. By this He obtains for us the estate of honor which Peter describes for us: "Ye are the chosen generation, the royal priesthood, the holy nation, the people of the possession" (1 Peter 2:9). He brought us the true white robe of innocence, with which we shall shine forever, as John says in his Revelation 7:9ff., when he sees in the Spirit the elect out of all manner of nations in white robes and with palms in their hands, standing in heaven before the throne of the Lamb, which is a sign of the perfect holiness and righteousness, the great joy and the glorious victory and conquest. He is led for us as a spectacle, like a Shrove Tuesday king and fool, throughout the whole city, that the devil may not make a spectacle of us before the holy angels and all creation, and mock us forever, but that we may rather strike a blow to them and their whole kingdom, and to the glory of God sing this joyful song of thanksgiving and victory: "O death, where is thy sting? O hell, where is thy victory? Thanks be to God, which hath given us the victory through Jesus Christ, our Lord" (1 Cor. 15:55, 57).

Over Christ the worst enemies, Pilate and Herod, become the best friends, as also our enemies and adversaries today, who usually hate each other with a passion, can easily join forces when it comes to the church of God. For the devil is a master of a thousand arts; he seeks and contrives in all places to join together against God and His Word those who wish but ill for each other, and ties them together like Samson's foxes, that they may kindle a fire. "For of a truth, both Herod and Pontius Pilate with the Gentiles and the people of Israel were gathered together against Thy holy Child Jesus, whom Thou hast anointed, for to do whatsoever Thy hand and thy counsel determined before to be done" (Acts 4:27–28). So the apostles pray after Psalm 2. But our Lord Christ thereby gained for us the power to have the holy, blessed friendship of God in heaven with the angels and all the elect through our faithful Savior, as Christ says: "I say not henceforth that ye are servants, . . . but My friends; for all things that I have heard of My Father I have made known unto you" (John 15:15). And St. Paul: "Therefore being justified by faith, we have peace with God through our Lord Jesus Christ, through whom also we have access by faith into this grace wherein we stand, and boast in the hope of the glory to come, which God shall give" (Rom. 5:1–2).

But since in the time of His Passion the Lord Christ was found in all respects innocent, and nothing could be laid to His charge in the religious, imperial, or royal court, this innocence of Christ also serves as a glorious comfort to us. For the innocent, faithful Savior suffered for us, and "is the Propitiation for our sins; and not for ours only, but also for the sins of the whole world" (1 John 2:2). His innocence doth bear my sin, and I am saved forever.

Prayer

O kindest Lord Jesus, I give heartfelt thanks to Thee that Thou didst not shun the mockery of Herod and his courtiers, that my honor might thereby be furthered, and I might be preserved from the mockery of hell! Grant me help, that for Thy sake I may in turn count as naught all the pride of the world and the reproach of the wicked for righteousness' sake, and rather choose to be abhorred by the ungodly than to be praised by dissemblers. Let me wisely shun the wisdom of this world, which is foolishness to Thee, and devote myself with a pure heart to Thee, who art true Wisdom. And if, when I live according to the new man, I am judged a fool by the world, let me not regard it, but always think of Thee, who willingly borest such mockery from the world out of love for me. O Lord Jesus, let this white robe cover my nakedness, and Thine innocence hide my guilt. Give me needful garments according to Thy will, and keep me from all pretension. Let my concern be to avoid defiling with sin the white robe that I received in Holy Baptism; and should this ever happen by the weakness or wickedness of my flesh, let me seek to wash it clean in Thy blood. So help me, O Jesus, and I shall be in Thee what I could never be in myself! Amen.

Mel.: Seelenbräutigam

Thou art First and Best,
Jesus, sweetest Rest!
  Life of those who else were dying,
  Light of those in darkness lying,
Ever be Thou blest,
Jesus, sweetest Rest.

Life, that died'st for me
And from misery
  To redeem us death hast tasted:
  Pardon life and blessings wasted,
Take away our load,
Lead us back to God!

Highest Majesty!
King and Prophet! see
  To Thy gentle rule submitting,
  At Thy feet like Mary sitting,
I would learn from Thee,
Highest Majesty!

O Thou Light Divine!
Make me wholly Thine.
  Wisdom by Thy Spirit knowing,
  With Thy love and ardor glowing,
Thou within me shine,
O Thou Light Divine!

DEVOTION 39

Christ Is Equated with the Murderer Barabbas

Mel.: Herzliebster Jesu, was hast du verbrochen

Holy Thou art, conceived by God the Spirit,
Splendid in robes of innocence and merit;
  Thou art than all the sons of men far Fairer,
  Free from all error.

How is it, then, that Thou shouldst be so treated,
As if Thou hadst a sin, and be so cheated,
  And as though naught more vile existed ever
  Than Thou, the Savior?

Thou as our Surety the price wouldst render,
Bearing the pain for man, the vile offender;
  Thus must He, who the debtor would be sparing,
  His debt be bearing!

I must pay that which I took not away. — Chastisement lieth upon him, that we might have peace.

Psalm 69:4; Isaiah 53:5

Now at that feast the governor, according to custom, must of necessity release unto the people a prisoner, whomsoever they desired. And he had then a notable prisoner, an evildoer and robber, who was called Barabbas, who with them that made insurrection had been cast into prison, who in the insurrection that was made in the city had committed a murder. And the people went up and began to desire Him *to do as he had ever done unto them. And when they were gathered together, Pilate answered them, saying, Ye have a custom, that I should release unto you one at the Passover; whom will ye that I release unto you? Barabbas, or Jesus, the King of the Jews, which is called Christ? For he knew that the chief priests had delivered him for envy. And when he was set down on the judgment seat, his wife sent unto him, saying, Have thou nothing to do with that righteous Man, for I have suffered many things this day in a dream because of Him. But the chief priests and elders persuaded and moved the people that they should ask Barabbas and destroy Jesus. Then the governor answered and said unto them, Whether of the twain will ye that I release unto you? And the people cried out all at once, saying, Away with this Man, and release unto us Barabbas! Then Pilate cried again to them, willing to release Jesus, and said, What shall I do then with Jesus, which is called Christ? They cried out again, Crucify, crucify Him! But he said unto them the third time, Why, what evil hath He done? I find no cause of death in Him; I will therefore chastise Him and let Him go. But they cried out the more exceedingly, saying, Crucify Him! And they pressed him instantly with loud voices, requiring that he might be crucified. And the voices of them and of the chief priests prevailed.*

Matthew 27:15–23; Mark 15:6–14; Luke 23:17–23; John 18:39–40

Pilate sees that he went too far when, in order to please the Jews, he chose to chastise Christ and let Him go; for he must again freely and openly confess that nothing can be brought against Christ. Why will he commit such a great injustice and let an innocent Man be scourged? Therefore, before the Jews can answer him, he thinks of other means. The Jews had a self-invented custom that the Roman governor must release unto them at the Passover a prisoner, by which they recalled how God redeemed them from Pharaoh's house of bondage in Egypt, which custom nevertheless ran directly counter to the command of God, who desired that what is wicked should be done away and evildoers be punished; for "cursed be he that keepeth back his sword from shedding blood" (Jer. 48:10). So also, God gave them another yearly memorial of this benefit, namely, the feast of the Passover, in which they had sufficient reminder. "In vain is God served with the statutes of men" (Matt. 15:9). Pilate is reminded of this custom of theirs, sets the murderer and seditious man, Barabbas, beside Christ, and it seems to him impossible that the people should ask for the murderer and rather reject Christ.

Now, before the Jews can answer Pilate's suggestion, the business with the dream of his wife Procla takes place, which without doubt was a divine dream. For she has her master warned of calamity, reminds him of his office, and has him told that he is not to let himself be persuaded by the reckless Jews to slay this righteous Man because of whom she has suffered so many things in her dream, nor to invite upon his conscience so heavy a debt.

But although Pilate accepts this testimony even by the dreaming of his wife, and seeks to move the people to ask for Christ, it is in vain. For from this hour the chief priests and elders incite the people so that they cry at the top of their lungs, "Away with this Man! Crucify, crucify Him! And release unto us Barabbas!" And so it was. So hostile is the devil and the world to the dear Lord Christ and His Holy Gospel that His own people, to whom He was promised and sent, desire rather to spare the greatest rogue and ne'er-do-well than to let innocent Jesus go free; yea, they would have asked for the devil himself to be freed rather than that the Son of God should be released. So it is still today and always. Great lords can tolerate Anabaptists, Sacramentarians, and other sects; but as soon as the Gospel is heard a little, there is fire in all the streets and no one will allow it. They also let Barabbas go free and crucify Christ, as the Jews did.

Long ago, King David sinned and the subjects were punished. Here, the subjects misbehaved and the King was taken to task. "O Thou Son of God, how deeply dost Thou humiliate Thyself! We did evil, and Thou bearest the punishment!" says Augustine. The first man let the devil deceive him in the garden of Eden, so that he rose up in seditious manner against God and His commandment, and in this insurrection he committed murder toward himself and all mankind. For "by one man came sin into the world, and death through sin, and so death spread to all men, forasmuch as they all sinned," says St. Paul (Rom. 5:18). *Barabbas* means approximately "son of the father," one whose nature resembles that of his father. O truly, truly do we all resemble our father Adam, for we are conceived and born in sin. Every desire and thought of our heart is evil from our youth up and continually (Gen. 6:5). We drink up iniquity like water (Job 15:16). There is none that doeth good, no, not one (Ps. 14:3; 53:3; Rom. 3:12). As often, then, as a man sins, so often does he rebel against God and become a murderer of his own body and soul. For God is not a God that taketh pleasure in ungodliness; he that is evil abideth not before Him (Ps. 5:4). Here we poor children of Adam ought to have been taken in bonds and suffered eternal death; for the wages of sin is death. But Barabbas and mankind are released, and Christ, the most holy Son of God, must pay the price and die. Why? St. Paul answers, "God made Him that knew no sin to be sin for us, that we might in Him be made the righteousness that availeth before God" (1 Cor. 5:21).

> As 'twas another's sin our race
>   In Adam all defilèd,
> So hath Another's loving grace
>   In Christ all reconcilèd.

This account also gives us two further things to consider: The first is the terrible, unprecedented ingratitude of the Jews. Our Lord Christ had led this people out of Egypt and delivered them out of the terrible house of bondage. He had preached His Holy Gospel to the inhabitants of Jerusalem, and in so doing performed great signs and wonders, healed all manner of diseases, and the like; even as His love is manifest in the heart-rending words, "O Jerusalem, Jerusalem! . . . how often would I have gathered thy children together, even as a hen gathereth her chickens under her wings, and ye would not!" (Matt. 23:37) What sort of thanks does He earn? He receives nothing but that they sing sorrowful song of murder, "Crucify Him!" and cast upon Him the piteous cry, "Away, away with this Man!"

The second is the inconstancy of the people. When Christ miraculously fed the five thousand men in the wilderness, they wished to take Him and make Him king; and behold, now they wish to know nothing of His being King of the Jews, but cry, "Away with this Man, and release unto us Barabbas!" Five days before they cried with a loud voice, "Hosanna to the Son of David! Blessed be He that cometh in the name of the Lord!" Now they cry at the top of their lungs, "Crucify, crucify Him!" Therefore do not trust in the praise and favor of the common people. How did it go with Paul? When he performed a miraculous work in Lystra, the people regarded him as a god and wished to offer sacrifices to him; soon after, they stoned him with stones and dragged him out of the city (Acts 14). When a viper attacked his hand on the island of Malta, the people said, "This man must be a murderer"—but when no harm befell him, they regarded him as a god.

Prayer

O Lord Jesus, the Love of the Father! Thou wast made the hatred of the Jews, the children to whom Thou wast sent. They complained to Pontius Pilate concerning Thee, the holy and righteous One, and asked to be given the murderer Barabbas. They rejected Thee, the highest Good, the Lord who is our Righteousness, and chose for themselves the highest evil, even wrath and damnation. Let me not become like them, nor reject Life and choose eternal death. In Holy Baptism I was pledged to Thee, and Thou to me; therefore I will remain Thine own in time and eternity. O my Surety and Substitute in the divine judgment, who wast made sin for me, that I in Thee might be made the righteousness that availeth before God: let me not fall away from the consolation of the right faith when my conscience and Thy Law accuse and condemn me! Thou who art the Light of the world, keep me, that I may not let myself be persuaded and moved by the wise and lofty of this world, nor prefer what is earthly, worldly, and sinful to Thee, but let me choose Thee, who of God wast made unto me wisdom, righteousness, sanctification, and redemption (1 Cor. 1:30). Though the world should do with me as it did with Thee, I know that the disciple is not above his Master. In the world I will gladly lie wherever it casts me and be as it regards me; let me only be made a companion of the elect in heaven, and I shall have what I hope for, and suffer gladly what I must suffer to Thy glory! Amen.

Mel.: Herzliebster Jesu, was hast du verbrochen

What strangest punishment is suffered yonder!
The Shepherd dies for sheep that loved to wander;
  The Master pays the debt His servants owe Him,
  Who would not know Him.s

(continued)

The sinless Son of God must die in sadness;
The sinful child of man may live in gladness;
  Man forfeited his life, and is acquitted—
  God is committed.

There was no spot in me by sin untainted;
Sick with sin's poison, all my heart had fainted;
  My heavy guilt to hell had well-nigh brought me,
  Such woe it wrought me.

O wondrous love, whose depth no heart hath sounded,
That brought Thee here by foes and thieves surrounded,
  All worldly pleasures, heedless, I was trying
  While Thou wert dying!

DEVOTION 40

Jesus Is Scourged and Crowned with Thorns

Mel.: Herr, ich habe mißgehandelt

Come with glances sad, astounded,
  Gaze upon thy Bridegroom-God,
See His back so scarred and wounded
  None can know it for the blood.
Come, the thorny crown descrying,
Round His ribboned temples lying.

Here a pauper slave He standeth—
  He, whom heav'n and earth adore;
Here He bears what Law demandeth,
  Stripes that should the servant score,
Here He suffers coronation
With the curse of all creation.

The plowers plowed upon my back: they made long their furrows. — I gave my back to them that smote me, and my cheeks to them that plucked me: I hid not my face from shame and spitting. — They shall deliver the Son of Man to the Gentiles, to mock Him.

Psalm 129:3; Isaiah 50:6; Matthew 20:19

Then Pilate took Jesus, and scourged Him. But the soldiers of the governor took Him into the judgment hall, and gathered together the whole band of soldiers, and stripped Him, and put on Him a purple cloak; and when they had platted a crown of thorns, they put it upon His head, and put a reed in His right hand. And they bowed the knee before Him, and mocked Him, and began to salute Him, saying, Hail, King

of the Jews! And they smote Him in the face and spit upon Him, and took the reed, and smote Him on the head therewith, and bowing their knees worshiped Him.
Matthew 27:27-30; Mark 15:16-19; John 19:1-3

Here Pilate makes an effort to set Jesus free by very improper means. For when the previous plan again falls apart, he causes the Lord Jesus to be treated so miserably that a hard stone in the earth would be moved to pity, doing so under the supposition that he will induce the people to compassion, break their wrathful heart, and set Christ free.

In their synagogues, those who sinned against the Law in some way were whipped by the Jews publicly before the congregation with thongs or whips of leather, and given forty lashes (Deut. 25:2-3; 2 Cor. 11:24). The Romans tied lawbreakers to a pillar, tore their clothes from their body, and abused them with rods and scourges in an abominable manner. So it was also with Christ, as Isaiah had prophesied beforehand: "I gave My back to them that smote Me, and My cheeks to them that plucked Me: I hid not My face from shame and spitting" (50:6), and, "He was wounded for our iniquity, and bruised for our sins" (53:5). But although Pilate gave out that it was only to be a chastisement, yet the soldiers, to please the rulers of the Temple, turned it into the most horrible spectacle of violence; for they used executioner's rods into which they wove thorns and cords and threaded iron hooks. With these they struck and scourged Him so that His veins were torn open and His scarlet blood flowed down His back in rivers, and no part of His body was left unscathed. O eternal Son of God, Jesus Christ, how is it that Thy heavenly Father caused Thee to be beaten so unmercifully with rods and scourges? How didst Thou ever deserve it? "Ah," says Anselm, "I see well what the cause is! Thou art the Lamb of God that taketh away the sins of the whole world. The Father cast upon Thee the iniquities of us all, the wrath of God so presses Thee that Thou must pay for us what we did merit!" In this I take comfort. Let this scourging of Christ also serve for patience. For since Thy Savior endured these sharp strokes of the lash with great patience, why would you murmur against God when He smites you a little with His rod of fatherly chastisement on account of your sins? Remember, troubled heart, that even under the rod you are His dear child. "Where is a son whom the father chastiseth not? But if ye be without

DEVOTION 40

chastising, whereof they all were made partakers, then are ye illegitimate and not sons" (Heb. 12:7–8).

After the *scourging,* the soldiers treated Christ mockingly, like someone who had claimed to be a king and was not. For this reason they put a *purple cloak* on Him in lieu of a royal robe. Because long ago, kings and chief priests used to be dressed in this way (1 Macc. 10:20; 2 Macc. 4:38), they pull out an old military cloak from under the bench and throw it over Him. This old, torn purple cloak and military garment was dyed outwardly with the blood of the worm from which purple dye used to be made, but inwardly with the blood of Christ, that that might be fulfilled which Isaiah said (63:2–3) and which is found written in Revelation 19:13, "Wherefore is Thine apparel red, and Thy garment like his that treadeth the winefat? I have trodden the winepress alone, and of the peoples no man is with Me." When Scripture speaks of great, terrible sins, it calls them bloodguiltiness and sins of blood (Ps. 51:14; Isa. 1:15). In these we all lay. But the Lord Christ, who here sprinkles His clothing with blood, washes and cleanses us from our sins. Though our sins be red as blood, yet shall they be white as snow, and though they be as scarlet, yet shall they be like wool (Isa. 1:18). He is the blood-red worm crushed for us, from which the blood was pressed by which all our bloodguiltiness has been dissolved. Hence He says, "I am a worm and no man" (Ps. 22:6). He wears the purple cloak, that He may put on us the robe of righteousness and the garments of salvation (Isa. 61:3). It is not His cloak, but that of another, to show that this was all done for our sake.

And that His head might also be wounded, they plait and weave a piercing crown of great, horrible *thorns,* such as grow in the Orient. They press it onto His head so that the blood flows out freely over His whole body, which was full of stripes, wounds, and bruises. The thorns and thistles are a fruit of the cursed earth (Gen. 3:17–18; Heb. 6:8). Likewise, we are all evil fruit, subject to the curse, and belong to hellfire. But as the goat or ram with its two horns stood in the hedge of thorns that Isaac might go free (Gen. 22:13), so here the Champion of two descents, God and Man, must stand in the crown of thorns that we might escape the eternal curse and obtain the crown of righteousness (1 Peter 5:4), the crown of life (James 1:12; Rev. 2:10), and the crown of pure gold (Rev. 4:4). We seized at the crown of our Lord God in paradise, and exalted ourselves so highly in our pride that, like Lucifer, we wished to be equal to the high Majesty. For this Christ makes atonement here. It says in the Song of Songs 3:11: "Go ye forth and see, ye daughters of Zion, King Solomon in the crown, wherewith his mother hath crowned him on the day of his wedding." Our faithful Savior is the true heavenly Solomon and eternal Prince of Peace, who here in the Passion celebrates His wedding feast, so that He strives with the devil in a bloody battle in which His own mother, the Jewish clergy, boldly lends a hand. By this He not only won for His bride, the holy Christian church, a beautiful wedding dress, which He dyed in His own blood, but also brought it about that God has crowned the earth and us all with grace and mercy (Ps. 68:10; 103:4).

The ungodly villains also put a *reed* in His hand instead of a golden scepter, that they might show that His kingdom cannot stand for long; it is like a reed shaken to and fro by the wind and swiftly broken. But we are to take comfort in the fact that the Lord Christ, our King, has a right scepter that cannot be bent like a reed, but is firm, strong, and exceedingly mighty (Ps. 2:9; 45:6; 110:2, 5–6). With it He can and will protect us from all our enemies. And as King Ahasuerus held his scepter out to his Esther as a sign of particular grace (Esther 5:2), so we also are to hold to the scepter of the divine promise and take comfort in the fact that the gracious King Jesus shall not wholly break the bruised reed nor quench the smoking flax (Isa. 42:3; Matt. 12:20).

Instead of royal *honor,* they give Him *mockery* in word and deed, as if performing a Shrovetide play, and smite and spit on His face. In Deuteronomy 25:9, it is established in the Law that the people are to be spit on before judgment. This reproach, scorn, and mockery the Lord Jesus receives to Himself, letting Himself be covered with spittle and filth for our sake, that He might renew in us the image of God in true righteousness and holiness.

Prayer

O Lord Jesus, most patient Redeemer! I thank Thee that for my sake Thou didst bear this abuse and mockery, this scourging and crowning, this spitting and reviling! I thank Thee that Thou didst suffer Thyself to be stripped of Thy garments and brought out naked, for now I shall be arrayed with the beautiful

DEVOTION 40

robe of righteousness, and my sinful nakedness shall be covered before God. I thank Thee that for my sake Thou didst suffer Thyself to be bound to a pillar and wounded and beaten without mercy, for now Thou wilt turn from me all the blows of God's wrath, and by Thy stripes and wounds make whole all the wounds of my sins. I thank Thee that Thou didst suffer Thyself to be clothed and wrapped with a purple cloak, for now I shall be dressed in the snow-white garment of innocence and holiness. I thank Thee that Thou didst suffer Thyself to be crowned with a crown of thorns, for now I shall receive from Thine hands the crown of glory, which in that Day Thou shalt set upon the head of all that love Thine appearing. I thank Thee that Thou didst will to take a reed in Thine hands, for now Thou shalt preserve me, who am a feeble reed and fragile vessel. I thank Thee that Thou didst suffer Thyself to be ridiculed, mocked, smitten in the face, and spit on, for now I shall not be spit on, smitten, and mocked in hell, but eternally honored, quickened, and gladdened in heaven. There I shall receive great honor, unspeakable bliss and joy, and the fullness of pleasures at Thy right hand forever and ever. Amen, Lord Jesus! Amen.

Mel.: Jesu, der du meine Seele
Or: Jesu, meines Lebens Leben

Hail, O Jesus, King of Glory
  In Thine hour of mockery!
Yet this is as naught before Thee:
  Hail, my God and Lord, to Thee!
For before Thy throne in heaven,
Crown and robe and scepter even,
  I fall down in heart and mind:
  Here Thy humbled servant find!

O Lord Jesus, my transgressions
  Surely brought Thee to this place;
I should bear these indiscretions,
  But Thou bor'st for me disgrace.

(continued)

Lord, Thy rightful crown pursuing,
Yet I see my sinful doing
  On Thy shoulders; my disgrace
  Mars not my, but Thy dear face.

When in sin I stand before Thee,
  Then I put Thee, Lord, to scorn;
When in my own self I glory,
  Then I plait Thy crown of thorn.
When I grieve Thy members lowly
Then my smiting fist I show Thee;
  When I sin with willful mind,
  Then, oh, then Thine eyes I blind!

Lord, alas! forgive and spare me,
  Look not scornfully at me,
From Thy crown let nothing tear me,
  Be my King eternally;
See how I with glad endeavor
Kneel before Thee, feigning never;
  Robes and wealth and earthly show
  For Thy glory I forgo.

At Thy feet I fall before Thee;
  Lord, my King, my Life, my Light;
I will kiss Thee and adore Thee
  Ere Thy wrath be kindled bright;
O my King, of might amazing,
I will Thee be ever praising;
  Through all scorn and mocking word,
  Thou shalt be my King and Lord!

DEVOTION 41

"Ecce homo! Behold, What a Man!"

Mel.: Was frag ich nach der Welt
Or: O Gott, du frommer Gott

See what a Man is this!
  O eyes with teardrops thronging!
O face reviled and scorned,
  O lips all full of longing!
O head with death-drops wet,
  O cheeks with spittle spread,
O heart, so full of blood!
  O limbs, distressed and dead!

See what a Man is this!
  Your tears in torrents offer:
It is your guilt that makes
  Christ's heart to bleed and suffer;
Oh, pass not by this scene,
  These pains which Him aggrieve,
But through His open side
  Your Jesus' heart perceive.

See, what a Man is this!
  Ah, yes, we would see ever
What men have done to Thee,
  O Friend of men, and Savior!
So long as eyes avail,
  So long that agony
Which Thou for us hast borne
  Shall still remembered be.

He had no form nor beauty; we saw him, but there was no form that should please us. He was the most despised and most abject; full of sorrows and sickness. He was so despised that our face was hid from him; therefore we esteemed him not.

Isaiah 53:2–3

Then went Pilate forth again, and said unto them, Behold, I bring Him forth to you, that ye may know that I find no fault in Him. Then came Jesus forth, wearing the crown of thorns and the purple robe. And Pilate saith unto them, Behold the Man! When the chief priests and officers saw Him, they cried out, saying, Crucify, crucify Him! Pilate saith unto them, Take ye Him, and crucify Him; for I find no fault in Him. The Jews answered Him, We have a law, and by that Law He ought to die, because He made Himself the Son of God.

John 19:4–7

Pilate presents Jesus to the Jews in His bloody form, removes the purple cloak from Him, shows them His stripes, wounds, and bruises, in the hopes that they might be moved to compassion, and cries, "'*Ecce homo! Behold what a Man!*' Do you not have pity yourself to see a Man treated so wickedly? I am sure you would have been appeased, contented yourselves, and released Him. But there is no pity among the Jews, though a heathen heart had pity. They cry with one voice, 'Crucify, crucify Him!'"

Now, even as this is very disgraceful and painful for Christ, yet it is very comforting to our heart.

Come, *people of little faith!* Behold what a Man! Here you can find joy. The tyrant King Rehoboam said to his subjects, "My father laid on you a heavy yoke; I will add to your yoke yet more. He chastised you with whips, I will chastise you with scorpions" (1 Kings 12:14). But the Lord Christ, our hereditary King, has no such scepter for the afflicted. The bruised reed He shall not wholly break, and the smoking flax He shall not utterly quench (Isa. 42:3). How comfortingly He says, "I look to him that is poor and of a contrite spirit, and trembleth at My Word" (Isa. 66:2). He helps not only the centurion of Capernaum, who had such strong faith, and the Canaanite woman, who had such great faith, but also willingly helps at once the father of the possessed boy, who calls his own faith unbelief, even as He does for the royal officer, who prescribes for Christ both time and measure. Simply sigh with the disciples, "Lord, increase my faith" (Luke 17:6).

Come, *arrogant fools of fashion!* Behold what a Man is Christ in this borrowed purple garment! With this He is made to atone for your pride and your vanity. This sin has now grown so common that many spend all their wealth on superfluous pomp and apparel. When they seek to exalt themselves by the beauty of their clothing, all their goods depart. "What madness," says the pagan Ovid, "to drag one's money about on one's body!" But the Lord God says by the prophet Isaiah:

> Because the daughters of Zion are haughty, and walk with stretched-forth necks, with wanton eyes, walking and mincing as they go, and having costly shoes on their feet, therefore the Lord will smite with baldness the crown of the head of the daughters of Zion, and the Lord will take away their jewelry, the beauty of their costly shoes, the clasps, the brooches, the chains, the bracelets, the mufflers, the bonnets, the rings, the headbands . . . And instead of sweet smell there shall be stink . . . and instead of a wide cloak a slender sackcloth; and burning instead of beauty. (3:16–24)

The first man to wear the purple in Rome was struck by lightning, as Pliny writes, and King Herod, who flaunted his haughty apparel on his throne, was smitten by the angel of the Lord and eaten by worms (Acts 12:23).

Christ here wears *another's* cloak. In this He might well be noted especially by *the German nation,* which above all other nations delights most in others' attire and others' ways. For this sin too Christ must make atonement here. He speaks to everyone in such foreign apparel, saying, "I will visit all them that wear a strange garment" (Zeph. 1:8). What is a strange garment? That which is not of your own country and estate. "Clothing is a sign of mortality," says Cyprian. Oh, whoever might think well upon this would not dress and adorn his mortal sack of worms to such excess!

Come, *troubled soul!* Behold what a Man this is! Here you can see not only how God is angry because of sin, but also how the heavenly Father sufficiently glorifies and demonstrates His heartfelt, unspeakable love therein, that for us, His enemies, He sets His only and obedient Son so deeply in such suffering. Whoever does not see and feel in these stripes and wounds and in this bloody form the boundlessness of God's fatherly heart, how else should that man know His fatherly love?

Come hither, *Christian bearers of the cross*—all you who are reviled, persecuted, and tormented for the sake of the Lord Christ! Behold what a Man Christ is, the Founder and Perfecter of faith. For as the Passion is played out with Christ, so is it for His church and congregation also. We are beaten and chastised, that we may not be condemned with the world. Before we attain to glory, we must also first suffer, for the crown of thorns precedes the crown of glory, and because we are conformed to the image of the Son first in His suffering before we are made like unto Him in glory, so we must also be made a spectacle unto the world (Rom. 8:29; 1 Cor. 4:9). Thus in Constance they set on the holy martyr John Hus a crown on which were painted many devils and the word "arch-heretic." Thus the Epicureans mock the messengers of God and despise His Word and imitate His prophets, until the anger of the Lord waxes upon the people. Yea, this also is the *Ecce homo,* when the world mocks us in our utmost distress, saying, "Aha, aha, we have seen it gladly!" (Ps. 35:21), and many of them have hearts of stone and adamant, who suffer themselves to be moved to no mercy, as among the Jews also there was no human pity at all for Christ, though Pilate cried, "See what a Man!" But for the faithful there follows upon this an eternal, unspeakable glory.

Prayer

O Lord Jesus, whose enemies saw Thee with evil and unrighteous eyes: open Thou mine eyes to behold Thee in right faith! Grant, I beseech Thee, that Thou mayest be my constant focus in my life, that I may look upon Thee and the mystery of Thy suffering for my instruction, to study it day and night; for the pattern of my life, in all points to walk in Thy bloodstained footsteps; and for my consolation, to be comforted and encouraged with Thee in all cross and suffering. Grant, I beseech Thee, that in death mine eyes may look upon Thee, that when they fail, I may yet see Thee in Thy bloody form, as Thou didst bow Thy head in death on the cross! Yea, grant me then the blessed sight that Stephen had in his death, when he cried out, "I see the heavens opened, and the Son of Man standing on the right hand of God!" Grant, I beseech Thee, that Thou mayest also be seen by me in eternity! There, there I will see Thee as the slain Lamb of God in the midst of the throne with the four and twenty elders, and intone to Thy glory an eternal Alleluia. Then, then I shall obtain the end of my faith: In my own flesh I shall see God, mine eyes shall behold Him, and not another. Amen, amen!

Mel.: Jesu, meines Lebens Leben

Thou hast borne the smiting only
  That my wounds might all be whole;
Thou hast suffered, sad and lonely,
  Rest to give my weary soul;
Yea, the curse of God enduring,
Blessing unto me securing.
  Thousand, thousand thanks shall be,
  Dearest Jesus, unto Thee.

Heartless scoffers did surround Thee,
  Treating Thee with cruel scorn,
E'en with piercing thorns they crowned Thee;
  All disgrace Thou, Lord, hast borne,
That as Thine Thou mightest own me,
And with heav'nly glory crown me.
  Thousand, thousand thanks shall be,
  Dearest Jesus, unto Thee.

DEVOTION 42

Pilate Is Afraid of the Son of God, but More So of the Jews

Mel.: O Durchbrecher aller Bande

Oh, how glorious was the ransom
  Giv'n to make us pure and free!
Deep and true as was Thy Passion
  Must our purifying be.
Holy, stainless, free, and perfect
  In the kingdom of the Lord
Shall the saved ones stand in glory,
  The redeemed and the restored.

Love, give us Thy deep communion;
  May we in Thy life arise,
Guided onward by Thy glory,
  To the depths of paradise,—
Deepen through the kindling heavens,
  Dawn of the immortal day!
As a dream shall heav'n entrance us
  And shall never pass away.

Great bullocks have compassed me, fat-fleshed oxen have beset me round; they spread their jaws before me as a roaring and a ravening lion.

Psalm 22:12–13

When Pilate heard that saying, he was the more afraid; and went again into the judgment hall, and saith unto Jesus, Whence art Thou? But Jesus gave him no *answer. Then said Pilate unto Him, Speakest Thou not unto me? Knowest Thou not that I have power to crucify Thee, and have power to release Thee? Jesus answered, Thou couldest have no power at all against Me except it were given thee from above. Therefore he that delivered Me unto thee hath the greater sin. From thenceforth Pilate sought to release Him. But the Jews cried out, saying, If thou let this Man go, thou art not Caesar's friend, for whosoever maketh himself a king is against Caesar. When Pilate therefore heard that saying, he brought Jesus forth, and sat down in the judgment seat in a place that is called the Pavement, but in the Hebrew, Gabbatha. And it was the preparation-day of the Passover, about the sixth hour. And he saith unto the Jews, Behold this is your King! But they cried out, Away, away with the Man, crucify Him! Pilate saith unto them, Shall I crucify your King? The chief priests answered, We have no king but Caesar.*

John 19:8–15

Because the Jews had finally brought the charge, "We have a law, and by that law He ought to die, because He made Himself the Son of God," Pilate is therefore struck with great fear at the new article of complaint, being concerned that this Jesus might possibly be a concealed, secret god whom he was eager not to mistreat, even as the pagans imagined that their gods sometimes walked on the earth, and as the people of Lystra believed that Barnabas was Jupiter and Paul was Mercury (Acts 14:11–12).

Now therefore, although Pilate is on the right path when, having heard this saying, he asks Christ Himself whence He is, he nevertheless had no serious intention of coming to true knowledge of Christ. And therefore Christ does not answer him. For there is no obligation to preach to scoffers and those who do not have sincere intentions, nor to answer their questions. What is holy is not to be given to dogs, nor pearls to be cast before swine, lest they trample them underfoot (Matt. 7:6). Whoever desires to seek and inquire after God inquires of His Word. And Pilate had heard this plentifully from the mouth of Jesus, and if he wished, he could have learned and found out a great deal long before this. In addition, Christ had openly confessed to his face who He was and how His kingdom is not of this world, from which he ought to have concluded that Christ must be from heaven. But when Christ said He was born and came into the world to the end that He might bear witness to the truth, Pilate cast this in His teeth, saying scornfully, "What is truth?"

But when Pilate, in response to Christ's silence, talks very boastfully and says that he has the power to chastise the Lord and also the power to release Him, the Lord can no longer remain silent, but rebukes him first on account of his boastful words, since he would have no power over Jesus if it had not been given him from above, and also on account of his sin, since he used the authority given him from above against Christ, adding, "Therefore he that delivered Me unto thee hath the greater sin." This is to be understood not only of Judas, who had delivered Jesus to the chief priests by his treachery, but also and especially of the chief priests, and then of all the Jews taken together. These all violated and sinned against Christ more than the governor Pontius Pilate. Judas sinned out of avarice, the chief priests out of envy, the people out of ignorance, yet Pilate out of fear and human weakness. Yet one sins more than another, for one sin is greater than another. Pilate does wrong to treat Christ so sternly and firmly, but the others far more by striking all the bells together, as it were, until they had handed over their faithful Kinsman to the Gentile Pilate.

Now therefore, when the Jews see how Christ's reminder to Pilate is so effective that he seeks to release Him, the Jews threaten Pilate by referring to Caesar, crying, "If thou let this Man go, thou art not Caesar's friend, for whosoever maketh himself a king is against Caesar." When Pilate hears this saying, he declines to release Christ, since he is afraid of being accused before Caesar by the malicious Jews. He thinks it more advisable to condemn an innocent man than to lose his office, dignity, and honor for the sake of such a man. But what the ungodly man fears befalls him. For, as Eusebius reports (bk. 2, ch. 7), Pilate not only fell into Caesar's disfavor within three years, but was also removed from his office and summoned to Rome to answer for himself. But while he is on the way, he falls into despair, runs himself through with his own sword, and thus dies in misery under the disfavor of God and Caesar. This was the just punishment for his injustice and ruthlessness. By this example, therefore, all judges ought to be moved to fear God more than man, that "the fear of the Lord may be with them" when they judge (2 Chron. 19:6), and that they may consider the outcome of trying to win the favor of those princes over them at the cost of an evil conscience. We also learn here that, once a man turns aside from the way of righteousness, a greater error soon follows. Pilate acted contrary to his conscience by delivering Christ to be scourged, when he ought to have pronounced Him innocent. Soon he is carried away so far into injustice that he gives up the attempt to release Jesus, since he wishes to appease the Jews, but especially because he does not wish to lose Caesar's favor.

Finally, we are also to be warned not to cast away Christ with His office and benefits, nor to despise Him, as the Jews did here when they cried, "We have no King but Caesar." These are terrible words, for with them they trample underfoot all the promises and all Holy Scripture concerning the Messiah to the greatest extent possible, condemn all their godly forefathers, who based their comfort, confidence, life, and salvation on Christ, and say, as it were, "We will not have this Nazarene as King or Lord. He shall not reign or rule over us. We have no interest in Him, for we have enough in Caesar Tiberius, whom we acknowledge as our lord." Very well, senseless, miserable Jews, you have hereby delivered up your heavenly, eternal King, and chosen to be imperial. You have become imperial, and so you must remain, for better or for worse. You have pronounced the sentence upon yourselves, and no doubt the emperor thanked you forty years later, and you will remember it daily still! Therefore we will not cast away the eternal Son of God, Jesus Christ, but rather embrace, yea, and kiss Him, lest He be angry and we perish on the way, for His wrath is soon kindled; but "blessed are all they that trust in Him" (Ps. 2:12). "Him that honoreth Him He will honor, and he that despiseth Him shall be despised in turn" (1 Sam. 2:30).

Prayer

O Lord Jesus, Thy own people, the Jews, and particularly their builders, refused Thee, the tried and choice Cornerstone and Foundation, and for all their heirs renounced the desire to have any part in Thee. Oh, the terrible, impudent renunciation! Yet, O Lord Jesus, be Thou to me for a strong Cornerstone and Stone of help, and enlighten me, that I may never be offended at Thee, but rather may be set upon Thee in true faith. Strengthen me, that the fearsome billows and stormy winds of tribulation may not prevail against me. If like Thee I too must be a despised man, rejected by the world, and tolerated nowhere, and must hear, "Away, away with this man!" yet raise up me, O Lord Jesus, set me as a seal, and comfort me, that I may count reproach and exile as nothing, and may rather take heartfelt comfort in the fact that my name is written in heaven and that Thou art my King in life and death. If Thy wayward children, the Jews, cried out as an exceptional mockery, "We have no King but Caesar! We would not have this Jesus of Nazareth to rule over us!" then I say from the bottom of my heart, "I have a King!" Thou David's Son of Jacob's race, my Bridegroom and my King of grace, for Thee my heart is pining: lowly, holy, great and glorious, Thou victorious Prince of graces, filling all the heav'nly places! If Thine ungrateful people, the Jews, cast Thee, the Bread of heaven, from the readied table of grace and trampled Thee underfoot, yet I will take care to lift Thee up and kiss Thee and find my refreshment and quickening forever in Thee! Let him go that thrusts Thee away, O Lord; Thou shalt remain my only comfort. I live unto Thee, I die unto Thee: whether dead or alive I belong to Thee, Lord Jesus! Amen.

Mel.: Seelenbräutigam

Brightness of His Face!
To redeem our race,
  Ere time was, Thou wast appointed
  And didst veil Thee, God's Anointed,
In our human race:
Brightness of His Face!

Conqu'ror, Thou alone
Hast the pow'rs o'erthrown
  Of the world, the flesh, the devil;
  Souls that once were slaves to evil,
Thou hast made Thine own,
Conqu'ror, Thou alone!

DEVOTION 42

Highest Majesty!
King and Prophet! see
  To Thy gentle rule submitting,
  At Thy feet like Mary sitting,
I would learn from Thee,
Highest Majesty!

DEVOTION 43

Pilate Condemns Jesus, and the Jews Take His Blood upon Themselves

Mel.: Herzliebster Jesu, was hast du verbrochen

O dearest Jesus, what law hast Thou broken
That such sharp sentence should on Thee be spoken?
 Of what great crime hast Thou to make confession,
 What dark transgression?

Whence come these sorrows, whence this mortal anguish?
It is my sins for which Thou, Lord, must languish;
 Yea, all the wrath, the woe, Thou dost inherit;
 This I do merit.

What strangest punishment is suffered yonder!
The Shepherd dies for sheep that loved to wander;
 The Master pays the debt His servants owe Him,
 Who would not know Him.

The sinless Son of God must die in sadness,
The sinful child of man may live in gladness;
 Man forfeited his life and is acquitted—
 God is committed.

*And it came to pass, when they were in the field, that Cain rose up against Abel his brother, and slew him. And the L*ORD *said unto Cain, Where is Abel thy brother? . . . The voice of thy brother's blood crieth unto me from the ground.*

Genesis 4:8, 10

DEVOTION 43

When Pilate saw that he could prevail nothing, but that a far greater tumult was made, he, willing to content the people, gave sentence that their request should be done, took water, and washed his hands before the people, saying, I am innocent of the blood of this just Man: see ye to it. Then answered all the people, and said, His blood be on us, and on our children. Then released he Barabbas unto them, that for sedition and murder was cast into prison, whom they had desired, but Jesus being scourged and mocked, he delivered Him to their will, to be crucified.

Matthew 27:24–26; Mark 15:15; Luke 23:25

Thus Pilate lets fear and selfish gain overcome him, which he esteems greater and higher than virtue and righteousness; for he sets men's favor over God's friendship and takes the temporal instead of the eternal. How terrible it is that a pagan man should, against his own will and conscience, sentence the Captain of Life, the Son of the living God, to death! Luther expresses the death sentence as it was spoken over Christ by Pilate in this manner: *"Quoniam Jesus,* etc. Whereas Jesus of Nazareth hath styled Himself King of the Jews and sought after the crown of Caesar, therefore I, Pilate, as steward and governor of the Roman Caesar in Judaea, hereby adjudge that He shall be crucified, as fitting and proper." With this he wished to put an end to the Jews' madness, that they might finally cease raving and be silent. For when Sir Multitude [i.e., the mob] is finally set in motion, he is never quiet again until he has accomplished and done his pleasure.

This sentence of death is passed upon Christ for our good. It is we that ought to die temporal and eternal death, and yonder hear with terror the ceaseless judgment, "Go, ye accursed!" But behold, here Christ stands in our place and lets the staff be broken upon Him before the whole council and all the people, that we might be absolved and pronounced free hereafter at the judgment seat of Christ before all angels and the elect, though we ought otherwise to have been damned and lost forever and ever according to the just judgment of God. But since Christ took upon Himself all our guilt and punishment and reconciled us with His Father, we are truly free and possess in true faith the righteousness restored by Christ, according to which no man can lay anything to our charge (Rom. 8:33–34). If judgment is still held against us, and the sentence of death passed on us for undeserved things, simply because of Christ and His Word, we should not let it bother us. And if it pains our flesh and blood, we should look to Christ, who also had to die so contemptibly because He testified to the truth, and we should rejoice for the rich reward to come, that we shall be worthy to suffer for the sake of Christ's disgrace.

Now, because Pilate must stand and confess that the blood of Jesus is the blood of a just Man, and his heart therefore trembles at this judgment, he has water brought to him and washes his hands as a sign of his innocence, before he leaves the judgment seat, thrusts it into the lap of the Jews, and wishes simply to be innocent. But whether he wishes to wash the innocent blood from his own hands, yet it remains upon his soul and conscience, and his washing is of no help to him, even if he were to pour the whole Jordan over his hands, since he delivers up to bloody slaughter the innocent blood of Christ over and against all justice.

But is it not wholly terrifying that the Jews wish to take the blood of Christ not only on themselves but also on their children and descendants? From this is seen what terrible foes of Christ's blood the Jews are. They have seen how much of the blood of Christ has been shed already, and yet are not satisfied. They wish to draw out the last drops of blood, and would give their own temporal and eternal salvation, along with that of their children and children's children, even to the thousandth generation, in exchange for it, and make a mockery of it, even as such bloodthirstiness is still practiced by the Jews and others who are heartily opposed both to Christ and to those who are washed and cleansed from their sins with the blood of Christ.

With this detestable wish the Jews became prophets of their own calamity to come, for what they wished for themselves was faithfully repaid them. For surely God will seek and avenge the blood of His saints; how then shall He leave the blood of His dearest Son unavenged? Without doubt, their wish was so truly granted, and the blood of Christ was so avenged, that fresh blood flowed down upon their own heads; for the blood-vengeance began shortly after the death of Christ, and God measured to them again with a full measure, so that many thousands of Jews went to sleep with bloody heads. And the curse would have come upon them without their willing it, for God punishes the sins of the fathers to the third and fourth generations (Ex. 20:5). Now, God visits the sins of the fathers on the children because of the parents, who wish to have it thus and no better, as the

Jews do here. In addition to the parents, the children all follow in their footsteps, for the apple falls not far from the tree. Their progeny proved this in deed when they persecuted the disciples and apostles of Christ with such bloodthirstiness that they finally slew them in cold blood.

Therefore let everyone look well lest he trample underfoot the blood of Christ, use it unworthily, or curse his neighbor with it. We should all rather call heartily upon our faithful Savior, that His holy, precious blood may come upon us and upon our children not for vengeance and punishment, as the Jews encountered in the destruction of Jerusalem and still feel it daily, but for our salvation, life, and blessedness, that we may be sprinkled with it and washed clean from all our sins (Ps. 51:2–7; Isa. 53:5; 1 John 1:7).

Prayer

O Lord Jesus, the Jews took Thy blood upon themselves and upon their children! They willfully desired that God should punish them and their children when Thy blood was shed unjustly and against propriety. Oh, the rash and thoughtless desire! O Lord Jesus, for this reason Thy blood came upon the Jews and their children in wrath, it came upon them as a curse. Oh, let Thy blood come upon us and our children, yet let it come in grace, let it come as a blessing! O Lord Jesus, let Thy saving blood come upon us, that we may be marked with it and the angel of death may pass over us! Let it come upon us, that it may deliver us from blood-guiltiness, and by it we may overcome all the enemies of our soul! Let it come upon us, that by it we may receive redemption and be saved and adorned for the wedding of the Lamb! Amen, Lord Jesus! Amen.

Mel.: O Jesu Christ, meins Lebens Licht

Lord Jesus Christ! Thy precious blood
Is to my soul the highest good:
  Of all my sins a perfect cure,
  It quickens me and makes me pure.

(continued)

Thy blood, my spotless glorious dress,
Thy innocence, my righteousness:
  Before my God I pardoned stand,
  And enter, crowned, the heav'nly land.

Lord Jesus Christ, Thou Son of God!
My Throne of Grace, my Staff and Rod!
  Thy precious blood, Thy quick'ning pow'r
  My spirit strengthen every hour.

Let me not draw my dying breath
In fear of Satan, hell, and death;
  O Christ! let this my comfort be:
  Thy blood from sin hath made me free!

DEVOTION 44

Christ Is Led out of Jerusalem Bearing His Cross

Mel.: An Wasserflüssen Babylon

A Lamb goes uncomplaining forth,
  The guilt of all men bearing;
'Tis laden with the sin of earth,
  None else the burden sharing;
It goes its way, grows weak and faint,
To slaughter led without complaint,
  Its spotless life to offer;
Bears shame, and stripes, and wounds, and death,
Anguish and mockery, and saith,
  "Willing all this I suffer."

This Lamb is Christ, the soul's great Friend
  And everlasting Savior;
Him, Him God chose, sin's reign to end
  And bring us to His favor.
"Go forth, my Son!" He said, "and bail
The children, who are doomed to hell
  But for Thine intercession.
The punishment is great, and dread
The wrath, but Thou Thy blood shalt shed,
  And save them from perdition."

"Yea, Father, yea, most willingly
  I'll bear what Thou commandest;
My will conforms to Thy decree,
  I do what Thou demandest."

(continued)

O wondrous Love! what hast Thou done!
The Father offers up His Son,
   The Son content descendeth!
O Love! O Love! how strong art Thou!
In shroud and grave Thou lay'st Him low
   Whose word the mountains rendeth!

All we like sheep were gone astray; every one looked to his own way. But the Lord *cast on him the sins of us all. When he was oppressed and afflicted, he opened not his mouth, as a lamb that is led to the slaughter.*

Isaiah 53:6–7

Then the soldiers took Jesus, and took His robe off from Him, and put His own raiment on Him, and led Him away to crucify Him, bearing His cross. And as they came out, they found a man who passed by, of Cyrene, Simon by name, coming out of the country, the father of Alexander and Rufus; him they compelled to bear his cross, and on him they laid the cross, that he might bear it after Jesus.

Matthew 27:31–32; Mark 15:20–21; Luke 23:26; John 19:16–17

When Jesus is made to change His clothes before being led to the place of execution, it is not without acute affliction to Him. For the purple cloak that was pinned to Him is torn from His mangled body by the soldiers with such great ferocity and violence that the wounds burst open again and the fresh red blood flows down over His scarred body. Now therefore, when Christ, our Savior, suffers His garments to be so unmercifully torn from His body and Himself to be treated in the most disgraceful and scornful way, this happens to merit for us poor children of Adam in turn the garments of salvation and the robe of righteousness. But when He is led away in His own garments, this happens according to God's counsel, that our faith in Jesus Christ, who was crucified in the manhood that He had assumed, might have the greater witness not only against those heretics who deny the true humanity of Christ, but also against Mahomet, who writes in his accursed Alcoran that Jesus was snatched away by God while He was led out, and that another who resembled Him was seized by the Jews and nailed to the cross.

Thus they lead Jesus out of the city and cast the natural Heir out of His vineyard with great tumult and terrible abuse. Behold, thus is Christ, your Savior, cut off out of the land of the living! (Isa. 53:8). But He is led out of the city for crucifixion, that He may fulfill the Scriptures. For just as those sacrificial beasts, the blood of which was carried by the chief priest into the most holy place, had to be burned outside the camp for the sins of the people, so "Jesus also, that He might sanctify the people with His own blood, suffered without the gate. Let us go forth therefore unto Him without the camp, bearing His reproach." (Heb. 13:12–13). Here goes godly Abel between unfaithful brothers, obedient Isaac as a burnt offering, the Lamb of God to the slaughter. He is led out with such disgrace from the earthly Jerusalem, that we may be led in with all the greater honor to the new and eternal Jerusalem. Adam was driven out of Paradise by an angel of God, and we too were to be thrust out of the New Jerusalem forever. But now Christ is led out of the earthly Jerusalem with disgrace by the messenger and instrument of Satan, that hereafter, on that day of His majestic coming, we may, by virtue of His contemptible extradition, be led into the heavenly paradise by the multitude of the heavenly spirits. Now therefore, if the world treats the servant no better than the master, if in every place all who glory in Christ and His Gospel, or will not and cannot take part in the false, invented worship of God, are thrust out of the city or land, persecuted and killed—patience, dear hearts! Simply go forth confidently, knowing that we have on our side the sun-bright truth, because of which we shall never be ashamed. For to follow Christ in cross and suffering is a more beautiful path of honor, and the first leap of joy into the heavenly and eternal life to come.

When Christ is thus led out with disgrace, He must bear His cross Himself, even as Isaac, foreshadowing this, bore the wood of his sacrifice (Gen. 22:6). This was done according to the custom of the Romans, who laid a cross on the back of their disobedient servants for their greater reproach and mockery, which they had to carry through the whole city. Hence they were also called *furciferi* (cross-bearing scoundrels), in which the Jews, however, out of devilish hatred, had all the greater joy. Now, this cross was not only a great and heavy piece of wood, but it also had on it the unbearable weight of the sins of all the world, the wrath of God, and the infinite pains of hell. Here consider how the dearest Savior must walk weighed down under such a burden, as He lamented long before, "O man, thou hast made labor for Me in thy sins, and hast made toil for Me in thine iniquities" (Isa. 43:24). But in this way He wished to unburden us from the unbearable burden of the yoke of the Law, and to free us from the curse of the Law by becoming a curse for us (Gal. 3:13).

Accordingly, because the cross of Christ was so great and heavy a burden, and He was entirely exhausted from the preceding pain and torment, the soldiers finally take the cross from Christ and compel the stranger, *Simon of Cyrene,* as he is coming in from the country and encounters the procession, to carry Jesus' cross after Him. This was of course done by the soldiers not out of compassion, but because they were unable to get on quickly enough with the weary Christ, and were worried that they would not bring Him yet alive to the place of execution. But God is so faithful that in His great anger and zealous wrath He imposes no more than he can bear, even as He permits none to be tested above his ability. Moreover, Christ was thus appointed and required to die by hanging on the tree (Deut. 21:23; Ps. 22:16).

This Simon is a true image of Christians, for they must all bend their back to the cross of Christ and take a little corner of it. Yet believing hearts do not choose such bearing of the cross for themselves, but it comes to them unawares and all of a sudden, and they are also, like the foreigner Simon, compelled and pressed into it. It often comes unexpectedly. Simon would certainly have supposed that heaven would sooner fall than that he should bear the cross of Jesus of Nazareth after Him. Yet a Christian is always to be prepared and ready for it, for he will hardly avoid the cross. No one, however, should carve for himself his own little cross, but everyone should bear with patience whatever God sends and lays upon Him, as our Lord Christ Himself bore His own cross. But how are we made fit for that? When God lays upon us merely a splinter of His cross, we turn reluctant and wish to leave our body at once, yet our cross is not even a piece of straw compared to the great tree of Christ's cross. On top of all this, our cross soon ceases, and provides for us an eternal and exceedingly weighty glory (2 Cor. 4:17). But alas! our flesh and blood are so perverse that though our suffering, however great it may be, can hardly be regarded as a shadow, yea, as nothing compared to the great and heavy sufferings of Christ, yet our old Adam always turns up his nose at it and refuses to move a step in any direction. So also Simon bristles at the idea and declines to bear Christ's cross after Him, so that they must even compel and force him to do so. Likewise, another had to gird up Peter's loins and lead him whither he would not go (John 21:18). Christians are to submit willingly to such things. It must be so; as Christ says, "And he that taketh not his cross, and followeth after Me, is not worthy of Me." (Matt. 10:38). But as unwilling as Simon is to take the cross upon him, so willingly did he then bear it after Christ. We are to do the same, and endure patiently in the cross and continue steadfast unto the end. But because the flesh and blood soon grow weak, even though the spirit is willing, we should therefore sigh and pray heartily to God, "O Lord, by Thy power prepare and strengthen the dullness of the flesh, that we may contend valiantly here and pass through death and life to Thee."

Prayer

O Lord Jesus, I thank Thee with mouth and heart that Thou didst bear out on Thy striped back the heavy tree of the cross to Calvary! By this Thou also bearest all my sins utterly away so that they shall never come before the face of Thy Father. Oh, let this Thy atoning labor be my comfort when, in my final anguish of death, Satan sets my sins before me and seeks thereby to frighten me! For because Thou hast borne my sins and wast pressed beneath the heavy tree of the cross by them, I am freed from the punishment of my sins, and shall no longer be pressed down into hell on account of my transgressions, but as Thou wast led out of the earthly Jerusalem under the heavy burden of the cross, so I, free and released from the heavy burden of sin, shall be led into the heavenly Jerusalem. As Thou wast killed outside the city of God, I shall live forever in the city of God which is in heaven. For the present, however, as long as I live in this world, I cannot be without cross and tribulation, but must with Simon of Cyrene bear Thy cross after Thee and take it upon me. Therefore assist me, I beseech Thee, with Thy power, and grant that I may gladly and willingly endure all the sadness and displeasure that Thou shalt lay upon me, and believe without a doubt that, as Simon bore Thy cross only so far as the Place of a Skull, so Thou shalt also set for my cross a certain bound, that I may not fall beneath it, but may at last lay aside the manifold hardships of the cross of this life and be transported into the everlasting rest and joy. Amen, Lord Jesus! Amen.

Mel.: Mir nach, spricht Christus, unser Held

Come, follow Me, the Savior spake,
  All in My way abiding;
Deny yourselves, the world forsake,
  Obey My call and guiding;
Oh, bear the cross, whate'er betide,
Take My example for your guide!

He that without Me thinks to find
  His soul, shall surely lose it;
He that to lose it hath a mind,
  In God shall introduce it;
Who takes no cross nor follows Me,
Deserves not Me nor heav'n to see.

Then let us follow our dear Lord,
  And take the cross appointed,
And, boldly clinging to His Word,
  In suff'ring be undaunted;
For who bears not the battle's strain
The crown of life shall not obtain.

DEVOTION 45

Jesus Preaches to the Lamenting Women

Mel.: So gehst du nun, mein Jesu, hin

So, Lord, Thou goest forth to die,
  For me the cross enduring;
For me a sinner willingly
  A blest release procuring.
Go forth, my Lord—
Be Thou adored;
  Thee may I follow weeping!
A flood of grief
Without relief,
  Watch o'er Thy sorrows keeping.

Lord Jesus, I, yes, I should bear
  Sin's price in pain and sadness,
In soul and body, flesh and hair
  I should be of all gladness
Fore'er deprived
And sore aggrieved,
  But Thou the debt dost sever;
Thy blood and death
Bring me by faith
  To God the Father's favor.

What for this love, O Lord, to Thee
  Can I be ever giving?
I know of nothing good in me,
  Yet will I, while here living
Be but Thine own, *(continued)*

To Thee alone
  Due service here to render,
And after time
In heaven's clime
  Serve Thee in greater splendor.

Behold, and see if there be any sorrow like unto my sorrow, which is done unto me. For the LORD *hath filled me with affliction in the day of His fierce anger.*

Lamentations 1:12

And there followed Him a great company of people, and of women, which also bewailed and lamented Him. But Jesus turning unto them said, Daughters of Jerusalem, weep not for Me, but weep for yourselves, and for your children. For, behold, the days are coming, in the which they shall say, Blessed are the barren, and the wombs that never bare, and the paps which never gave suck. Then shall they begin to say to the mountains, Fall on us; and to the hills, Cover us. For if this is done in the green tree, what shall be done in the dry?

Luke 23:27–31

A great company of people goes with Christ as He is led out of the city. Among them are found several godly women who are greatly troubled, and sigh, lament, and weep, "Oh, how pitifully the faithful preacher Jesus is abused and His whole body covered with wounds! Oh, shall the great, innocent Man, who has done great good for the whole land, die such a contemptible and cursed death? God in heaven, have mercy!"

To these godly women the Lord Jesus turns and gives them a memorable farewell sermon, saying, "'Daughters of Jerusalem, weep not for Me'—I will soon sing the joyful *Consummatum est* (It is finished)!—'but weep for yourselves, and for your children.' Repent of your sins and take comfort in My bitter suffering and dying. Ye have cause to be sorrowful and to lament, for a storm of wrath shall come upon you and all the Jewish people, so that many a mother might wish that she had never borne nor given suck to any child at her breast. Yea, then shall the people cry for great anguish, 'O ye mountains, fall on us; and ye hills, cover us!'"

Here learn how you are to contemplate the Passion of Christ fruitfully. Let this be a heart-rending *repentance sermon* for you. Do not be enraged at Judas, who betrayed Jesus, nor at the chief priests, who falsely accused Him, nor at Pilate, who unjustly condemned Him, nor at the unmerciful soldiers, who nailed Him to the cross, but weep heartily and sorrowfully for your own sins and the sins of your own, and say with King David, "We have committed iniquity and done wickedly." For your and my iniquities are the sharp nails wherewith the Lord Jesus was nailed to the cross. It was for your iniquities that He was wounded, and for your sins that He was thus beaten. Nazianzen and Jerome report that the Jews are supposed to have gathered yearly at the place where Jesus stood and there observed together their days of lamentation. But as for you, dear man, weep for your own wickedness and say with Daniel, "Alas, O Lord, we have sinned and committed iniquity and done wickedly!" But you, O man, are the unfruitful fig tree that deserved the curse. You are the dry tree of sin which is to be cut down and cast into the fiery furnace of hell.

Yet do not despair, dear soul. Take comfort in the Lord Jesus, who is the green Tree, whom God the heavenly Father caused to be cut down for you. He is the Tree of Life; if in true faith you lay yourself under His spreading branches of grace, you will have shade and shelter from the fire of God's wrath, yea, from the heat of hell's brimstone. Thus if with Mary Magdalene you pour out your tears of repentance, and with the lost son (Luke 15:17–21) seek for grace, you will be comforted and be a dear child of God. "God is ready to turn away the punishment, if you will simply lay aside your wickedness by true repentance," says Ambrose. Yea, the Lord will be your shade and your protection in the heat of all crosses, and will sustain you like godly Noah, Lot, and David. And though you die, yet shall nothing be able to separate you from His love and grace.

But whoever will not bewail his sins, let him know that the Lord of Sabaoth with the sharp axe of His anger will cut him down as the dry tree of sin and cast him into the furnace of hell. For if this is done in the green tree, what shall be done in the dry? If the righteous must suffer many things, what shall become of the ungodly and sinner? (Prov. 11:32). If you hide in the cave with the kings of

Canaan, or hide in a dark cellar with Johann the German, to escape the thunder, yet the heavenly Joshua shall find you there. Think of the terror that all the ungodly shall feel when they cry, "O mountains, fall on us!" In the morning they shall say, "Would God I might live till even!"; and in the evening, "Would God I might live till morning!" (Deut. 28:67). Therefore turn during your time of grace. For "God is a just Judge, and a God that threateneth every day. If they turn not, He hath His sword whetted and His bow bent" (Ps. 7:11–12). "Upon the ungodly He shall rain lightning, fire, and brimstone, and shall give them a tempest for a reward" (Ps. 11:6). He that hath ears to hear, let him hear!

Prayer

O my Lord Jesus, if only I had water enough in my head and my eyes were fountains of tears, that I might sufficiently bewail day and night my great sins and their terrible punishment! For it was my sins, O my Lord Jesus, that cast Thee into this distress and this misery, by which Thou art now compassed round about! My sins are the stinging thorns in the crown that stung Thy sacred head. My sins are the fetters and bonds in which Thou sufferedst Thyself to be pulled and pressed on Thy way to Mount Calvary. My sins are the whips with which Thou wast smitten whenever Thou didst stumble and sink to the earth for great weariness. My sins are the heavy tree of the cross lying upon Thy bloody back. And shall I not groan at this? Shall I not lament at this? Shall I not weep bitterly at this? O Lord Jesus, Thou green Tree, Thou fruitful Tree of all virtues! If Thou art thus afflicted, thus beaten, thus spit on, thus mocked, thus reviled, thus aggrieved, thus tormented for the sins of others, oh, what shall become of me, a fruitless, dry tree, doubly dead to every good, because of my own and manifold iniquities? Alas, what anguish and distress, what pain and agony, what grief and sorrow I deserve! Therefore, O Lord Jesus, make me to know, repent of, mourn, and bewail my sins in this time of my life, that I may blessedly enjoy for the eternity to come Thy perfect satisfaction, which Thou hast made for the sins of the whole world. O Lord Jesus, let me sow bitter tears of sorrow in this life, and reap with rejoicing hereafter! Amen, Lord Jesus! Amen.

Mel.: Der am Kreuz ist meine Liebe (p. 323)
Or: Freu dich sehr, o meine Seele

To the place of skulls then follow
  Mournful in thy Savior's train,
While in truth, not accents hollow,
  Thou dost pray amid thy pain
That the Father in His Child
May behold thee reconciled,
  In Thy Ransom sin atoning,
  Mercy to thee, needy, loaning.

Must I, Jesus, thus perceive Thee
  In Thy toil and sorrow here?
Can I nothing better give Thee
  Than my unavailing tear?
Lamb of God! I weep for Thee,
Weep, Thy cruel cross to see,
  Weep, for death o'er death victorious,
  Weep, for Life immortal, glorious!

DEVOTION 46

Christ Wills Fully to Taste Death for Us

Mel.: O Jesu Christ, meins Lebens Licht

Lord Christ, dear Savior of all men,
Creator of the earth and heav'n:
  In favor hear our heartfelt plea,
  Who with due praises worship Thee!

By kindly grace Thou bor'st the cross
Whereby Thou didst repair our loss,
  From Adam's sin and bonds that weighed,
  Thou, wounded, hast our freedom made.

Thou madest heaven's starry span,
Yet art the very Son of Man,
  Nor dost refuse for us to die
  And in most shameful death to lie.

*The Lord, the L*ORD*, hath opened mine ear, and I am not rebellious, neither do I turn away back. — They give me gall to eat and vinegar to drink in my great thirst.*
Isaiah 50:5; Psalm 69:21

And there were also two others, malefactors, led with Him to be put to death. And they brought Him unto the place which is called in the Hebrew Golgotha, which is, being interpreted, The Place of a Skull. And they gave Him vinegar or myrrhed wine to drink, mingled with gall; and when He had tasted thereof, He would not drink it.
Matthew 27:33–34; Mark 15:22–23; Luke 23:32–33; John 19:17

DEVOTION 46

Here begins the account of the crucifixion of the Lord Christ.

First, we are here told of the *place* where Christ was led to be crucified. This was the hill on which wicked men used to be put to death, and was called Golgotha, that is, The Place of a Skull, because the skulls and bones of those executed lay scattered about on it. In this contemptible place Christ must die. This is a reproach and shame in the eyes of the world, but with God His heavenly Father He has no dishonor. He still remains God's Son and an innocent, holy Man. The sun shines even on the gallows and the breaking wheel, yet the sun is not thereby diminished. So also, an honorable, godly man may come to such a disreputable and dishonorable place, yet it is no dishonor for him as long as he does nothing froward and has committed nothing worthy of punishment. And the same reproach and disgrace is frequently cast on believers by immoderate religious zealots who act violently and fill every prison and dungeon with innocent hearts, and to some extent even drag them to the place of execution, as seen by countless thousands of martyrs as well as the holy apostles.

But Christ, in this His place of execution, atones for our father Adam's guilt and his great fall into sin by which he profaned the beautiful, glorious garden of Eden and ushered in death, so that now the whole earth has become the place of a skull, in which the bones of all men lie and rest, and where the blood of Christ drips from the cross upon the dry, mouldering bones of men, so that they are quickened thereby and made alive. But at the same time He also sanctifies with it the grievous scaffold of the martyrs, where they sacrifice their lives, suffer, and die for Christ in the confident hope that, hereafter, the Lord Jesus will grant them a glorious place of honor in heaven.

Second, the *refreshing draft* is described for us, which was given to Christ before He was nailed to the cross. No doubt they remembered Lemuel's wise proverb concerning a refreshing draft for evildoers who are to be put to death, where he says, "Give strong drink unto them that are to perish, and wine unto the afflicted souls, that they may drink and forget their misery, and remember their misfortune no more" (Prov. 31:6–7). So also Christ, when He comes to the place of execution, is given a refreshing draft, yet not of fresh water, much less of invigorating wine, but rather (from malice and wickedness) of vinegar, myrrh, and gall. With these they fulfilled what Christ had long since lamented through the mouth of David: "They give Me gall to eat and vinegar to drink in My great thirst" (Ps. 69:21). Gall is a poisonous, bitter herb which they used to put in the drinks of criminals that they might feel less their agony and that their life might be shortened. When Demosthenes was about to be killed, he sucked up poison by a reed that he might not die a contemptible death. But Christ cannot drink this drink made bitter with gall, for He does not wish to numb His profound suffering, but to remain obedient to His Father unto death, and to atone and suffer perfectly for us; He also wishes not to shorten His life by this draft, but willingly to die on the cross and rather to lay down His life (John 10:18), thus He also wishes to await the hour when He will be able to speak the comforting "*Consummatum est* (It is finished)!"

Prayer

O Lord Jesus, what a bitter draft of vinegar mingled with gall and myrrh was maliciously and wickedly poured for Thee in the place of a skull, that I might not be made to drink only pitch, brimstone, and hellfire forever! Yet Thou dost not ask for such a draft, for Thou wilt drink to the dregs the cup that Thy Father poured Thee for our sake. For our sake Thou didst offer Thyself as a guilt offering once for all, and didst enter into this hour of torment; therefore Thou hast no desire to be excused from this sorrow, nor prematurely to seize Thy death, nor to take Thine anguished soul from the wearied body and thereby to release it from all sorrows before it pleases Thy Father. Only then dost Thou desire willingly to follow, only then dost Thou desire gladly to die. O Lord Jesus, plant such devotion in my heart, that when I too fall into anguish and sadness, sorrow and sickness, I may not wish for my own death out of reluctance and impatience, much less take my own life, but may willingly suffer all things as long as it pleases Thee, and gladly forsake this temporal life when it pleases Thee. O Lord Jesus, let it be unto me as Thou wilt; Thy will is best! Amen.

Mel.: O du Liebe meiner Liebe
Or: O Durchbrecher aller Bande

O Thou Love wherewith I'm lovèd,
  Source of all my happiness;
Thou, O Love, by mercy movèd,
  Tak'st upon Thee my distress:
As a lamb led to the slaughter
  Goest to the cross's tree,
Seal'st Thy love with blood and water,
  Bear'st the world's iniquity.

Love, whose heart in humble silence
  Bravely bore disgrace and shame,
Love, who through the worst revilements
  To the end wast e'er the same;
Love, who didst not cease Thy pleading
  To the last expiring breath,
Kindly for me interceding
  When Thy head was bowed in death!

Love, who as my bleeding Savior
  Didst my heart in righteousness
Unto Thee betroth forever,
  Ah, I thank Thee for Thy grace!
Love, who thus Thyself engagèd,
  Let my mis'ry and my smart
Now be utterly assuagèd
  In Thy wounded, bleeding heart.

DEVOTION 47

Christ on the Cross

Mel.: Der am Kreuz ist meine Liebe (p. 323)

Oh, how is my Love suspended,
  How the spotless Lamb must be
Like a thief that had offended,
  Nailed upon the cursèd tree!
See what sin hath pow'r to do,
For it pierceth Jesus through—
  Prophet, Priest, and King of heaven—
  To the cross it naileth even!

Oh, that death so dread mysterious,
  Cross with strength and wisdom filled,
By thee only is the serious
  Wrath of God the Father stilled,
And the rod of Moses cracked—
This the writing doth redact—
  Yea, this dread device of mourning
  Kills the flesh's passions burning!

Come, ye foes which torment bring me—
  Worldly pleasure, greed, and pride,
Which to very hell would sting me—
  With me to the gallows stride;
Work no more your fears within,
For I have been purged of sin
  By the off'ring of these ashes;
  Jesus' blood me wholly washes.

Hell and Satan may affright me
   For my great iniquity,
And my conscience gnaw and bite me
   And my burden heavy be;
Yet my Jesus' cross's load
Gives me rest and peace with God.
   Hell and Satan here He showeth
   That my sins no more God knoweth.

And as Moses lifted up the serpent in the wilderness, even so must the Son of Man be lifted up, that whosoever believeth in Him should not perish, but have eternal life. — For dogs have compassed me: the assembly of the wicked have inclosed me: they pierced my hands and my feet. — Therefore will I divide him a portion with the great, and he shall divide the spoil with the strong; because he hath poured out his soul unto death: and he was numbered with the transgressors; and he bare the sin of many, and made intercession for the transgressors.

John 3:14–15; Psalm 22:16; Isaiah 53:12

And they crucified Him in the place Golgotha, and two malefactors with Him, one on the right hand, and the other on the left, and Jesus in the midst. And the Scripture was fulfilled, which saith, He was numbered with the transgressors.

Matthew 27:35; Mark 15:22, 27–28; Luke 23:33; John 19:18

The crucifixion of Christ happens as follows: The executioners strip Jesus naked and lay Him on the cross as upon the rack. They spread His tender body in such a way that all His bones may be counted. They pierce His hands and feet and nail Him with sharp nails to the cross, at which He again bleeds, so that all His powers are dried up as a potsherd. Finally, they lift Him up, hanging so disgracefully on the tree, and by this He is raised up from the earth according to the pattern of the brazen serpent in the wilderness, which Christ Himself related to His own death (John 3:14). There, then, He hangs between heaven and earth as the only

Mediator who will make peace between angered God in heaven and fallen mankind on earth (Col. 1:20). He suffered Himself to be nailed hand and foot to the tree of the cross for our sins and iniquities, and with His pierced hands canceled and blotted out the handwriting that was against us (Col. 2:14), and took them from our midst and affixed and raised them to the cross, that they should nevermore be remembered. He wishes to die on the accursed tree (as it is written, "Cursed is he that hangeth on a tree") to deliver us from the accursed death of everlasting damnation.

Oh, see, dear soul! Oh, see how lamentably Christ your Savior is stretched out! How His body is spread utterly wasted upon the cross! How His tender eyes break! How His crimson mouth grows pale! How His stiffened arms are held fast! How His stiffened legs hang down! How the holy blood runs down His arms and feet! See, there He hangs full of sorrows, full of stripes and wounds from head to toe. Wherever He turns, His wounds are torn open again. What unprecedented pains! Pains from within, pains from without—oh, the painful body of torment! See the brazen serpent raised up, see the innocent and blameless sacrificial Lamb dying on the cross, dying an accursed death to deliver us from the accursed death of everlasting damnation! For this perfect sacrifice, dear Father, for Christ's perfect merit forgive that sin! Forgive us all—us, whom He bought and redeemed so dearly by His painful sufferings! For He died for me, that I might live, and as in the fruit of the beautiful tree Eve ate death, so in the dry tree of the cross Christ slew death, destroyed the devil's kingdom, opened hell, and restored everlasting life. Therefore, although the crucifixion of Christ is offensive to the Jews and foolish to unbelievers, yet by the strength and light of the Holy Ghost we draw from it vigor and power in life and death, soar into His outspread arms, and wish with Augustine to fall blessedly asleep therein.

Now, the evangelists report two different things here: first, that Christ was crucified not alone, but in the midst of two *malefactors*. The Jews do this to Him as a mockery and disgrace, yet by doing so they only fulfill the Scripture, for Isaiah prophesied, "He was numbered with the transgressors," and God long foresaw it, and indicated it to us with beautiful figures. Joseph lies captive between two transgressors, of whom one perishes, but the other is freed and released (Gen. 40). Likewise, Christ hangs here between two evildoers, of whom one is preserved and blessed, but the other perishes and is destroyed. Christ occupies with honor this middle position, for He is the worthiest among all and above all, God and Man in one person. Theophylact interprets it to mean that Jesus Christ was crucified between two crowds of people, Jews and Gentiles, who are represented by the two robbers. Those on the left hand of Christ slandered Him and were rejected, but those on the right hand knew Him and were received by Him. Yet these two evildoers are also a good example of all men, who are evildoers and deserving of eternal death because of sin. But there hangs Christ in their midst, stretching out His arms and desiring to bring all men to Himself (John 12:32), and stretching out His arms all the day (Isa. 65:2). Therefore we should all go out to meet Him with outstretched hands, and embrace Him together with His cross, saying, "Draw us to Thee: we'll follow Thee!" And because He suffered so much for us that even all blades of grass, all flowers and leaves, if they were utter tongues, yea, all angels of heaven, could never fittingly express the distress and torment that He suffered on the cross—therefore we also should for His sake suffer patiently, and most of all crucify our flesh together with its lusts and desires.

Prayer

O Jesus, Son of the living God and Captain of Life! Thou wast stripped naked in the place of corruption on Golgotha, pierced in hand and foot, and hung up like a cursed worm between heaven and earth to redeem us from the ancient, venomous wound of the serpent in Eden and from the curse of the Law, and instead to bring us the eternal blessing! Alas, my faithful Savior, how great Thy suffering is, how heavy Thy pain, how numerous Thy torments, how deep Thy wounds, how bitter and stinging Thy death! And yet how fervent Thy love! O my Lord Jesus, who didst patiently die for me on the cross and gain me salvation, and the eternal kingdom of heaven for us all: draw me to Thee, as Thou didst say of Thy crucifixion, "I, when I am lifted up from the earth, will draw them all unto Me." Fix me to Thy holy cross by true faith and fervent love. For the sake of Thy bloody crucifixion help me to crucify my sinful flesh together with its wicked lusts and desires, that they may not have dominion in me with their power. Comfort me also when for the sake of Thy holy Word and name I am afflicted, tormented, and crucified by the world, and pierced through with venomous nails of falsehood, or else hindered, hemmed in, and constrained in my calling and Christian resolve. Oh, how can I grow reluctant or fainthearted in my cross when I see Thee on the cross, since Thou hast blessed my cross with Thy cross, and made it a holy thing? Surely it is better to suffer with Thee and afterward to reign with Thee forever than to have good days with the world and afterward to go to the devil. O Lord, by Thy cross and death strengthen me in all distress, and deliver me from everlasting death. Amen, Lord Jesus! Amen.

Mel.: Der am Kreuz ist meine Liebe (p. 323)

O communion of this Passion,
  O mysterious death profound!
Thou dost give me jubilation
  When my soul by grief is drowned!
Oh, what pleasure it will bring,
At the cross by faith to cling
  To my Savior Jesus solely,
  There my life surrend'ring wholly!

Come, my feet, no longer languish,
  Christ my Savior's cross pursue;
He without the gate bore anguish,
  His disgrace I'll carry too.
Jesus' life and death and pain
All my cross and crown remain.
  With Him dying, one in Spirit,
  I with Him will life inherit.

DEVOTION 48

Christ Prays for His Enemies
(First Word)

Mel.: O Welt, sieh hier dein Leben
Or: O Welt, ich muß dich lassen

See, world, thy Life assailèd,
  On the accurs'd tree nailèd;
Thy Savior sinks in death!
The mighty Prince from heaven
Himself hath freely given
  To shame, and blows, and cruel wrath!

Come hither now and ponder,
  'Twill fill thy soul with wonder:
  Blood streams from every pore!
Through grief whose depth none knoweth,
From His great heart there floweth
  Sigh after sigh of anguish o'er!

He made intercession for the transgressors.

Isaiah 53:12

And it was about the third hour when they crucified Him. And Jesus said, Father, forgive them; for they know not what they do.

Mark 15:25; Luke 23:34

The holy evangelist Luke reports particularly that as soon as Christ is nailed to the cross and the cross is raised with Him, He immediately and before all else begins to pray, saying, "Father, forgive them; for they know not what they do." These words testify clearly that now, as He hangs high on the cross, He is in His true priestly office and accomplishing His work for which He came to earth, not only with His suffering, by offering Himself up, but also with *prayer*. For these two things, *offering and praying,* are the works of a priest. The offering is properly seen, as He says in John 17, in His willing to sanctify Himself for us, that we might be sanctified in truth and truly; likewise in John 10, in His giving Himself for the sheep. Of such sayings you find many more, which all testify that His suffering is to be a suffering for us, not for Himself or for His own sake. This work and sacrifice He carries out in such earnest that He also prays that the Father will forgive those who are crucifying Him, nor punish their sin, but will pardon them, that everyone may see why He came to the cross, and take comfort in that. Therefore you are first to learn from this prayer that our dear Lord Jesus is a Priest, and here on the cross has performed His priestly office.

However, the Lord does not pray thus generally, but makes a distinction with respect to those for whom He prays, saying, "Father forgive them; *for they know not what they do.*" With this He wishes to show that there are two kinds of sinners. Some know that they do wrong, and do it without any hesitation; this is called sinning against the Holy Ghost, when they wish to persist in such knowing sin, will not confess, will not depart from it, and will not pray for forgiveness for it. Other sinners are those who sin *unknowingly*. But this is not to be understood as though, e.g., David did not know that it was a sin to take Uriah's wife and to let him be slain. He knows it very well, but therein sin and the devil drive and compel him so vehemently that he falls into such sin before he properly considers what he is doing. Afterward, however, he confesses it, is sorry for it, wishes he had not done it, and asks for grace. We all carry such sins on our neck and are easily taken unawares and fall, sometimes out of fear like Peter, sometimes out of incaution and weakness, sometimes out of presumption. Such sins Christ hangs on the cross with Himself, and prays for them; for they are such sins as are not contrary to grace, since they are acknowledged and confessed, and forgiveness is sought for them. Thus we often see that fornicators and scoundrels, murderers and other wicked men come to grace, for they know that they have done wrong and have no wish to defend it.

Those sins which are confessed have this sacrifice between them and God, so God will not count them against us. But those who knowingly sin and wish to defend their sins resist the Holy Ghost and deny the grace of God. Christ does not pray for them here, but rather for those who "know not what they do," and fall through weakness. They are to take comfort in this sacrifice and intercession, and know that their sins are forgiven. For it is for these that Christ prayed here, and what fruit this prayer had then we shall hear afterward in the thief, since this prayer was his Gospel, and a sermon from which he learned to know the Lord Christ, that He is the Son of God and hung on the cross to pay for the sins of all the world, and after the death of body will live and reign with God His Father forever. Therefore we are not to doubt, but to take comfort and rejoice in Him, and to follow His example and walk in His footsteps, loving our enemies, doing good to those who hate us, and praying for those who injure and persecute us.

Prayer

O Lord Jesus, as the true High Priest in Thy blood-red priestly garment Thou didst pray for the evildoers crucifying Thee, crying at once with a loud voice on the high altar of the cross, "Father, forgive them; for they know not what they do!" In so doing, Thou didst pray also for me, for I too am a great evildoer, and with my sins brought Thee down from heaven to the cross, to the spilling of Thy precious blood, to the loss of Thy life, yea, even into the grave. But because Thou didst pray for evildoers so heartily, I too will surely benefit from Thy powerful intercession. O Lord, enlighten and govern me, that according to Thine example I too may with all my heart forgive mine enemies and persecutors and make intercession for them, and some day with a forgiving heart bid this world farewell and depart for my heavenly home in peace. Amen.

Mel.: O Welt, sieh hier dein Leben
Or: O Welt, ich muß dich lassen

I'm bound, my Savior, ever,
By ties most sacred, never

(continued)

Thy service to forsake;
With soul and body ever,
With all my pow'rs t' endeavor,
   In praise and service joy to take.

Not much can I be giving
In this poor life I'm living,
   But one thing do I say:
Thy death and sorrows ever,
Till soul from body sever,
   My heart remember shall for aye.

Of sin how great the danger,
How it excites God's anger,
   How doth His vengeance burn,
How sternly He chastiseth,
How His wrath's flood ariseth,
   Shall I from all Thy suff'rings learn.

From them shall I be learning,
How I may be adorning,
   My heart with quietness,
And how I still should love them
Whose malice aye doth move them
   To grieve me by their wickedness.

When tongues of bad men grieve me,
Of peace and name deprive me,
   My restive heart I'll still;
Their evil deeds enduring,
Of pardon free assuring
   My neighbor for his ev'ry ill.

DEVOTION 49

Jesus of Nazareth, the King of the Jews

Mel.: Wer nur den lieben Gott läßt walten

The King who blood and life hath given
  To save the life of all His own
Be glorified in earth and heaven!
  His praises evermore intone!
Sing all the wonders of our God,
Yet over all extol His blood!

My heart hath found that King victorious,
  Where else but there on Calv'ry's mound?
There from His wounds flows healing for us,
  There my redemption too is found;
He let His life for me outflow
While I was yet His fervent foe.

To whom else should I then surrender,
  O King that dièdst on the tree?
My blood and life to Thee I tender,
  My heart pours out itself to Thee;
I to Thy crossèd banner swear,
Thy citizen and soldier e'er.

Behold, my servant shall deal wisely, and shall be exalted and extolled very high. — His name shall abide forever; as long as the sun endureth, his name shall extend unto them that come after, and they shall be blessed in him; all nations shall glorify him.
Isaiah 52:13; Psalm 72:17

And Pilate wrote a title, having written whereof He was accused, even the cause of His death, and set it on the cross over His head. And it was written: Jesus of Nazareth, the King of the Jews. This title then read many of the Jews, for the place where Jesus was crucified was nigh to the city. And it was written in Hebrew, and Greek, and Latin. Then said the chief priests of the Jews to Pilate, Write not, The King of the Jews; but that He said, I am King of the Jews. Pilate answered, What I have written I have written.

Matthew 27:37; Mark 15:26; Luke 23:38; John 19:19–22

Since, according to Roman custom, the sentence and transgression of criminals was either read aloud by the bailiff or written on a tablet that was carried around before them, or possibly set over their heads, therefore Pilate also set over Christ's head this title of the cross: JESUS OF NAZARETH, THE KING OF THE JEWS. And although Pilate might well have been mocking Christ or the Jews by doing so, yet he also thereby gives Him His due honorific title. And although the Jews desire a change to be made, and that it might be written that He *said* He is the King of the Jews, yet with Christ, *to say* is also *to be*. What Christ said of Himself He truly was as well. So in truth, and to the eternal mockery and shame of the Jews, this title stands there in different languages, that all tongues might testify to the Jews' great treachery, and acknowledge that they were the actual murderers of their own King. But for us, this title is salvation and consolation, indeed, a true cancellation of the handwriting and bill of debts for all our sins. For the devil had (to say with St. Cyril) a bill of debts against us, and was the curse upon the transgressors of the Law, in which all mankind was condemned. Now therefore, Christ took this with the title of His cross and canceled and blotted it out. Hence He is also extolled as the Savior who endured a horrible punishment for our transgressions. And although only One suffered for all, yet as the true Son of God He was higher and worthier than all creatures, and His life more glorious than the lives of all men.

Now, Pilate's use of the *three chief languages* in this title happened by special provision of God, that Christ's death and suffering might be announced to each nation in its mother tongue throughout the world, even as the apostles began to do on the feast of Pentecost, declaring the wonderful works of God, every man in his own tongue wherein he was born (Acts 2:8, 11), and as David also foretold: "There is no speech nor language where their voice is not heard" (Ps. 19:3). And this prophecy has also been fulfilled according to Paul's testimony, "and their sound has gone out into all lands, and their words into all the world" (Rom. 10:10). This is still preached in many languages, and Christ's title on the cross is spread throughout the world, so that both Jews and Gentiles can hear and perceive plentifully concerning His death and the cause thereof, to which end God's Holy Scripture is also translated in so many languages, among all of which Dr. Martin Luther's translation, with its fine marginal glosses, is an admirable light and key of understanding.

Pilate wrote this title of the cross doubtless unwittingly and unintentionally by the instigation of the Holy Spirit, who guided his heart, hand, and pen to give a glorious testimony to Christ, and made him to persevere therein against the will of the Jews. And Christ bears this title with great honor. Neither will He give this honor to any other, for He is the true *Jesus,* a Help in the great distresses that have befallen us—particularly in the great distress of sin, when a man is altogether anxious and fearful—that we may recall the first word on the title of the cross and of this name *Jesus,* which was given to our Bridegroom in His salutary circumcision, in which He shed His first drops of blood for our redemption and salvation. Now on the cross, when His holy blood is drained from His body even to the last drop, this name is repeated on the cross to testify that He is the steadfast Jesus and shall remain our Life until the end. Him we are to write in our heart and always have in our remembrance, doing all things in the name of Jesus (Col. 3:17), if our deeds are at all to have fruit and to turn out well. He is also the true *Nazarene* vowed and set apart from all sinners, who made a vow to His dear heavenly Father to accomplish His holy will and to carry out the high work of the redemption of mankind. He also is and remains *King* not only of the Jews but also of the Gentiles, as said above, who now walk in His light and say, "My King and my God!" He must also remain King forever, no matter how it pains the devil and his whole infernal horde. And some day who refused to know or kiss this King shall see and know with fear and terror His mighty power and glory, .

Prayer

O my most faithful Immanuel! Write Thy most holy name *Jesus* in my heart, and let it be engraved therein, that no anguish or distress, sorrow or death may pluck it away! Assure me thereby that Thou art my gracious and almighty King, who canst not only mightily protect me against all mine enemies bodily and spiritual, but art also ready to do so. O crucified Love, Lord Jesus Christ! What man can fathom and express the length, breadth, depth, and height of Thy love, who not only reignest with grace and mercy over Thy faithful and elect as a loving and gracious King, but also makest them kings and priests? Oh, grant me by the perfect merit of Thy blood and death that I may be pleasing to none more than Thee, my King and Lord, to whom alone all honor, praise, and glory belong, who art the King of the Jews, yea, not only the King of the Jews, but also the King of the Gentiles, and with Thy blood hast bought us for God out of every tribe and tongue and nation and people! Sprinkle me continually with Thy precious blood, that I may belong to the chosen generation, the royal priesthood, the holy nation, and the people of the possession, and may show forth the praises of Him who hath called me out of darkness into His marvelous light, until I leave the valley of sorrows and come to Thy hall of gladness! Amen, Lord Jesus! Amen.

Mel.: Valet will ich dir geben

In this my heart embedded,
   Thy name and cross alone
Gleam through all trials dreaded;
   Therein all bliss I own.
O Lord, so let me see Thee
   When great distress is nigh,
As on the cross Thou freely
   Didst bleed for me, and die.

So write my name most kindly
   Within the Book of Life,
And in that bundle bind me
   Of victors in the strife,
Above in heaven dwelling,
   And flourishing in Thee;
Thy faithful heart excelling
   I'll praise eternally!

DEVOTION 50

The Parting of Jesus' Garments

Mel.: Der am Kreuz ist meine Liebe (p. 323)

He who on the cross did love me
  Is my Friend, my Love, and All.
From that Love may nothing move me,
  Which all pleasure gives my soul!
This shall be eternally
Ever new and true to me!
  Christ, the Crucified, shall ever
  Be my loving Lord and Savior.

Well I know both eve and morrow
  This Love's struggle, toil, and sting:
Persecution, scorn, and sorrow,
  Cross and suff'ring doth it bring;
Yea, if my Belovèd will,
Bitt'rest death may meet me still;
  Yet the Crucified shall ever
  Be my loving Lord and Savior!

With my Lord I choose forever,
  Cross and Passion, pain, and woe;
Earth's most valued pride and pleasure
  Gladly I for Him forgo.
Though they scorn me and deride,
I shall stay at Jesus' side:
  Christ, the Crucified, shall ever
  Be my loving Lord and Savior.

(continued)

At the last this Love, rewarding,
  To the Father's house doth bring,
Wreath and crown to us according
  After this world's toil and sting;
Oh, that all the world might write
On their heart with letters bright:
  Christ, the Crucified, shall ever
  Be my loving Lord and Savior!

They part my garments among them, and cast lots upon my vesture.
Psalm 22:18

The soldiers, when they had crucified Jesus, took His garments, and made four parts, to every soldier a part; and also his coat. Now the coat was without seam, woven from the top throughout. They said therefore among themselves, Let us not rend it, but cast lots for it, whose it shall be: that the Scripture might be fulfilled, which saith, They parted My garments among them, and for My coat did they cast lots. And sitting down they watched Him there; these things therefore the soldiers did. And the people stood beholding.
              Matthew 27:35–36; Mark 15:24; Luke 23:34–35; John 19:23–24

When a sick man lifts merely one arm out of his warm bed and bares his head, his head begins to shiver. And Christ, who had lost all His powers in the painful scourging and coronation, to say nothing of His cold sweating of blood, is nailed *naked* to the cross. By this baring on the cross, however, Christ wished to atone and cover to the uttermost the shame and barrenness of our first parents. For Christ's innocence and righteousness are our most beautiful garment of honor in which we please God and of which we all, yes, all, have need, because we are all by nature wretched and miserable, poor, blind, and naked. Here we are not helped by fig leaves or seeking to excuse our sins; they must wither away in the heat of the fiery burning of God's wrath. The spider webs of good works clothe us poorly (Isa. 59:6). The garments of salvation, however, are the robe of righteousness

(61:10) made by Christ on the cross, which covers the shame of our nakedness. We put it on along with our baptismal gown in Holy Baptism, and it remains the best death-shroud of all believers, in which they can fall asleep in all gentleness and blessedness. But hereafter we shall be clothed with the beautiful radiance of heaven and be made like the glorified body of Jesus Christ (Phil. 3:21) and like the angels, and surpass the glory of all the stars (Matt. 22:30) and the glory and beauty of the grass. Then we will joyfully sing with David, "Thou hast put off my sackcloth and girded me with gladness" (Ps. 30:11).

What is here stripped from the Lord Christ was His everyday clothing, besides which He had "not where to lay His head" (Matt. 8:20). By His meager wardrobe, Christ wishes to leave to His believers an example and pattern, that they may learn to be humble and rid themselves of superfluous fashion and finery. Many of them go about in far too much splendor; many even exercise great frivolity in their dress, thereby exposing their detestable mind and deformed manners. As is commonly said, a bird is known by his song and a maiden by her walk, and superfluous finery is commonly a harbinger of great punishment. For "he that shall be destroyed first groweth proud, and haughtiness goeth before the fall" (Prov. 16:18).

But Christ's feet were not yet cold when the soldiers struck in and began *dividing the inheritance.* Men do not usually seize upon the garments of evildoers with great relish, but here it is otherwise. The garments of Christ are not thrown to His dear mother as His next of kin, but the soldiers greedily seize them and part them under the cross of their own accord, and with laughing lips cast lots for His seamless tunic, since they cannot divide it. Here nailed to the cross naked and bare, the Lord Christ is made to witness this great wantonness of the wicked villains. This was done that the Scripture (Ps. 22:18) might be fulfilled, yet also for our consolation, and as an example to us, since the world treats His Christians not a hair better, not only persecuting and hunting them down because of their confession, but also with laughing lips treating their goods and possessions with all manner of insolence and malice. Whoever is made to suffer such things, let him mark how Jesus is made, amid such great sorrows, to look down from the cross at this parting of His garments, and so let him overcome all temporal loss with great patience and longsuffering in view of the hundredfold restoration to come (Matt. 19:29).

This seamless coat of Christ's relates perfectly to holy, divine Scripture, which is in all points consistent and cannot be divided without loss. The soldiers, that is, false teachers and erring spirits, gamble for it when with great mischief and wantonness they use it as a cloak for their sin and yet do not desire to further their own or others' salvation thereby. Such wantonness is also perpetrated when in times of persecution the goods and possessions of Christians are divided out, as already said, or when the goods of the church are seized by those who, like the feathers of an eagle, devour and consume all things round about them. For such people finally end up like the vulture in the fable which stole a piece of meat from a sacrifice made to Jupiter and brought it into the nest of her young; but because a glowing ember still clung to it, she thereby set the nest on fire and burned up herself and her young. There are also many examples of men who have burnt their fingers by grasping brashly and irreverently at this coat of Christ's. No less are Christ's garments parted when, as the children of this world say, "the priest's roomy skirts are trimmed a little," that is, when their salaries and incomes are diminished and reduced. When the least problem arises, they seize at Christ's coat, as it were, and wish to take something from the preacher. Then those who minister to school and church must relinquish a portion of their wages, or the budget, it is claimed, can no longer be maintained. But God knows well how to inquire into these things, so that such sophists are often made to throw ten times more down the gullets of soldiers and others than they have torn from the teeth of poor preachers and ministers of school and church, as is, alas (God have mercy!), all too plain and clear.

Prayer

O Lord Jesus, Thou wast born in great poverty! Thou sayest Thyself in what great poverty Thou didst bear Thy preaching office: "The foxes have holes, and the birds under heaven have nests, but the Son of Man hath not where to lay His head." And now, my Lord Jesus, Thou diest in great poverty also, and art left not even a piece of cloth to cover Thy beaten, scourged, wounded, and torn body on the cross and in Thy death. O Lord Jesus, Thou tookest this upon Thee, that Thy poverty might become my riches! Let me, who am by nature poor, naked, and bare, be made rich by the merit of Thy poverty! Clothe the nakedness of my sins with the garment of Thine innocence and righteousness. But if I am persecuted for Thy name's sake, and deprived of my loved ones, help me to suffer with joy the deprivation of my goods, comforted in the promise that it will be restored to me a hundredfold here and I shall have everlasting life hereafter; or if I must pass my days on earth in poverty and care, let Thy great poverty in which Thou didst live here below be my greatest comfort, and graciously grant to me and all the faithful and God-fearing poor that, as we are conformed unto the likeness of Thine image in this temporal life, so we may be made like unto Thee in heavenly riches in the life eternal. Amen, Lord Jesus! Amen.

Mel.: Herr Jesu Christ, meins Lebens Licht

Lord Jesus Christ, Thy precious blood
Is to my soul the highest Good;
  Alone this strengthens, feeds, and cleans
  My heart from all its guilty sins.

Thy blood—my crown and glorious dress—
Thine innocence and righteousness
  Help me before my God to stand
  And enter heaven's blissful land.

DEVOTION 51

Jesus Takes Care of Those Left Behind
(Second Word)

Mel.: Herzlich thut mich verlangen

My Shepherd, now receive me!
  My Guardian, own me Thine!
Great blessings Thou didst give me,
  O Source of gifts divine!
Thy lips have often fed me
  With milk and sweetest food;
Thy Spirit oft has led me
  To stores of heav'nly good.

Here I will stand beside Thee,
  From Thee I will not part;
O Savior, do not chide me!
  When breaks Thy loving heart,
When soul and body languish
  In death's last fatal grasp,
Then, in Thy deepest anguish,
  Thee in mine arms I'll clasp.

Naught ever so much blesses,
  So much rejoices me,
As when in Thy distresses
  I take a part with Thee.
Ah, well for me, if lying
  Here at Thy feet, my Life,
I too with Thee were dying,
  And thus might end my strife!

DEVOTION 51

And Simeon blessed them, and said unto Mary His mother, Behold, this Child is set for the fall and rising again of many in Israel, and for a sign which shall be spoken against; yea, a sword shall pierce through thine own soul also, that the thoughts of many hearts may be revealed.

Luke 2:34–35

Now there stood by the cross of Jesus His mother and His mother's sister, Mary the wife of Cleophas, and Mary Magdalene. When Jesus therefore saw His mother and the disciple standing by, whom He loved, He saith unto His mother, Woman, behold, this is thy son! Then saith He to the disciple, Behold, this is thy mother! And from that hour that disciple took her unto his own home.

John 19:25–27

Here is the most notable mother on whom the sun has ever shone. With what an afflicted heart and many sorrows do you think she stood under the cross and looked upon her dearest Son? That Son of whom the angel preached so many glorious things, from whom she had seen so many and various wonders, in whom she had the greatest hope—this dear Son of hers she must see dying on the cross, so full of disgrace, so full of torment, so full of misery! This must have pierced her heart right through, more sharply than any piercing sword, even as old Simeon had told her some thirty years before. It would be no surprise if she fell into one faint after another for sorrow. But she does not act powerless in the situation, though she is heartily troubled, and weeps and waits till He has taken His last breath and the pain departs, as an example to all Christian parents that, when God sends them cross and suffering in their children or otherwise, they may possess their souls in patience, and in true faith, fervent prayer, and strong hope stand firmly in God.

In the midst of His own pains, therefore, the condition of His dear mother grieves Him most. Now therefore, lest she be utterly without comfort during the three days when Christ lay dead in the tomb, and waste away for great sorrow, He entrusts her to His beloved disciple John, to regard her as a mother; John, conversely, He gives to His mother, that she may in turn treat him in a truly motherly way. And this is the third point of His last will and testament. For first, He had bequeathed poor sinners to His heavenly Father and besought grace for them; then His garments are parted by the soldiers; and now He also provides for His mother and entrusts her to John for good, so that he is to take her faithfully into his charge, though John out of humility omits his own name. Father and mother are to be honored and treated well, especially when they become old and feeble. For children can never repay their parents what they have received, even if they do them every good. And because the elderly commonly become infantile and often quite unpredictable, they are to be treated with compassion. Yet how many wicked children there are who honor their parents no better than a dog does a nettle-bush! What they do, they do with groaning and reluctance. They even let loose with stern words and only seek, after collecting their little treasure, to turn their little scorn to pleasure, and even wish them an early death and lay every wicked curse on their head. This should not be so, for the Lord wishes the father to be honored by the children and the children to show their parents all due obedience, helpfulness, and faithfulness. And whoever honors father and mother is honored in turn, and inherits the blessing of God, even as God promises good children blessing and life forever and ever. But those who do the contrary are ungodly and accursed children who will not find the fruit that they seek, for God will turn their blessing into a curse because they are acting contrary to His will and commandment.

But the Lord Christ, by entrusting His *mother* to John, also reminds us that all faithful teachers and preachers should heartily take up the church and congregation of God by teaching and protecting her, and that every Christian ought personally to attend to the salvation and welfare of all, as David prays, saying, "Redeem Israel, O God, out of all his troubles" (Ps. 25:22), and "Wish happiness for Jerusalem; let them prosper that love thee" (Ps. 122:6). Likewise, by entrusting His beloved *John* to His mother, and saying, "This is thy son," the Lord thereby suggests that parsons and pastors are to attend to the congregation of God as their own dear sons. For the church, next to God, has her comfort, protection, and help from faithful teachers of the Word, for which reason she ought rightly to hold them in esteem and to love and support them. Land and people are in full flower and are richly graced and gifted with all manner of blessing as long as godly and faithful Johns, teachers, and preachers find room and lodging among them, and churches and schools exist in prosperity and peace, and repentant and believing hearts cling to Christ. There God and all good reside and such wonderful people can, like Moses, still forestall calamity and stave off punishment for a time, because they make up the hedge and stand in the gap, and are the true Atlases who help to carry it all so that it does not fall to pieces. Accordingly, where these pillars and columns are not held in esteem, but cast down, and now this, now that pastor is promptly lost from churches and schools, the foundations of the earth must shake and one thing after the other must fall to ruin.

Prayer

O Lord Jesus, Thou hangest on the cross naked and bare, and under the cross Thy mother stands sorrowful, grief-stricken, and comfortless, and in her is fulfilled the word that was told to her, "A sword shall pierce through thine own soul." But Thou, O Lord Jesus, even though Thou hast need of help Thyself, yet Thou desirest to provide all help to Thy beloved mother. Thou turnest to her Thy loving eyes and entrustest her to the faithful hands of Thy faithful disciple, that she may not be left alone and without all consolation. So, Lord Jesus, Thou bringest me also under Thy dear cross from time to time, and I must often feel grief and sorrow in my heart. Therefore I sigh and beseech Thee, Lord Jesus, forget me not, but turn Thy gracious face upon me also, as Thou didst to Thy mother, and uphold, comfort, and provide for me! For if Thou upholdest me, I shall sink in no cross; if Thou comfortest me, I shall despair in no sorrow; if Thou providest for me, I am truly well provided for. Amen, Lord Jesus! Amen.

Mel.: Was mein Gott will, das gscheh allzeit

O faithful heart! Thou car'st for all
  Thine own, who truly love Thee;
Thou see'st when they in trouble fall,
  The sight doth deeply move Thee;

(continued)

A Friend in need,
In word and deed,
  E'er at their side appearing,
Thou dost by grace
Find them a place,
  Them to good souls endearing.

DEVOTION 52

Christ Mocked and Reviled on the Cross

Mel.: O Lamm Gottes unschuldig

Lamb of God, pure and holy,
  Who on the cross didst suffer,
Ever patient and lowly,
  Thyself to scorn didst offer.
All sins Thou borest for us,
Else had despair reigned o'er us:
  Have mercy on us, O Jesus! O Jesus!

Lamb of God, pure and holy,
  Who on the cross didst suffer,
Ever patient and lowly,
  Thyself to scorn didst offer.
All sins Thou borest for us,
Else had despair reigned o'er us:
  Have mercy on us, O Jesus! O Jesus!

Lamb of God, pure and holy,
  Who on the cross didst suffer,
Ever patient and lowly,
  Thyself to scorn didst offer.
All sins Thou borest for us,
Else had despair reigned o'er us:
  Thy peace be with us, O Jesus! O Jesus!

But I am a worm and no man, a mockery of men and a despising of the people; all they that see me mock me, they shoot out the lip and shake the head, saying, Let him cry unto the Lord, *that He may help him and deliver him, if He delighteth in him.*

Psalm 22:6–8

And they that passed by slandered Him, shaking their heads, and saying, Fie on Thee! How well Thou destroyest the Temple, and buildest it in three days; save Thyself. If Thou be the Son of God, come down from the cross. Likewise also the chief priests mocking Him among themselves with the scribes and elders and the people, said, He saved others; Himself He cannot save. If He be Christ, the King of Israel, the Chosen of God, let Him now come down from the cross, that we may see and believe Him. He trusted in God; let Him deliver him now, if He delighteth in Him, for He said, I am the Son of God. The thieves also, which were crucified with Him, cast the same in His teeth, and reviled Him. And the soldiers also mocked Him, coming to Him, and offering Him vinegar, and saying, If Thou be the King of the Jews, save Thyself.

Matthew 27:39–44; Mark 15:29–32; Luke 23:35–37

The Lord Christ's sufferings on the cross are also multiplied with manifold mockery and words of slander. For although He was assailed before with all manner of reviling and slander in the palace of Caiaphas the high priest, at the royal court of Herod, and in the judgment hall of Pilate, His heart is also afflicted now in its greatest anguish with all manner of vile reproaches and scornful gestures. And this is done not only by the uncomprehending masses and the pagan soldiers and executioners, but also by the chief priests, scribes, and elders. "O blind and foolish multitude of priests!" says Ambrose on Matthew 27:41, "was it not possible for Him to come down from a little stump of wood who came down from the height of heaven? Or could thy cords contain Him whom the heavens cannot contain? He came not to free Himself, who was not under bondage, but to deliver and redeem us from bondage." Yea, Christ, in suffering for all, willed also to suffer for each man; therefore the number of those who slander Him is also joined by "the thieves which were crucified with Him." But the fact that Matthew and Mark use the plural, while Luke speaks of one only, is interpreted in distinct ways. Theophylact says that at first, both malefactors abused Christ, but soon the one thought better of it, and confessed Jesus to be the Christ, a King, in which case his conversion would be an extraordinary example of divine mercy, like the conversion of Saul, who had viciously opposed Christ. Augustine and others, however, think that Matthew and Mark used the plural according to the common, customary manner of speaking, instead of the singular, and Augustine also deduces this from the fact that the evangelists wish to indicate not so much the persons but rather the *type and classification* of thieves, and to say how no class of the people failed to injure Christ with mockery and slander, not even the malefactors who hung on the cross with Him and were half dead, so little was He spared by any man. For this reason no man is to exclude himself from His merits; "God cast on Him the sins of us all" as a heap (Isa. 53:5).

It should especially be noted here that those who slander the Lord Christ always reiterate that He said He is the Son of God. So hostile is the devil to the article of the Godhead of our Lord Christ that he was always eager not only to persuade everyone that Christ is not the true and eternal God, or Son of God, but also to bring Christ Himself into doubt whether He were the Son of God or not. For he knows that everything for us men depends on this article, since eternal life stands on our knowing God and Him whom He has sent, even Jesus Christ, and if this foundation of Christianity is laid low, he knows that the salvation of the whole world is simultaneously overthrown. This is the rock on which the Lord builds His church, that is, St. Peter's confession, "Thou art Christ, the Son of the living God" (Matt. 16:16). Now therefore, because the evil foe knows that all emphasis lies on this point, he has at all times stirred up heretics to fight against this necessary article and thereby cast many men into eternal perdition; as in the time of the apostles he stirred up Cerinthus and Ebion, who denied the Godhead of Jesus Christ, and afterward brought the Arian heresy to the stage, and from it created the false Turkish religion and numerous other factions and sects which the crafty and evil foe has renewed in these latter days, and tempted men with this very temptation, whether this Man Jesus Christ is truly the Son of God or whether He is only bound together with Him, so that the Son of God bears this manhood, which could not otherwise exist for itself if it were not thus borne by Him, and gives to it created gifts and imputed authority, but otherwise does not really and truly share with it His infinite Person nor His Majesty and divine working. By this temptation the way is paved to wholesale denial of the person of Jesus Christ, our Redeemer and Savior.

Prayer

O Lord Jesus, how the ungodly Jews with their chief priests and elders shoot at Thee with their many slanderous words as with sharp and pointed arrows! They wickedly pervert Thy words, and what Thou saidst of the temple of Thy body they twist to mean the great edifice of their Temple. They cast it in Thy teeth before Thy cross and maliciously bid Thee come down "if Thou be the Son of God." They reproach Thy miracles as though performed out of season, and say that now it is time for Thee to work a miracle and come down from the cross. They call Thy benefits shown to others mere sleight of hand, for if it were all true, according to their thinking, Thou wouldst now save Thyself first. They despise Thy trust which Thou didst put in God Thy Father. And what do the soldiers do? They revile Thee as a poor, forsaken, helpless King of the Jews. O Lord Jesus, most gracious Savior, grant me Thy grace that I may never forget Thy patience and meekness with which Thou didst bear the slander of Thine enemies, but following Thee, may cheerfully resist all reproaches and abuse, mightily overcome them, and firmly believe that Thy scorn is my crown, Thy disgrace my honor, Thy despising my redemption—yea, that I may be delivered by Thee out of the mockery of the world and brought to the glory of heaven. Amen, Lord Jesus! Amen.

DEVOTION 52

Mel.: Jesu, meines Lebens Leben

Heartless scoffers did surround Thee,
  Treating Thee with cruel scorn,
E'en with piercing thorns they crowned Thee;
  All disgrace Thou, Lord, hast borne,
That as Thine Thou mightest own me,
And with heav'nly glory crown me.
  Thousand, thousand thanks shall be,
  Dearest Jesus, unto Thee.

Thou hast suffered great affliction
  And hast borne it patiently,
Even death by crucifixion,
  That Thou might'st atone for me;
Thou didst choose to be tormented,
That my doom should be prevented.
  Thousand, thousand thanks shall be,
  Dearest Jesus, unto Thee.

DEVOTION 53

The Conversion of the Thief on the Right
(Third Word)

Mel.: Vater unser im Himmelreich

As truly as I live, God saith,
I do not wish the sinner's death,
  But rather that he turn betimes
  From all his evil ways and crimes,
With true repentance come to Me,
And live to all eternity.

O man, this word prevail with thee,
Despair not in iniquity,
  Lay hold on this free offered grace
  Confirmed by surest promises,
Nay, sealed with God's most solemn oath;
Blest, all who their transgressions loathe!

O blessed Jesus, grant I may
Return to Thee this very day
  And live in constant penitence,
  Till death appears to call me hence,
That I in every time and place
Be well prepared to end my race.

As truly as I live, saith the Lord, the Lord, *I have no pleasure in the death of the ungodly, but that the ungodly turn from his way and live. Turn ye then from your evil ways! Why would ye die, O ye of the house of Israel?*

Ezekiel 33:11

DEVOTION 53

And one of the malefactors which were hanged slandered Him, saying, If Thou be Christ, save Thyself and us. But the other answering rebuked him, saying, And dost thou not even fear God, seeing thou art in the same condemnation? And we indeed be justly therein; for we receive the due reward of our deeds; but this Man hath done nothing amiss. And he said unto Jesus, Lord, remember me when Thou comest into Thy kingdom. And Jesus said unto him, Truly, I say unto thee, Today shalt thou be with Me in paradise.

Matthew 27:44; Luke 23:39-43

As the first evildoer lived, so he died. There is no remorse for sin there, no fear of hell, no longing for heaven. He would gladly have come down from the cross that he might further satisfy his lust and exercise all manner of mischief and impudence. And thus, in a word, he is ill prepared for death. For he is unbelieving, regards the Lord Jesus as a mere man and his equal, who may have claimed to be the Christ and boasted much, but is now caught in distress with himself and the other evildoer. And in this unbelief he stubbornly persists until with horror he meets his end.

It is quite otherwise with the second thief, till now this wicked fellow's companion; for he changes his mind very much for the better. It sorely pains him that this wicked villain so terribly and disgracefully reviles the innocent Lord, therefore he defends Christ's innocence, rebukes his companion's recklessness, and acknowledges himself deserving of punishment. Yet with this penitent heart he also promptly turns in true faith to the Lord, praying, "Lord, remember me, when Thou comest into Thy kingdom!" Oh, what an unexpected statement from a man who was so many years, and even till this moment, a thief and a robber! He is not offended by the fact that the Lord Jesus, hanging on the cross, is now to die, but he recognizes Him as a King and Lord who after this life also has another and eternal kingdom—one that He will and can share with others who desire it. The Pharisees and scribes did not understand this, much though they read Moses and the Prophets; yea, even the disciples did not grasp it, though they were in Christ's school for three and a half years. For they hoped for an earthly kingdom, but this man awaits the kingdom of God and longs to be a fellow heir with Christ and a member of His kingdom after his death. Christ on the cross touched his heart and thus, even in his deepest humiliation, caused him to see a beam of His divine power piercing through, and showed him His free grace.

What this robber seeks in Christ he also finds, namely, a gracious God who forgives him his sin and gives him eternal life; for he promptly says to him, "Truly, I say unto thee, today shalt thou be with Me in paradise." O sweet, O friendly Lord Jesus! Wilt Thou let into heaven such an accursed and arrant knave, and put such a noxious plant in paradise? A fine adornment for heaven he would make, I should say! Yet even he is to be with Him in paradise, and be brought in as the firstfruits of His blood-draining labor of the cross, that all the world may know how Christ came into the world to save all poor sinners, and He is truly in earnest when He says, "All that My Father giveth me, cometh unto Me, and whosoever cometh unto Me, him will I not cast out" (John 6:37). From this we plainly and clearly see how a poor sinner is justified before God and saved, namely, not by his own merit and works. For the thief was an ungodly man, but he was justified out of pure grace through the most precious merit of Christ, of which he takes hold in faith.

Now therefore, no man may despair in his sins, since God promises paradise and the kingdom of heaven to such a man, insofar as he repents and asks for grace. Today (to borrow the fine thoughts of Chrysostom) Adam is driven out of paradise, and today a robber is let into paradise. One thief goes out, the other goes in; for the former had stretched out his hand for the forbidden fruit, and the latter, for the purse of many a traveler. Oh, the saving grace of God! Who can despair in his iniquities, since the thief on the cross was saved?

But just as we are reminded in this example of the thief that no one is to despair in his sins, so we are also to be warned in the example of the other robber not to put off our repentance and conversion to the last hour. It is true, no man has sinned so long and so much that he should despair, since this penitent thief, who was always a wicked villain before, is received into grace. Nevertheless, as Sirach (5:7) reminds us, we ought not to tarry to turn to the Lord, nor to put off our repentance from day to day. For He who promised the penitent man grace did not promise the negligent man a tomorrow. And it is certainly true that no repentance comes too late if it is in earnest; yet the late repentance is seldom an earnest repentance. Therefore today, if we will hear the Lord's voice, let us not harden our hearts (Ps. 95:8), lest if this time of grace be neglected, another time come when the previously offered but thanklessly rejected grace is sought after but not found, as the threat of Proverbs 1:24–30 reads.

Finally, we have a reminder here that there are only *two estates of souls* when they depart this life, namely, salvation or damnation, paradise or hell, even as there are two kinds of men: believing, who are not judged but immediately pass through death into life (John 5:24), and unbelieving, who are damned (Mark 16:16). The papistic inventions of purgatorial fire and of the abomination of masses for souls come largely from the apparitions of devils and malevolent spirits, even as the whole papacy is, according to the description of John (Rev. 18:2), a "habitation of devils, and the hold of every foul spirit and hateful bird." We are to know that nothing else can purge and cleanse us from sins than the blood of Christ alone, which also frees and releases us from all punishments of sins, but especially from punishment after this life; for Isaiah (53:5) says, "Chastisement lieth upon Christ, that we might have peace."

Prayer

O Lord Jesus, with what an exceedingly remarkable example Thou dost confirm Thy precious oath, which Thou didst once declare: "As truly as I live, I have no pleasure in the death of the ungodly, but that the ungodly turn from his way and live"! My Lord Jesus, I too am a great sinner; "mine iniquities have gone over my head, and as an heavy burden they are too heavy for me" (Ps. 38:4). Oh, let me be blessed and be made a partaker of Thy grace and mercy! Look upon me, Lord Jesus, with the gracious eyes with which Thou didst look upon the believing thief, and forgive me my sins. Oh, wake me today, even now, while I yet live and am not so near the end as the thief was then! Oh, wake me, that I may not delay to turn to Thee, nor wait until death for my correction! But when it is time for me to die and depart, oh, then be with me, Lord Jesus, and forsake me not! Grant me then to hear the comforting word that Thou spakest to the thief, and say to my soul, "Be of good cheer, believing soul! Truly, I say unto thee, today shalt thou be with

Me in paradise!" Oh, yes, Lord Jesus, remember me in my last distress of death! O Lord Jesus, when death closes my eyes, do not depart from me! Amen, Lord Jesus! Amen.

Mel.: Singen wir aus Herzensgrund (p. 324)

Jesus Christ, Thou King supreme,
Great and fearsome dost Thou seem,
  Yet Thou grantest every Christian
  Healing, life, and sin's remission:
Fountain whence all good is giv'n—
Grant me, too, the joys of heav'n!

Faithful Shepherd, hear my plea,
And remember graciously
  Thy uniting with creation,
  Suff'ring bitter pain and Passion,
That we may on yonder Day
Safe escape from all dismay.

Never didst Thou rest or sleep
Till Thou found'st Thy wand'ring sheep,
  But Thou bor'st the cross to save me;
  Thus Thy death my freedom gave me:
Oh, may all Thine agony
Never prove misspent on me.

Mary found Thy grace immense
Through her tearful penitence;
  And the thief, contrite in dying,
  Mercy found in Thy replying.
May I also, as is just,
Fix on Thee my hope and trust.

DEVOTION 54

Christ Forsaken by God
(Fourth Word)

Mel.: Jesu Leiden, Pein und Tod

Jesus cried, "My God, my God!
  How am I forsaken!
How I feel Thy grievous rod,
  By distress o'ertaken!"
So, O man, in agony,
  Cry, and God will hear thee;
Though He seem so far from thee,
  He will still be near thee.

Jesus Thou who once wast dead,
  But now ever livest;
Who in ev'ry time of need
  Kindly me relievest,
And dost help to me afford:
  Faithful Lord and Savior,
Give me what Thy death procured,
  And I'm rich forever.

My God, my God, why hast Thou forsaken me? I wail, but my help is far off.
Psalm 22:1

And when the sixth hour was come, there was darkness over the whole land until the ninth hour, and the sun was darkened. And about the ninth hour Jesus cried with a loud voice, saying, Eli! Eli! Lama azabthani? which is, being interpreted,

My God, my God, why hast Thou forsaken Me? And some of them that stood there, when they heard that, said, This Man calleth for Elias.
Matthew 27:45–47; Mark 15:33–34; Luke 23:44–45

"The sun is the eye of the world," says Sirach 42:16. "She giveth light unto all the world, and her light is the brightest of all." But before Christ departs on the cross, a great darkness befalls her, of which Phlegon also writes, "About the sixth hour, the day turned into a dark night, so that the stars could be seen in the heavens." The Jews used to divide the day into twelve hours, and to begin at sunrise. Now when the sun had shone six hours and stood at her highest, this great light in the heavens was suddenly and unexpectedly darkened, and according to the reckoning of our clock, continued thus from high noon until about three o'clock, all of three hours, as God had caused to be prophesied by the prophet Amos. This, then, occurred not by natural causes, as do eclipses of the sun and moon, but beyond and contrary to the course of nature. Normally, if the sun is to be darkened, it must happen when the moon is new, as experience proves. This darkness, however, fell when the moon was full, from which it may therefore be seen that Christ was crucified on the feast of the Passover in accordance with the evangelists' account, which feast had to be held on a full moon according to God's ordinance (Ex. 12:14). From this it must be concluded that it was supernatural and a miracle. Furthermore, this darkness fell over the whole land or earth. This is apparent not only from the writings of the evangelists, but also from other writers. Suidas writes, "At the time of the holy suffering of Christ, Dionysius the Areopagite and the orator Apollophanes lived concurrently in Heliopolis (or 'the city of the sun') in Egypt. And when the darkening of the sun occurred contrary to nature, Apollophanes said, 'O renowned Dionysius, a change in the heavens must certainly have taken place.' To which Dionysius replied, 'Either God Himself is suffering, or He is mourning the afflicted state of one who is suffering, or the world is about to end.'" Orosius writes that the darkness was also seen in Rome.

From this miraculous darkness it is evident that God had good knowledge of Christ's suffering, since here the very thing comes upon Christ that was prophesied of Him before by the mouth of His spiritual prophets. And if so many different wonders had not occurred before the departure of Christ, there would have been no end of slander, and the Jews would have repeatedly claimed that God knew nothing about Him. But now nature shows to great excess that Christ is more than a man, and is thus infallibly true, essential God. This was a sign from heaven, even as the Jews had once asked for a sign, but now they do not regard it and are not troubled. Therefore they do not see either that Scripture is fulfilled thereby. For as Moses had to spread his hands toward heaven that there might be darkness throughout the land of Egypt for three days, such that no man saw nor arose from the place where he was for three days, so also Christ spreads His arms on the tree of the cross and then a great darkness falls throughout the land. Immediately thereupon, the Passover Lamb is slain, and Christ brings His faithful out, as Moses brought the people of Israel out of Egypt.

In this terrible darkness, however, Christ sees nothing above Him, nothing below Him, nothing around Him, nothing within Him but the anguish of hell, torment of hell, fire of hell, and the merited, unbearable pains of hell, so that these lamentable words are pressed from Him: "My God, my God, why hast Thou forsaken Me?" These nine words which Jesus spoke in the ninth hour a Christian heart should ponder well. They are taken from the Psalter (Ps. 22:1) and are found nowhere else in holy, divine Scripture; so incomprehensible and unfathomable in meaning, so profound and great, that no creature, neither angel nor man, can grasp nor fathom, much less express, the great anguish into which Christ came for our sins, such that He even cries that He is forsaken, though He is the Son of the living God and is true, essential God. Here without doubt the devil and his minions did not rest, but as may be supposed, exerted all their power and utmost abilities herein. As a result, Christ came according to His manifold, unspeakable sufferings into the most extreme distress and oppression, where the Godhead rested and, as it were, slept in Christ, so that the human nature no longer felt any cooperation with it, as a man who lies unconscious has no sensation of his life, despite the fact there is still life in him.

This suffering in each and every point is for our good. Our ancestral parents were dear children of God, but they willfully forsook God and made the acquaintance of and befriended the serpent. For all of this Christ now atones, and laments that He is forsaken by God, that we might not be forsaken by God in any trouble, however much we give God cause to forsake us with our sins, for these separate us from our God and conceal His face from us. Therefore we are to keep ourselves diligently from sin, since nothing can be more terrible than when a man is forsaken by God, for God is opposed to him, the holy angels resist him, the devil afflicts him, the worm of the consciences gnaws at him, and all creatures are against him and must serve as a curse to him. In short, there is no more miserable creature under the sun than such a man, as we see in the example of Judah the betrayer. But now, since Christ has indubitably been made to know and to feel in His soul how a man must feel who believes himself forsaken by God, we are to take hearty comfort in this, and in cross and distress rightly to learn to know God our dear Father, who always first brings His dearest children into hell and causes them to know much and great anguish before He brings them into heaven.

Prayer

O Lord Jesus, though the misery that befell Thee before this was already so great, the reproach that was poured upon Thee was already so unspeakable, the torment with which Thou wast tormented and tortured was already so painful—nevertheless Thou madest no complaint about any of it. But now, when Thou hast little time left to live, Thou beginnest to lament, to complain, to weep, and to wail, to cry out, because the wrath of God surrounds Thee on the tree of the cross in terrible darkness, and powerfully afflicts Thee, so that for peace Thou hast great bitterness. Now therefore, O my Lord Jesus, I thank Thee for all this bitterness and dread of Thy soul and for the anguish of Thine heart! I thank Thee for this with all the power of my soul and from the depths of mine heart. For now I know and believe confidently that I shall never be forsaken by my God and Thy Father, since Thou, Lord Jesus, His one and only beloved Son, wast forsaken by Him on the tree of the cross for my sins. Oh, yes, Thou comforting and helping Lord Jesus! Let me feel Thy presence, let me sense Thy comfort, let me see Thy help when I am forsaken by all men in the world! Graciously take up my cause now and forever, and deliver me! Turn from me the murderous darts of hell's tribulations, and defend me. O Lord Jesus, by virtue of Thy meritorious forsakenness let me never be forsaken by Thee! Forsake me not, O Lord, my God! Be not far from me; hasten to help me, O Lord, my Help! Amen, Lord Jesus! Amen.

Mel.: Wer nur den lieben Gott läßt walten

My God, Thou never wilt forsake me,
  For I rely alone on Thee,
In faith upon Thy pledge I stake me!
  Thy pitying eye consoleth me:
For my salvation Christ supplied
When on the cross for me He died.

When He, weighed down with our transgression,
  No helper had in agony,
This was His greatest lamentation:
  My God, why hast forsaken Me?
Yet at this last and mortal pain,
New comfort filled His heart again.

Now, Father, hear my supplication:
  I pray Thee through this anxious cry
Of Him who died for my salvation:
  Be with me when distress is nigh!
My plaints Thou know'st ere sigh I make:
My Father, do not me forsake!

DEVOTION 55

Jesus' Thirst on the Cross
(Fifth Word)

Mel.: Seelenbräutigam

Prince of Peace once curst,
Heavy was Thy thirst
  To save man from his affliction,
  When amidst Thy crucifixion,
Thou didst cry, "I thirst!"
Prince of peace once curst.

Grant Thy peace, O Lord,
Of Thy love outpoured
  Unto us of Thy confession,
  Who by name are Thy possession;
To Thine own adored,
Grant Thy peace, O Lord.

Here through scorn and frown,
There the glorious crown;
  Here in hoping and believing,
  There in having and perceiving;
For the glorious crown
Follows scorn and frown.

Reproach breaketh my heart and afflicteth me. I wait for some to take pity, but there is none; and for comforters, but I find none. And they give me also gall to eat, and vinegar to drink in my thirst.

Psalm 69:20–21

DEVOTION 55

After this, Jesus knowing that all things were now accomplished, that the Scripture might be fulfilled, saith, I thirst. Now there was set a vessel full of vinegar. And straightway one of them ran, took a sponge, and filled it with vinegar and hyssop, and put it on a reed, and put it to His mouth, and gave Him to drink, saying with the rest, Let be, let us see whether Elias will come and take Him down.
Matthew 27:47–49; Mark 15:35–36; John 19:28–29

Even John had no wish to omit the fact that our dear Lord Jesus Christ, in His last throes of death, laments in few words His unbearable thirst, which becomes so great that He forgets all other pains. Such a thirst came upon the Man who made the oceans and all the springs of water, who gives both men and cattle to drink.

Now although the physical thirst may have been great, as may easily be estimated if one ponders at all what pains He endured throughout the night, shedding His blood and hanging in the dry air, yet this is not chiefly a matter of external thirst; rather, He is tormented by the inner thirst of the soul. He thirsts for the salvation and blessedness of poor, lost man, and He has such heartfelt longing to restore lost mankind that we too might hunger and thirst for His righteousness. For thereby Christ's spiritual thirst of His soul is stilled, when we believe in Him and trust in Him, and acknowledge and perform His holy will, as He also says of Himself, "My meat is that I do the will of Him which sent Me" (John 4:34). Those accordingly who leave Christ thus hungering and thirsting do not do according to His Word nor perform His holy will, and they shall be made in turn to hunger and thirst after Christ for eternity.

Now, the Lord Jesus is given vinegar in His great thirst so that the Scripture might be fulfilled, in which David said before in the Psalter, "They give Me gall to eat and vinegar to drink in My great thirst" (Ps. 69:21). This drink goes around the table and shall also come to us. This is His cup of the cross, poured full to the brim with the vinegar and strong wine of grief and sorrow. While it is sharp and bitter enough, yet it must serve them well that love God, and be for their best. And the most delightful thing is that at the bottom, in the dregs, lies our highest comfort, namely, that Christ with this sour vinegar and bracing, bitter draft of gall extinguished and atoned for the eternal, inescapable thirst of hell, which the ungodly, especially with their inhuman drunkenness, had more than merited. Now therefore, when in much cross and suffering we find no refreshment or quickening, we ought to think of Christ's bracing draft of refreshment. For the world honors Christ and His saints no better, nor does He desire to serve them anything else than sour vinegar and bitter gall. Therefore, O fainting souls, bring hither your hearts panting for comfort, for here we find Christ, the true, living, and truly life-giving water, who by the great thirst that He suffered on the cross slakes and stills all the thirst of our soul and quickens again our wearied soul!

But because Christ is given His sharp draft with much mockery and scorn, as though He were waiting for the help of others, and till Elias should come and take Him down, therefore we are to learn here how it goes no better for godly, Christian hearts in the world. For not only must they dip their sponge in the vinegar when others have full abundance and the unruly swine of the world pour the best down their gullets and out again before the pigs, but what is more, this draft of vinegar is also filled with gall for them, and they must hear the scornful and mocking words, "Let be! Let us see, where is thy God?" David knows how to sing of this, and says, "It is as murder in my bones, that mine enemies reproach me, while they say daily unto me, Where is thy God? (Ps. 42:10). "Many say of my soul, There is no help for him in God. Selah" (Ps. 3:2). This is the mischief and wickedness of the ungodly, the bearing of which calls for patience. Here, it is the comfort of the godly that some day, their sharp cup of the cross shall be filled full with the sweet wine of joy, for God shall give them to drink of pleasures as a river, in which they shall be truly joyful, and shall shout for joy with a goodly mind, while conversely the scoffers and ungodly hereafter shall, with eternal mockery and scorn, be made to give an account for the dregs which they left behind, and shall drink of the wrath of the Almighty.

Prayer

O most gracious Lord Jesus, I thank Thee with all my heart for Thy thirst on my behalf! By this Thou didst dry up the sea of my sins, so that I can find the way to heaven without tarrying. Oh, that my soul might hunger and thirst after Thee as I wish! O Giver of all gifts, grant me a loathing for all that is in the world, and a hunger and thirst for what is of heaven, especially for Thee, my Love, and for the grace that is in Thee, and for righteousness, sanctification, and the Holy Ghost, for the eternal God and His kingdom. But if I must also suffer according to Thy will, help me to possess my soul in patience, to do according to Thy will, and to receive the promise. And when I am anxious for comfort and I thirst as a hart after fresh water, then quicken my soul with Thy grace and let me drink confidently the cup of the cross in the hope of everlasting joy, where my soul shall be satisfied with heavenly pleasure when it awaketh after Thy likeness (Ps. 17:15). Bring me out of the pit wherein is no water (Zech. 9:11), and bring me at last to the place where I shall hunger and thirst no more! Amen.

Mel.: Jesu, der du meine Seele

Let Thy holy thirst avail me,
   Which Thou on the cross didst know;
When unholy lusts assail me,
   When my sins are haunting so,
Let me share Thy holy thirsting,
Let Thy wells of life be bursting.
   Oh, Thy Passion's fright'ning pain
   Let my heart fore'er retain!

DEVOTION 56

Christ, Dying, Proclaims His Victory
(Sixth Word)

Mel.: Gott sei Dank durch alle Welt

Jesus Christ hath finished quite
What saves sinners from our plight;
  This word from His mouth makes known
  What bequest He makes our own.

Lo, He spoke this word for thee,
Spoke it for all men and me:
  All, yes, all is finished quite
  That saves sinners from our plight!

All He did for which we yearned,
All atoned, all for us earned;
  All that God of us demands
  Now forever certain stands.

All our sins and death as well,
All that threatens us with hell,
  All that can cause us dismay—
  Blotted out and done away!

Seventy weeks are determined upon thy people and upon the holy city, then shall the transgressor be prevented and sin sealed up, and iniquity reconciled and everlasting righteousness brought, and the vision and prophecies sealed up and the Most Holy anointed. — When Jesus therefore had received the vinegar, He said, It is finished.

Daniel 9:24; John 19:34

Before, Christ did not wish to drink the draft of gall, lest He should seem afraid of death; now He receives the vinegar, that He might refresh Himself and at the same time taste the bitterness of our sufferings. With this, all was finished and nothing that He was to do for our redemption was left that He had not done. The sacrifice for sin is finished. His earthly life now ends, and hereby the whole Scripture is fulfilled in all its foreshadows and prophesies. Now is sin, the sin of all mankind, superabundantly paid for! Now is the wrath of God assuaged, the Law fulfilled, and its curse abolished, the head of the ancient serpent of hell crushed, hell harrowed, death swallowed up, life restored, and heaven opened. O blessed hour! O comforting words, for which all the saints of the Old Testament waited with longing and sighs some four thousand years! O glorious word of victory, for the enemies are laid low and the battle is won! O sweet word of comfort, for salvation belongs to us all! O powerful word of defiance! It is finished! Far be it that any of His enemies should stir! What the heavenly Father determined for His Son from eternity is finished. His promise and pledge are finished; the wrath and wickedness of the Jews are finished; toil and labor are finished; war and victory are finished: the work of redemption is finished. Through our Lord Jesus Christ, blessedness is ours, and we will enter into the joy of our Lord!

Now therefore, whoever believes in this crucified Jesus is considered in God's sight as perfect as Christ the Lord, even in His entire obedience, suffering, and death. For His obedience which He rendered to the heavenly Father under the Law is ours; He did not need it, but what He did and suffered He did and suffered in our place and for our sake. If therefore it is finished, how can there be anything condemnable in those who are in Christ Jesus?

Men often undertake to do a great deal, but as with spun cloth, so is it often with their thoughts. They cannot do, fulfill, and carry out all that they desire. Likewise, the tyrants and enemies of the Gospel may undertake to destroy the church of God and to lay waste the vineyard which His right hand hath planted, but God disappointeth the devices of the crafty so that their hands cannot perform their enterprise. The undertaking of Christ, however, shall prosper by His hand. He had undertaken to merit salvation for men, whom He desires to transport from hell into heaven, which He procured for them by His bitter sufferings and death, and by His Word He still causes them to be readied, strengthened, fortified, and grounded, till they all come in the unity of the faith, and of the knowledge of the Son of God—until that *final* "It is finished!" comes to pass, and He welcomes us into heaven—and the corrupted Adam comes unto an entirely other being and "a perfect man, unto the measure of the stature of the fullness of Christ" (Eph. 4:13).

Prayer

O Lord Jesus, how heartily glad I am that Thou, my Treasure, the Alpha and Omega, the Beginning and the End, before Thou didst commend Thy Spirit into the hands of Thy Father, didst speak the glorious, powerful word of triumph and victory, *"Consummatum est* (It is finished)!" with a loud voice. Now, Lord, Scripture is fulfilled. Now Thy Father's wrath is stilled. Now we, sunk in corruption, have eternal, full salvation. Now all pain of heart is o'er; thanks be to Thee forevermore! O Lord Jesus, Founder and Perfecter of our salvation, there is still great controversy today over the article of our justification and salvation, for our opponents wish to add all manner of extraneous, worthless merits to Thy most holy and perfect merit. But I hold to Thy clear Word, believing firmly that with Thy single, bloody sacrifice on the cross Thou hast finished all, and hast found an eternal redemption—even if I must suffer not only bonds and imprisonment but also death itself. Grant me Thy grace that I may valiantly finish my course and remain faithful to Thee to the last sigh. Amen, Amen! Come, Thou beauteous Crown of glory, wait no longer; daily grows my yearning stronger! Amen.

DEVOTION 56

Mel.: Es ist genug

"'Tis finished now!" The Lamb of God doth cry
  When vinegar He tastes,
And so He sings upon the Cross-tree high
  Another hymn of praise.
The Scriptures now are all fulfillèd,
His blood the Father's wrath hath stillèd.
  'Tis finished now! 'Tis finished now.

For this dear word, O Thou my Champion true,
  My all, my thanks I show:
It is my balm and comfort ever new
  Amid this world of woe!
Some day, whenever death shall find me,
Then let Thy Spirit's cry remind me:
  'Tis finished now! 'Tis finished now.

DEVOTION 57

Jesus Dies
(Seventh Word)

Mel.: Es ist gewisslich an der Zeit

I thank Thee for Thy death endured,
  Lord Jesus, and adore Thee
For all Thy pains of heart conferred
  By those who beat and tore Thee!
Grant that the merits of that pain
May for my soul refreshment gain
  When death my eyelids closeth.

I thank Thee for Thy loving grace
  Which Thou to me displayest
When Thou dost bow Thy holy face
  And all my debt repayest;
Incline to me, my God, as well
When I am faced with death and hell,
  That I Thy grace may savor.

My soul let in Thy favor go
  From all its griefs here tasted,
That of Thy precious, costly woe
  Naught may on me be wasted.
Receive my soul to heaven's heart,
Where Thou, its dearest Jesus, art,
  And let me live forever.

Into Thine hands I commend my spirit; Thou hast redeemed me, O LORD, Thou faithful God.
Psalm 31:5

DEVOTION 57

And again He cried with a loud voice and said, "Father, into Thine hands I commend My spirit." And having said thus, He bowed His head and gave up His spirit.
             Matthew 27:50; Mark 15:37; Luke 23:46; John 19:30

This is the seventh and last word of Christ on the cross, and is as if He should say: "Nothing more is left than My soul, and that will I now breathe out. But to whom shall I yield this immortal treasure? To none more safely than to Thee, my dear, heavenly Father. 'Into Thine hands I commend My spirit!'" He cries this word with a loud voice not for the sake of His Father, who always hears Him, but because it was said in Psalm 69:3 that He would wail and cry, that He would cry Himself hoarse and weary, so that even His eyes would fail because of it. This Scripture Christ also had to fulfill.

Approach, dear soul! Approach the cross of Christ, behold and consider how your Savior falls asleep on the cross and yields up His spirit. He bows His head, for He wishes to retire to His rest after the toil and labor which we made for Him with our sins. But behold and attend, for here Life dies! The Captain of Life yields up His spirit! The Son of God, who made the whole world, who gave natural life to all creatures, dies. But He dies according to the flesh because the essential Word that was made flesh has taken His rest and consented to die, and yet has remained personally and inseparably with the flesh, that Christ, after death, might at the right time be able to overcome according to the flesh and thus with a glorious victory rise again from the dead the third day. And this was His deepest humiliation, when He became obedient to His Father unto death, even the death of the cross, died for us ungodly, and gave His life as a guilt offering for many.

Therefore there has never been a worthier or more glorious departure since the beginning of the world than Christ's death and departure on the cross. There He bows His head and shows hereby that He also consents to the heavenly Father's eternal counsel and will, according to which He decided from eternity that Christ must die. According to this He also desires, as it were, to beckon to death and to yield Himself as spoils; for until Christ yielded His will and cast His life into the arena, death could not lay a finger on Him, but Christ falls asleep when He wills, and demonstrates that, as the one with all authority over death and life, He has the power to take life up again. Accordingly, because the work of redemption was finished with great toil and labor, He commits Himself to rest, dies, and with His death fulfills the Scripture, which had clearly foretold of the Messiah that He must be put to death (Dan. 9:26). And hereby He confirms His testament, bequeathing to His believers the forgiveness of sins and everlasting life. This glorious and heavenly bequest could be effected in no other way than by the death of Christ.

Yet by this death He took death's power, even as He had threatened that He would be a poison unto death (Hosea 13:14). Here, therefore, He lets death swallow Him up, that death may in His death devour its eternal death. Who now will condemn? Christ is here, who hath died (Rom. 8:34), who hath redeemed us from hell and delivered us from death. He hath swallowed up death in victory (1 Cor. 15:54), He hath abolished sin and death, and hath brought life and immortality to light! (2 Tim. 1:10). But because death is the wages of sin (Rom. 6:23), and we poor sinners must all die, we may bow our head joyfully and confidently when temporal death knocks at our door, for by death we go from this temporal misery to eternal rest, from the storming, tumultuous waves of this world to the safe harbor of everlasting life in heaven—in a word, from cross and suffering to glory. Therefore, when the hour of our departure is at hand, we too may commend our poor soul into the faithful hands of God, for He is the Creator of souls, who breathed into man the breath of life, and into His fatherly hands true, believing hearts have commended their souls in turn, and like Stephen following the example of Christ, heartily sighed, "Lord Jesus, receive my spirit!"

Prayer

O Lord Jesus, Thou bowest Thine head before Thou diest, desiring thereby to offer me a kiss of Thy love in parting and to assure me that Thou lovest me unto death. O Lord Jesus, let me love Thee in turn, let me love Thee unto death! And when on my sickbed and deathbed I am no longer able to raise my head, then let my heart be directed to Thee, that with it I may take hold of Thee, with it

DEVOTION 57

embrace Thee, with it hold Thee and not let Thee go till Thou bless me. O dearest Lord Jesus, grant me Thy grace, that the last word that Thou spakest on the cross may also be my last word when I die, and that as my soul departs the body, I may commend it into the faithful hands of Thy Father and Thee! Oh, yes, Lord Jesus, take up my soul then and present it to Thy heavenly Father, and say to Him, "Behold, dear Father, this is a soul that Thou hast created; this is a soul that I have redeemed; this is a soul that is washed with My blood. Do Thou, My Father, therefore graciously accept and receive this soul." O Lord Jesus, with what shouts of joy and triumphant rejoicing, with what praise and adoration, my soul will exalt Thee when it shall be thus received by Thy Father and by Thee to eternal glory! Surely, it will take Thy word from Thy lips, address Thee with it, and boldly declare, "Yes, Lord Jesus! It is finished! O Lord Jesus, all my sorrow and misery has come by Thee to a blessed conclusion! For this Thou shalt be praised forever." Amen, Lord Jesus! Amen.

Mel.: Herzlich thut mich verlangen

What language shall I borrow
  To thank Thee, dearest Friend,
For this Thy dying sorrow,
  Thy pity without end?
Oh, make me Thine forever,
  And should I fainting be,
Lord, let me never, never
  Outlive my love to Thee.

My Savior, be Thou near me
  When death is at my door;
Then let Thy presence cheer me,
  Forsake me nevermore!
When soul and body languish,
  Oh, leave me not alone,
But take away mine anguish
  By virtue of Thine own!

(continued)

Be Thou my consolation,
  My shield when I must die;
Remind me of Thy Passion
  When my last hour draws nigh.
Mine eyes shall then behold Thee,
  Upon Thy cross shall dwell,
My heart by faith enfold Thee.
  Who dieth thus dies well.

DEVOTION 58

The Miraculous Signs Following Jesus' Death

Mel.: Ach Gott, erhör mein Seufzen und Wehklagen (p. 321)

Alas, shall thus my dearest Life be dying?
Yea, it is done, He makes His final sighing.
  My Lord is dead,
  O grief! O dread!
Can any man in pain like mine be lying?

The Dayspring from on high His setting keepeth,
The early-hunted Hind to slumber creepeth.
  Let tears not fail!
  My Crown bewail!
Oh, that I could not join Him where He sleepeth!

He lieth stiff, at whom hell stands affrighted,
Before whom heaven high bows down delighted;
  The soul's great Friend,
  Death's Bane and End
Is laid by death within the tomb benighted.

Ye graves, be split! Ye flinty rocks, be broken!
Be dim, thou sun! Earth shake, thy grief betoken!
  O sky, O sea—
  Star-canopy—
All creatures, to your Lord's lament be woken!

His rest shall be glorious. — I seek not Mine own glory, but there is One that seeketh and judgeth.

Isaiah 11:10; John 8:50

And, behold, the veil of the Temple was rent in twain from the top to the bottom, and the earth did quake, and the rocks rent, and the graves were opened, and many bodies of the saints which slept arose, and came out of the graves after His resurrection, and went into the holy city, and appeared unto many.

Matthew 27:51–53; Mark 15:38; Luke 23:45

All these wonders, and others following besides, testify that God well knows of the suffering and death of His beloved Son, even as He also caused that suffering to be announced before by all His servants the prophets. Now they have also been made to come as witnesses to the innocence of Christ for the hardened people. And because the Lord Jesus is Lord of all things, therefore all creatures also exhibit their sympathy and serve Christ in His suffering, death, and dying; yea, all the bells of nature toll as one to ring their Lord and Maker to the grave.

The first miraculous sign by which God honors His Son is *the rending of the veil of the Temple.* The veil, one of the chief appointments of the Temple's furnishings, wrought in very fine and sumptuous manner of yellow silk, scarlet, crimson, and twisted white silk, created a proper distinction between the Holy of Holies, in which the high priest might enter only once a year, and the Holy Place, where the priests and Levites attended to their work; and it covered the ark of the covenant along with the mercy-seat and other holy vessels, lest they should be seen. But behold, this veil of the Temple is rent in twain, so that it is possible to see right into the Holy of Holies. God does this first as a sign of His wrath, in which He also earnestly visits the Jews afterwards, rending in twain and tearing apart Temple, city, and government, and abolishing His worship among them, as Christ had also threatened before, saying, "Your house shall be left to you desolate," which desolation now commences.

Second, God also desires by this wonder to show that Jesus Christ is the true and only High Priest, who entered once into the Holy of Holies not by the blood of goats or calves, but by His own blood (Heb. 9:12) and thereby made for us free access to God. Now laymen and simple hearts know the Way to Life and have a free, open access to God, as the priests never had before; for Christ has made us all kings and priests before God and all the people, in whose name we also make our prayer and offer without fear the sacrifice of our lips. And now that the veil is rent apart, both Jews and Gentiles belong to the kingdom of Christ and of God. Now the Holy of Holies, even heaven, stands free and open to all men! Now we can see God with unveiled faces in the clear light of the Gospel (2 Cor. 13:18), and now we may come with all confidence and boldness unto the mercy-seat and without hindrance enter into everlasting glory and majesty in the heavenly and eternal existence.

Next, God causes the death of His Son to be announced to all the world by a *terrible earthquake,* in which all the foundations of the earth were so shaken that even the hard rocks split open with a great crack, which happened not only in Judaea but over the whole face of the earth. For as Eutropius writes, on this day the greatest part of the city of Nicaea in Bithynia fell, and many cities in Asia were shaken and reduced to rubble, so that the Roman Emperor was made to waive the customary tribute. On that day, a cry was supposed to have been heard on the sea, saying, "The great God, who was all things, has been destroyed!"

Through this wondrous work, God wishes to terrify the murderers of His Son, so that they consider how easily and quickly He can command the earth to open her jaws and swallow them up as the rebellious horde. He wishes to show hereby that the salutary teaching of the consolation of Christ crucified shall be proclaimed by the apostles in all the world, and stony hearts shall be softened and brought to the Christian faith. Yea, because the lifeless things of creation have neither tongue nor mouth with which to lament the painful death of Christ on the cross, they wish to manifest their due sympathy by this shaking and shuddering, cracking and crashing, and since men are silent, the stones must proclaim the innocence of Christ (Luke 19:40). "All creation sympathizes with Christ and His death; only poor man, for whom alone Christ suffers, has no sympathy," laments Jerome. O dear man, if the earth shook, oh, then tremble much more at the wrath of God and your own wickedness! If the hard stony rocks were rent, then rend all the more your own heart by true repentance and amend your life!

Finally, God points all the world to the death of His Son by causing all *the closed tombs to burst open,* in which the holy patriarchs, fathers, and prophets and those of their company lay, so that their dead bones were seen lying inside the hollows of the tombs. These go forth out of their tombs alive with Christ in His joyous resurrection, appear to the apostles and many other friends of Jesus in Jerusalem, and hold sweet converse with them for those forty days until they go with Christ up into heaven.

Here we see that Christ Jesus is the Lord who can and will open the tombs and wake the dead. If He did this in His deepest humiliation, oh, how much more shall He demonstrate it on the Last Day, when as the appointed Judge of the whole earth He appear in the open and cry aloud, "Arise, ye dead, come unto the judgment"? Therefore, dear heart, do not recoil at death, but say with Job in expectation of the Last Day, "I know that my Redeemer liveth; He shall raise me up out of the earth, and I shall be encompassed with mine own skin, and in my flesh I shall see God. Him shall I see for myself, and mine eyes shall behold Him, and not a stranger" (Job 19:25–27).

Prayer

O Lord Jesus, eternal Son of God, to whose innocence all creatures bear witness: be gracious to me, a poor sinner, and forgive me all my sins for the sake of Thy suffering and death! O Jesus Christ, for whose innocence the earth is shaken: help my heart also to be shaken in true remorse and sorrow for my sins! O faithful Savior, for whose innocence the rocks are rent: break and bend my rock-hard heart also, that with joy I may discover the power of Thy death! O everlasting Savior, for whose death the veil was rent in twain and the Holy of Holies laid bare to all men: help me in Thy name to come boldly to the mercy-seat, that I may obtain mercy and find grace in the time when help and comfort shall be needed! O Jesus Christ, whose mighty death opens the graves and raises the dead: raise me also on the Last Day, that I too may go forth from my tomb and come into the eternal holy city, to appear before God and all His angels and saints! Amen, O Jesus! Amen.

DEVOTION 58

Mel.: Alle Menschen müssen sterben

Rocks, be rent! and earth, be quaking!
  Sun, thy splendid labor quit!
All the world with grief be shaking,
  For my saving Rock is split.
At the lashing strokes He crieth
As the fairest body dieth,
  Deathly pale and bloody red—
  Jesus, my Belov'd, is dead!

I'll die fearless, then within me
  Shall be manifest the Life
Which hath died, new life to win me;
  Though I suffer, yet the strife
Ceases when life's woes desert us;
Death itself shall never part us,
  'Neath Christ's burial stone for lee,
  With Him I will buried be.

DEVOTION 59

The Wonderful Effects of the Death of Jesus on Men's Hearts

Mel.: Jesus, meine Zuversicht

Go, my soul, to Calv'ry's brow!
  Rest beneath the Cross of Jesus!
There in deep contrition bow!
  He who healeth thy diseases,
Doth for all thy guilt atone!
Canst thou be unmoved as stone?

See the martyred Son of God,
  Hangs twixt heav'n and earth suspended!
See the streams of precious blood!
  Nails and thorns His flesh have rended!
See His stripes, His riven side!
O my soul, thy Lord has died!

Holy Lamb of God, so pure,
  Thou didst die for my transgression!
For my guilt Thou didst endure
  All the anguish of Thy Passion
That I might not suffer loss
Thou didst die upon the cross!

Spotless Lamb without all dross,
  I Thy love with praise receiving
Pray Thee, look down from Thy cross,
  See how I for Thee am grieving.
Thy dear heart in blood immersed,
Makes me feel the more accursed.

DEVOTION 59

Therefore will I give him great multitudes for his portion, and he shall have the strong for his spoils; because that he hath given his life unto death and was numbered with the transgressors, and he bare the sin of many, and made intercession for the transgressors. — And I, when I am lifted up from the earth, will draw them all unto Me.
Isaiah 53:12; John 12:32

And when the centurion, which stood over against Him, and they that were with him, watching Jesus, saw that He so cried out and gave up the ghost, and saw the earthquake and those things which were done, they feared greatly and glorified God, saying, Truly this was a righteous Man, and the Son of God.
Matthew 27:54; Mark 15:39; Luke 23:47–48

That everyone might know why such glorious wonders happened at the death of Christ, the *pagan centurion* stands here under the cross, and must explain and expound these wonders and their meaning. For he paid great heed to them above all others, and concluded from them that this Jesus of Nazareth must have been not only innocent, but also the Son of God, confessing openly and freely, "Truly, this was a righteous Man, and the Son of God."

And this was the sermon for Christ's funeral, which this pagan centurion preached by instigation of the Holy Ghost. Thus God often wonderfully converts people if they simply attend to His Word and wonders. With the centurion under the cross, Christ's blood began at once to work and bear fruit. Moreover, it is seen here particularly how God most wonderfully appoints the holy preaching office. The pagan centurion herein surpassed all the priests of the Israelites. And this is God's common way of filling His pulpit and altar. He once took prophets from behind the plow and shepherds from behind the sheep, and by the same appointed the holy ministry and preaching office when the great prelates in Jerusalem would not duly oversee the office entrusted to them. But the centurion in these few words encompasses unfathomable heavenly wisdom, so that one might well say of this funeral sermon, as Bartholomew did of the Gospel, that it is both brief and long: brief in words, long in sense, inasmuch as he here makes a good, brief summary of the whole doctrine of Christ's person, office, and innocence. For he explicitly calls Him *a Man*, by which he emphasizes His manhood, wherein He suffered and died on the cross. No less does he preach of Christ's *Godhead,* for he calls Him the Son of God, perhaps because he has heard how He had publicly confessed that He is the Son of God. Now then, since so many supernatural wonders were added to this, and he heard the voice of Christ and saw His reasonable and gentle ending, he turns within himself and concludes that Christ must be more than Man, and so without doubt, as He had taught, the Son of God, so that Christ in life and death is and abides the living Son of God. Next, we see in what wonderful ways God knows how to convert men through His strong Word and mighty wonders. Let every man take heed to these salutary means of salvation above all, that he may hear with devotion the proclamation of Christian preachers, and faithfully take heed to the wonders of Christ, if the power of Christ is to work in such a way that we may believe rightly and be saved eternally.

But as seldom as a man dies or is deprived of his life without leaving behind some souls to mourn his death, so also here in the death of Christ on the cross there are *sympathetic mourners* who help the deeply afflicted mother of God bear the sorrow, bewail His death, and grievously lament. These are not only His relatives and acquaintances, but also His enemies and those who had helped to nail Him to the cross—these are sincerely afflicted by it. They could not deny the deed, for the crucified, tortured body hung before their eyes. The wonderful works they could not despise, they were far too great and terrible. The centurion's sermon they could not reproach, for it was far too scriptural and confirmed by so many unprecedented wonders. They find themselves conquered in their own conscience, which bears witness against them that Christ has been wronged and abused. This accordingly grieves them in their heart, so that they smite their breast, bearing witness that they have transgressed, that they are heartily sorry, and that they wish it had never been done. And to the extent that they doubtless remember His glorious sermons, His great and excellent wonders, and the many poor, crippled souls to whom He did good, they find in their own selves how here He has been repaid evil for His good. As much as in them lies, they would rather have Him alive and bring Him again with glory, accompanied by jubilant shouts of Hosanna, into the city and into the Temple, whether the chief priests liked it or not. But because they can do so no more, they smite their own breast and, full of contrition and pain, turn again to Jerusalem.

This is an admirable mirror of repentance for all men: When they become aware of their sins, that they also smite their breast, for there lies the heart as the seat of the desires, out of which, as a harmful vapor and mist, arise evil thoughts: murder, adultery, fornication, stealing, false witness, slander, and so on, as Christ teaches. Now therefore, whoever feels his sins, let him hear God's Word, which is the Word of Life, and is sheer Spirit and life, and gives life to the world. But whoever has remorse and sorrow for his sins and departs from evil and turns to good, God will turn to him also, and he will be free from his sins and eternally saved.

Prayer

O most holy Redeemer, who by one offering hast perfected all them that are sanctified, how universal and boundless is the power of Thy blood! No man is barred from it, not even those who put Thee on the cross. Thou didst pray for them on the cross when Thou didst shed Thy blood for them and us all. And that Thou didst not shed it in vain is shown at once by the conversion of the centurion and the other confessors. O Lover of Life, how clearly even in death itself Thou showest that Thou delightest not in the death of the ungodly, but that he may turn and live! How Thou fulfillest what Thou didst promise, that Thou wouldest draw all men unto Thyself when Thou shouldst be lifted up from the earth! Thou drawest to Thyself even Thy worst enemies, so that they run to confess Thee, and that the mouth that slanders Thee may praise Thee again. Thus didst Thou give Thy life as a guilt offering, that Thou mayest have seed. It sprang up even on the rocky soil, so that out of Thy worst enemies have come Thy boldest confessors. O my crucified Love, Lord Jesus, who doest such wonders in death: give my heart that blessed fearlessness to confess Thee continually, and to let myself be taken from Thy truth by no danger! Direct mine eyes and my heart to Thy cross, that I, like the centurion, may regard Thee in faith, contemplate Thy wonders, and courageously confess Thee in life and in death. Help me, with those who stood around Thy cross, to smite my breast and with heartfelt contrition for my sins to recoil at the wrath of God. Strike my heart Thyself with the hammer of Thy Law, yet also bind again my wounds which Thou hast inflicted. Let me never doubt Thy grace, which Thou didst not withhold even from the soldiers, but let me confidently draw from the fountain of Thy blood, which stood open also to those who crucified Thee. Help me, O Lord Jesus, to overcome all the offense of Thy cross and to confess Thee not only in my heart, but also before all the world with my mouth, until some day I shall glorify Thee forever with all the saints, and as a living member in Thy body triumph over death and sin. Amen.

Mel.: Christus, der uns selig macht
Or: Jesu Leiden, Pein und Tod

Grant, O Christ, God's very Son,
  By Thy bitter Passion
That all evils we may shun,
  As Thy faithful nation;
Grant us fruitfully to think
  On Thy death and suff'ring,
And for that, though oft we sink,
  Bring Thee thankful off'ring!.

DEVOTION 60

The Kinsmen and Friends of Jesus at the Cross

Mel.: Liebster Jesu, wir sind hier

O my soul, awake thee now,
  On the love of Jesus ponder.
Upward to Mount Calv'ry's brow
  Let thy meditations wander.
Know how boundless is His favor,
And adore thy faithful Savior.

Crowned with thorns, the Son of God
  On the cross for thee is dying.
See His body stained with blood,
  Hear Him in deep anguish sighing.
Oh, how deep His love's emotion!
Canst thou fathom His devotion?

Lost in sin, thy penalty,
  O my soul, is death eternal;
Hell's dominion yawns for thee
  With its vast abyss infernal;
But thy Lord for thee doth suffer,
Grace and life to thee to offer!

Jesus, Savior without peer,
  Wholly I to Thee commend me,
That from Thee, my Portion dear,
  All dissemblers may not bend me;
Unto Thee all things I tender,
Life and death and self surrender.

My dear ones and my friends stand aloof from my sore; and my kinsmen stand afar off. — Thou hast put away mine acquaintance far from me.

Psalm 38:11; 88:3

All His acquaintance, and many women that followed Him from Galilee, stood afar off, beholding these things, among whom was Mary Magdalene, and Mary the mother of James the less and Joses, and Salome, the mother of Zebedee's children (who also, when He was in Galilee, followed Him and ministered unto Him), and many other women which came up with Him unto Jerusalem.

Matthew 27:55–56; Mark 15:40–41; Luke 23:49

When the evangelists spoke of the centurion, the soldiers, and the people who stood near the cross, they took the opportunity also to mention the kinsmen of Christ and those godly women which had followed Him from Galilee and had ministered unto Him of their own substance. The centurion, the soldiers, and the rest honored Christ in His death, but the godly women readily loved Him while He lived as well as when He was dead. While He lived they ministered unto Him with their gifts and abilities, and when He hung dead on the cross, the disciples fled away, but they stood near Him. All of them, as many as there were, were Christ's kinsmen, friends, and acquaintances, among whom His mother Mary and His disciple John are distinguished (John 19:25), and they stood afar off, beholding all, that is, observing closely and carefully what took place during the crucifixion of Christ. The love of Christ, which drew them from Galilee to Judaea, now drew them also to the cross. That they stood afar off cannot be attributed to some wicked fear or lack of faith, for if they were afraid, they would have remained at home or hidden themselves among the multitude, especially since, as Galilaeans, they were unknown to the Judaeans standing beside the cross. Among them was Mary Magdalene, Mary the mother of James the Less and of Joses, and Salome the mother of Zebedee's children, which had also followed Him in Galilee and "ministered unto Him of their substance," as it says in Luke 8:3. "For there was a custom among the Jews," writes Jerome, "and it was regarded by ancient people a blameless thing for women to give teachers food and clothing." The evangelists, however, wished to mention these godly women here to show that the prophecy of Psalm 38:11 was fulfilled: "My dear ones and My friends stand aloof from My sore; and My kinsmen stand afar off." Christ was forsaken by all, that we might not be forsaken by God. Not a little, moreover, did it multiply the bitterness of that suffering that He had to endure so shameful and disgraceful a death and to have such blasphemies heaped upon Him, not simply in the presence of strangers and enemies, but even before friends and acquaintances, and that all His friends stood afar off. For although it was a sign of faith and love in these women that, while the disciples had fled in their fear, they followed Christ to His death, yet it seems that there was a certain weakness of faith in that they remained standing afar off, since the psalmist says they "stand aloof from my sore." But Christ forgives them this, and after His resurrection shows Himself to them, which serves for our comfort when we too contend with weakness of faith (2 Cor. 12:9). Therefore, when in our greatest troubles we are forsaken by our family and friends, we are to take comfort in Christ's example and to say with David, "My father and mother forsake me, but the LORD taketh me up" (Ps. 27:10).

But here it also becomes quite clear what outcome carnal thoughts of earthly glory and happiness receive in Christ's kingdom. These women went with Christ to Jerusalem to ask for temporal honor and dignity (Matt. 20:21), but behold, they not only forfeit the honor hoped for, but must also see Christ covered with the greatest shame and disgrace. Thus do those regularly end in shame who seek in Christ what is perishable and do not know the nature of His kingdom.

Prayer

O Lord Jesus, Lover of life! Help me to follow Thee throughout my life, and to be a living member in Thy body that shall never be torn from Thee. Live in me, that I may not love myself, but as Thou hast loved me and given Thyself into death for me, I may in turn heartily love Thee and devote myself to Thee even unto death. Let no danger frighten me from Thee, but let me always follow Thee with the faithful women wherever Thou goest, however sorrowful and troubling the way may be. If Thou seest in me much weakness still, as there was in them, then have patience with me, I beseech Thee, O patient Jesus, and deal with me as Thou didst with them, whose sorrow and doubt were dispelled by the brightness of Thy resurrection! Cast me not away when I heap up errors in my weakness, but remember that Thou art a Shepherd to carry the weak sheep and to straighten the weary knee! Behold the heart of Thy servant (maidservant), who loves Thee, and through Thy death forgive me whatever sinfulness and imperfection still cling to me! O Lord Jesus, if Thou wilt break the earthen vessel in which we carry our treasure, how shall we stand before Thee? But spare us for Thy mercy's sake. Pour the oil of Thy grace into our lamps and trim them anew, that we may be pleasing to Thee! Let us seek what is above, and not what is on earth. Let Thee be found, O my Help, when my soul seeketh after Thee; and when it has mourned Thee as lost, as did Mary Magdalene, show Thee alive to it again, and never let me go disconsolate from Thy presence! Amen.

Mel.: Jesu, komm doch selbst zu mir

Standing under Jesus' cross,
Gazing on His wounds and loss,
  'Tis a place of blessedness,
  Here doth faith its joy possess.

Singing 'neath the dreadful rod:
"Lo, it is the Lamb of God!"
  Here my faith doth comfort take:
  All these wounds are for my sake.

When I die, pray, bring Thou me
'Neath Thy cross to rest with Thee,
  Let me stand before Thy throne
  Gazing on those wounds alone!

DEVOTION 61

Jesus' Side Is Pierced

Mel.: O Jesu, du mein Bräutigam
Or: Nun laßt uns den Leib begraben

Thy soul, O Jesus, hallow me,
Thy Spirit steep me all in Thee,
   Thy body, pierced by ruthless steel,
   My wretched soul and body heal.

The water from Thy side that poured
For me a cleansing bath afford,
   And all Thy blood, with life divine,
   Revive this weakened heart of mine.

The sweat of death upon Thy face
Deliver me from death's embrace,
   And all Thy passion, cross, and pain,
   With strength my feebleness sustain.

O Christ, turn not away from me,
Receive and hide me all in Thee,
   Within Thy holy wounds enclose,
   And keep me safe from all my foes.

In death's dark hour with me abide,
And place me, Savior, at Thy side,
   Where with Thy saints I shall adore
   And praise Thee, Lord, forevermore.

Ye shall break no bone thereof (i.e., of the Passover lamb). — And I will pour upon the house of David, and upon the inhabitants of Jerusalem, the Spirit of grace and of supplication; for they shall look upon me, whom they have pierced, and they shall mourn for him, as one mourneth for his only son, and shall be in bitterness for him, as one that is in bitterness for his firstborn.

Exodus 12:46; Zechariah 12:10

And the Jews, because it was the preparation day, that the bodies should not remain upon the cross on the sabbath day (for that sabbath day was great), besought Pilate that their legs might be broken and that they might be taken away. Then came the soldiers and brake the legs of the first and of the other which was crucified with Him. But when they came to Jesus and saw that He was dead already, they brake not His legs: But one of the soldiers with a spear opened His side, and forthwith came there out blood and water. And he that saw it bare record, and his record is true; and the same knoweth that he saith the truth, that ye also may believe. For these things were done that the Scripture should be fulfilled, Ye shall break no bone of Him. And again another Scripture saith, They shall look on Him whom they have pierced.

John 19:31–37

God had earnestly commanded the Jews to leave no one who died on a tree hanging overnight, but to bury him the same day. In order to follow this divine command, they go to Pilate and beseech him in accordance with his office as judge to give orders that the bones of the crucified might be broken, their life shortened, and their bodies taken down and buried. The governor causes this to be done. Now therefore, when the soldiers had broken the legs of the two robbers, and coming to Christ see that He is already departed, they do not break His legs (that the Scripture may be fulfilled), but one of the soldiers, to learn for certain whether there is any life in Him, pierces His holy side with a lance or spear; instantly blood and water flow forth separately. This is a remarkable *wonder,* that water and blood should abundantly run out of a dead, lifeless body. This is why St. John confirms it with utter words of authority: "I saw it with my own eyes," he says, "I speak what is true, and knowingly testify to the same before all the world, that all may contemplate this profound wonder and know this crucified Jesus as the Son of God and the Savior of the world.

To speak *figuratively* of this wound of His side, the pious ancients connected this to the two covenants: the blood in such a way that the old covenant with its bloody sacrifices was abolished, while it was with the Holy Baptism of water that the new covenant was begun. But by the fact that both water and blood flow *simultaneously,* we are reminded that both Sacraments point alone to Christ and must be understood of Christ alone, as He who in the first by blood, but in the second by the holy water of Baptism, set apart for Himself a church and congregation. And indeed, as God made for Adam his Eve out of the rib of his side when he was dead and fallen asleep, as it were, so here the second Adam, Christ, falls asleep on the cross and causes blood and water to issue from His side, out of which He builds for Himself the Christian church as a new bride and congregation, which He builds for Himself and cleanses her for Himself by His precious blood and the choice water of His side, that she may be glorious, not having a spot or any such thing, but that she may be holy and blameless (Eph. 5:27). Thus this wound of His side is opened for our eternal salvation, so that all believers draw salvation and comfort from it as from an open fountain of salvation. For here is the Fountain of Life, an open Spring against all sin and uncleanness, out of which our soul is nourished and inwardly quickened; yea, by His wounds we are made whole and saved. In short, the wound in Christ's side avails against all deficiencies: By the wound in His side He opens to us the gate of heaven. The wound in His side bears witness that He is the Savior of all the world, and came into this world by water and blood; not by water only, but by water and blood (1 John 5:6–8), which has its wonderful power and effect even after His death and until the end of the world.

For by the fact that water and blood, visibly distinguished, flowed simultaneously in an altogether supernatural manner, it is indicated that by the Holy Baptism of water, the blood of Christ also is appropriated to us, and by it we have been washed and cleansed from sin. Thus both the washing of our purification as well as the blood of the new covenant spring forth out of the heart of Christ. For by these two things, the holy Christian church is sustained: by the water of Holy

Baptism we are born again, and by the blood we are given to drink in the Holy Supper. Hence Theophylact says, "When thou goest to the Cup of the Communion of Christ, let it seem to thee not otherwise than that thou drinkest out of the open wound in the side of Jesus Christ." Then come, weary, panting, thirsty soul, come and draw a powerful draft of refreshment from the heart-quickening fountain of salvation and comfort, from the open wound of the heart of Jesus dead on the cross, and in so doing consider how, of the piercing that opened that side, it was prophesied many centuries before, "They shall look on Him whom they have pierced" (Zech. 12:10).

Prayer

O Jesus, sweet Spring and Source of Life! How full of love Thy heart is, that even after death it lets the stream of comfort flow. My soul is quickened when I remember Thee, and death becomes acceptable to me when I contemplate Thine unspeakable love which Thou hast shown me in death. Thou callest to me and to all who are weary and heavy-laden to come unto Thee, and Thou wilt refresh them. I come to Thee, my Rock, drawn by Thyself. Oh, refresh me, I pray, and let me find rest in Thine open side! Wash me with Thy blood, that I may be white as snow and come holy and clean before Thy face. Thou didst come by water and blood, that Thou mightest cleanse and reconcile us. Thou comest to us with the water of life in Holy Baptism, which is the washing of regeneration and renewing of the Holy Ghost. In it our souls are washed from our sins and cleansed from our iniquity. Oh, that we might never treat this purity lightly, nor put on again the polluted garments of sin! Thou makest us to receive Thy shed blood with our mouth in the most Holy Supper, and with this draft of immortality Thou refreshest our weary soul. Oh, that we might recognize Thy love from this, and in faith and love cling firmly to Thee! Water my heart with this stream of life, which is better than that water that flowed in the Garden of Eden. With Thee is the living spring that stands eternally open to the house of David and all the citizens of Jerusalem for the washing away of their sins. This spring does not dry up, even if all the rivers in Syria should dry up, and the well of Jacob should give water no more. Stir up in me, Lord Jesus, a holy thirst, that as the hart crieth for fresh

DEVOTION 61

water, so my soul, O God, may cry for Thee! Cleanse and reconcile me, and let the blood of sprinkling that speaks better things than the blood of Abel cry for me and procure grace from Thy Father. Amen.

Mel.: O Jesu Christ, meins Lebens Licht

O let Thy holy wounds for me
Clefts in the rock forever be,
  Where as a dove my soul can hide
  And safe from Satan's rage abide.

And when my lips grow white and chill,
Thy Spirit cry within me still,
  And help my soul Thy heav'n to find,
  When these poor eyes grow dark and blind!

Lord, from Thy nail-prints let me read
That Thou to save me hast decreed,
  And grant that in Thy opened side
  My troubled soul may ever hide.

Ah, then I have my heart's desire,
When singing with the angels' choir,
  Among the ransomed of Thy grace,
  Forever I behold Thy face!

DEVOTION 62

Joseph Begs for the Body of Jesus

Mel.: Es ist genug

My Jesus rests! How great His battle fought!
  How great His agony
Which He endured! Yet pleasant is that lot!
  We're saved eternally.
God's Son, our Abel, had to bear it
That we might heav'nly bliss inherit.
  My Jesus rests! My Jesus rests!

My Jesus rests, released from all the load
  That He for us must bear.
O man, behold! Thy sinful breach with God
  Thou couldest not repair:
Thy faithful Jesus must be broken
O work, O never-witnessed token!
  My Jesus rests! My Jesus rests!

I am glad and rejoice in Thy mercy, for Thou considerest my trouble and knowest my soul in adversity, and deliverest me not into the hands of the enemy; Thou settest my feet in a large room.

Psalm 31:7–8

After these things, at even, because it was the preparation day, that is, the day before the sabbath, there came Joseph of Arimathaea (a city of the Jews), an honorable counselor, a good man and a just, which had not consented to the counsel and deed of them, which also waited for the kingdom of God, being a disciple of Jesus, but secretly for fear of the Jews—he went in boldly unto Pilate and besought him that he might take away the body of Jesus. And Pilate marveled if He were already dead, and calling the centurion, he asked him whether He had been any while dead. And when he knew it of the centurion, he gave the body to Joseph, and commanded the body to be delivered unto him. And Joseph bought fine linen. And there came also Nicodemus, which at the first came to Jesus by night, and brought a mixture of myrrh and aloes, about an hundred pound weight.

Matthew 27:57–58; Mark 15:42–46; Luke 23:50–52; John 19:38–39

That the Messiah's rest would be His glory was already prophesied in Isaiah 11:10, and was not only fulfilled by the wonderful works which followed upon His death but also demonstrated by the fact that His burial was so honorable and splendid. Of the two chief undertakers, one was Joseph of Arimathaea, a secret disciple of Jesus, an honorable counselor, who waited for the kingdom of God, who also went in boldly unto Pilate and begged for the body of Jesus. And Nicodemus also came, which at the first came to Jesus by night.

Joseph of Arimathaea was at least as unknown in Jerusalem as his native city was, but he showed the Savior more love in His death than any in Jerusalem, indeed, even than His own disciples. They fled, and it seems as if, with the death of Christ, their faith also was dead. Here at the death of the Savior, the faith of Joseph of Arimathaea comes to life, and this secret disciple puts the open disciples to shame. So God has His hidden saints who are often unknown to the world, but more acceptable to heaven than those who, having a form of godliness, deny the power thereof (2 Tim. 3:5). He who at the time of Elijah still had seven thousand left Him who had not bowed the knee unto Baal still has His adherents here and there (1 Kings 19:18). "The Lord knoweth them that are His" (2 Tim. 2:19), and "there is a book written before Him for them that fear the Lord and that think upon His name" (Mal. 3:16). The secret disciple is bold to approach Pilate to ask him openly for the body, who beforehand was not bold to come to Jesus secretly. How God is able to preserve the smoking flax of faith and by His power to make it into a great, shining light! How He is able to strengthen weary knees and to bolster wavering hearts, that they may stand firm like the cedars of Lebanon!

Joseph of Arimathaea begs for the body of Jesus and receives it at once from Pilate, who does not know what a treasure he is giving away in this poor Man, and what life in this dead Man. How the world treats Christ! Judas sells Him for thirty pieces of silver; Pilate gives Him away for nothing. The Lord of Glory was valued so little, that He might make us glorious with His Father. But He whose value Pilate did not perceive was a precious and invaluable possession to Joseph of Arimathaea. Thus the manna that Israel only loathes becomes like honeycomb in the mouth of a stranger, and what to the one is the savor of death unto death, to the other is the savor of life unto life (2 Cor. 2:16).

Joseph of Arimathaea was a rich man, yet richest of all when he received from Pilate Him "in whom are hid all the treasures of wisdom and knowledge" (Col. 2:3). Riches in themselves do not hinder godliness; the gold of faith can exist with your earthly gold. But like Joseph of Arimathaea, you must have Christ in your heart and the gold only in the coffer. Mammon must not be so dear to you that you would not gladly use it for the glory of Christ, nor gladly sacrifice all that is yours to gain Christ. Joseph of Arimathaea goes in boldly, risking all that is his for the sake of Christ, yet loses not a farthing. Whoever seeks the kingdom of God, to him shall the temporal be added, or yet maintained. A rich undertaker might well befit this dead Man, who made us eternally rich, and who was made poor that we might have plenty. He also had to be buried as a rich man (Isa. 53:9). Blessed are the rich who do works of mercy and lay up for themselves treasures which neither moths can devour nor thieves dig up and steal! (Matt. 6:19). So does this rich man. He seeks with great eagerness the pearl of the kingdom of heaven. He does not let himself be kept from his enterprise by all the impurity of the pagan house of Pilate, for he seeks purity in Christ. He does not fear the unrighteousness of the judge, for his heart does not condemn him. He does not turn aside from the hatred of the council, for he is assured of the love of his Master. Shame in the sight of the people he counts as naught, for his glory is in being called a disciple of Christ. The loss of his goods he counts a light thing, for he waits for the heavenly goods in Christ. Oh, that our soul might feel so much faith and love, so much frankness and faithfulness, so much zeal and hope in Christ! How desirous should we not be to be partakers of the body of Jesus, who was crucified for us, that we might bury Him in us by faith? Run, my heart, to the cross;

take Him down likewise, bear this sweet burden in the arms of faith, hold Him fast and treasure Him more highly than all the treasures of earth. This dead Man can bring you to life, for His death is the source of life. The death of Christ truly brought to life those whose faith was dead before! Nicodemus came to Christ by night when He was alive; now, when He is dead, he comes by day. Because the night of doubt for him was past, he no longer avoids the danger of the day. Thus is the strength of the Lord able to make our weaknesses strong!

Prayer

O Lord Jesus, Thou art my heart's only Comfort, and my Portion! What do I care for heaven and earth, if I have but Thee? (Ps. 73:25–26). I have and hold Thee, and will not let Thee go until I bring Thee into the chamber of my grave. However little Thou wast accounted by Thine enemies, and however scornfully Thou wast given away by Pilate, nevertheless I have in Thee my soul's greatest riches, my glory, and my joy. I go in my mind to Thy cross, I take hold of Thee in the arms of my faith, I press Thee to my heart, I seek in Thee, the dead Man, life. Oh, forsake me not, my Confidence and my Help, and despise not the heart that is filled with Thy love! I will go with Thee whither Thou goest; I will boldly risk all for Thy glory, I will gladly take upon me the reproach of Thy cross! I will not let myself be separated from Thy love! O Lord Jesus, strengthen my resolve, preserve me in blessed communion with Thee, and let me constantly be a living member in Thy body! And because Thy love is so great, that the very body that Thou gavest into death for me Thou givest to me for food in the most Holy Supper, therefore help me with faithful desire to long for this food, and not to cease showing forth Thy death. Let me be made a partaker of all the benefits which Thou hast won for me by Thy death on the cross, and ground my heart in faith, in love, and in hope, that I may overcome all that is in the world and finally pass through death and life to Thee. I think with joy on the grace and strength shown by Thee to Thy friends in Thy death, whose weakness Thou madest to be strong, and whose courage Thou madest to live. Thou makest me, poor man that I am, to have sure hope that out of the riches of Thy mercy Thou shalt give me new powers, forgive my frailty and fear, anoint me a believing confessor of Thy name, and finally bestow on me the kingdom as Thy Father bestowed it on Thee.

Mel.: O Traurigkeit, o Herzeleid

See, stained with blood,
The Lamb of God,
  The Bridegroom, lies before thee,
    Pouring out His life that He
  May to life restore thee.

O Ground of faith,
Laid low in death!
  Sweet lips now silent sleeping!
    Surely all that live must mourn
  Here with bitter weeping.

O Virgin-born,
Thy death we mourn,
  Thou lovely Star of gladness!
    Who could see Thy reeking blood
  Without grief and sadness?

DEVOTION 63

Jesus' Body Is Taken Down from the Cross and Readied for Burial

Ach Gott, erhör mein Seufzen und Wehklagen (p. 321)

The Shepherd for His sheep to death is wearied;
Come, Joseph, let His body thus be carried
  With gentle hands
  In spice and bands,
Within the tomb, that He may be well buried.

Dear Jesus Christ, I too would thank Thy favor,
Would give to Thee the spice of faith's behavior:
  Repentance true.
  My heart anew
Will bury Thee within this tomb, my Savior.

To seal this tomb, Thy Spirit send from yonder;
Let faith be firmly set, and love grow fonder.
  Abide in me,
  Let me on Thee
And on Thy faithfulness devoutly ponder.

His rest shall be glory. — Thy garments are all myrrh, aloes, and cassia.

Isaiah 11:10; Psalm 45:8

Then took they the body of Jesus, which was taken down, and wrapped Him in a pure linen wrapping, and bound Him in linen clothes with spices, as the Jews were accustomed to bury.

Matthew 27:59; Mark 15:46; Luke 23:53; John 19:40

All those attending at the cross saw that Christ died on the cross, saw how He bowed His head and gently departed. But in addition to all this, and as a further testimony of it, the body of Jesus cannot be taken down until He has been legally pronounced dead in the presence of Pilate by both Joseph and the centurion who had been appointed to the execution by Pilate. For because it is a most comforting article of our faith that Christ truly died, God desired that it should be attested in so many and various ways.

Here, then, the body of Jesus, piteously beaten and taken down from the cross, lies in the bosom of His mother—so the ancients sublimely imagined it, and such beautiful images and paintings are still to be found showing how, as soon as He was let down from the cross, Mary clasped Him in her arms and pressed Him to her bosom. If this happened (although the evangelists make no further mention of her in the Passion History), then among all her sorrows, this would have been the greatest and most poignant, which must have pierced her unmercifully. See and consider His pitiful visage, how it "was so marred more than any man, and His form more than the sons of men" (Isa. 52:14). See His deformed body, black and blue, covered with stripes and wounds. His hair hangs down, matted with trickling blood, His gracious face is covered with dirt, blood, and spittle. See the wounds on His feet and hands, His thigh covered with congealed blood. A heart of stone would surely sweat, to say nothing of pouring tears. For although the Jews laid their hands on Christ and took hold of Him, falsely accused Him, and finally delivered Him to death, and although the pagans carried out this brutal murder: yet the source of this all is our sin. This deformed body we abused with our own sins.

Now therefore, because Joseph and Nicodemus must hasten the burial because of the approaching Sabbath, and yet they lay great importance on the work, Christ is first wound in clean linen clothes and bound with linen strips; for when someone dies, it is, as it were, implanted in man by nature to be busied and to seek day and night that his deceased may be buried with all honor. If men give each other such honor, which they often do not deserve, it is far more fitting and far, far more decorous to show honor to the most holy body of Jesus. — Figuratively speaking, the linen clothes are the books of holy, divine Scripture, which are to be unwound and diligently searched and examined, for it is they which testify of Christ (John 5:39). Thereafter He would not need the linen clothes, for which reason He left His burial clothes in the tomb, for we are to see Him face to face, as He is. But by His merit Christ has cut for us a beautiful death shroud from His burial clothes, which cover us better than the lambskins of Adam; for here is the Lamb of God slain from the beginning of the world, which clothes us in His merit and holy innocence, and with this He covers the guilt of our sins.

Next, since Joseph and Nicodemus are prevented from embalming the body of Jesus on account of the approaching Sabbath, they only lay the various costly spices at the body of Jesus in the meantime until the good women can prepare their costly anointing. Thus they did not understand the saying of David: "Thou shalt not permit Thy Holy One to see corruption," for otherwise they would not have had so much toil and care to prevent the corruption. Christ had no need of such spices; His "garments are all myrrh, aloes, and cassia" (Ps. 45:8). Now then, as God had commanded costly incense to be prepared from good, powerful spices and holy anointing oil of balsam and pure incense, so the Gospel of Christ is a pleasant-smelling power that gives a sweet savor both "in them that are saved, and in them that are condemned, to the one a savor of death unto death, but to the other the savor of life unto life" (2 Cor. 2:15). But thanks be to God, who has revealed to us the fragrance of His knowledge in every quarter!

Prayer

O Lord Jesus, Thou didst suffer Thyself to be wound, like us, in burial clothes, that Thou mightest sanctify our burial shroud and take away what was detestable therein, even the fear of death. Now I see my shroud as a beautiful, splendid robe in which I will be brought unto Thee, my Bridegroom. Burial clothes shall not conceal me forever, nor the bonds of death keep me perpetually in the dust. I will go free from these bonds on that Day. And as Thou, my Redeemer, didst at the awakening of Thy friend Lazarus cause his linen cloth with which he had been bound hand and foot, and the napkin with which his face was concealed, to be loosed and untied, Thou wilt also loose and untie the bonds of my mortality on that great Day by the hand of Thy almighty power. Thou didst suffer Thy body to be anointed for Thy burial, although Thou wast not to see corruption, that Thou mightest teach us that Thou didst for us what was unnecessary for Thee. Yet in this anointing there arises for me a fragrance of life unto life, which takes from me all fear of death and awakens in me the hope of the life to come. For in truth, Lord Jesus, I am a member of Thy body; so shall I also be a partaker of Thy glory. Even if my body wastes away and there is no balm in Gilead to free me from the rottenness of the flesh, yet I know that this corruption shall put on incorruption, and this mortality shall put on immortality. All the odor of death and horror of the tomb shall be dispelled by the balm of Thy body, for in Thy dead body also I find the balm of life. Collapse, O my ruinous tent! I know that I have a better building in heaven. But Thou, O Lord Jesus, my Life and my Confidence, fill my heart with the balm of Thy comfort! Thou art anointed with the oil of gladness above Thy fellows (Heb. 1:9); yet give to Thy fellows only a few drops of comfort from Thine inexhaustible fount of grace, and with them let me, Thy poor servant, never go comfortless from Thee! I hold Thee, my most precious Savior, and will not let Thee go. I love Thee, I hope in Thee; let me never be ashamed! Amen.

Mel.: O Traurigkeit, o Herzeleid

O darkest woe!
Ye tears, forth flow!
 Has earth so sad a wonder?
  God the Father's only Son
 Now is buried yonder!

DEVOTION 63

O sorrow dread!
Our God is dead,
  But by His expiation
    Of our guilt upon the cross
    Gained for us salvation.

Yea, blest is he
Whose heart shall be
  Fixed here, who apprehendeth
    Why the Lord of Glory thus
    To the grave descendeth.

O Jesus blest,
My Help and Rest,
  With tears I now entreat Thee:
    Make me love Thee to the last,
    Till in heav'n I greet Thee.

DEVOTION 64

Jesus Is Laid in the Tomb

Mel.: Der Tag ist hin, mein Jesu, bei mir bleibe (p. 323)

O Lamb! That with my sinful debt was sifted,
And as a curse upon the cross was lifted,
  Now art Thou taken toward the eventide
  And borne away to Joseph's tomb untried.

O soothing sight! O sign where mercy reigneth!
Of which but faith alone a glimpse attaineth;
  The curse is gone, the ground is therefore clean,
  So Thou must buried be—here this is seen.

Thy Word in Thee could suffer no molesting,
Therefore Thy body must in earth be resting;
  By Daniel and by Jonah was foreshown
  What, Savior, now I see in Thee all done.

Therefore my heart is glad, and my glory rejoiceth: my flesh also shall lie securely. For Thou wilt not leave my soul in hell, nor let Thine holy one see corruption. Thou makest known to me the way to life; before Thee is fullness of joy, and pleasure at Thy right hand forevermore.

Psalm 16:9–11

Now, in the place where He was crucified there was a garden, and in the garden a new tomb, which was Joseph's, which he had caused to be hewn in a rock, in which no man was yet laid. There they laid Jesus because of the day of preparation of the

DEVOTION 64

Jews, since the sabbath was approaching and the tomb was close at hand, and they rolled a great stone before the entrance of the tomb, and went away.
                              Matthew 27:60; Mark 15:46; Luke 23:53–54; John 19:41–42

We are to contemplate the tomb of Christ, for it is not without reason that it has been described in such detail by both evangelists.

Regarding its location, the tomb of Christ was in a garden. By this we are reminded of our first parents' dire fall into sin, for that happened in the garden of Eden. Now as the corruption of man began in the garden, Christ desires likewise to conclude and end in the garden the work of our redemption, which He also began in the garden (as we were informed above) with travail and trembling, to indicate that He has now perfectly atoned for and expiated the guilt incurred in the garden by our first parents, and has opened to us all the garden of heavenly paradise. We cannot all be buried in such a garden; but as in the spring the flowers and grasses flourish and bloom, so our bodies, in whatever place they have their burial, and our bones also, will flourish and bloom like the green grass. For this reason we make plans for a decent burial, just as here Joseph, who had his own tomb, precedes us with an admirable example.

Regarding its *condition,* the tomb of Christ was, first, *a new tomb,* and not without reason, for the end of His earthly life had to agree with the beginning thereof. When He came from heaven to earth, He lay in the chaste *virginal* womb of Mary; when He goes out of the world to the Father, He has His rest and repose in a new tomb in which no man ever was laid, to indicate that through Christ we would become a new creation. At the same time, He also obtained by this a *new name* for our burial sites and graves, so that they are no longer to be or be called nests of serpents and toads, but soft and sweet sleeping chambers and beds of rest. Second, the tomb of Christ was also a *strange* tomb, belonging to another, for it was Joseph's, even as Christ had not so much of His own in this world where He might lay His head. So also, Jacob was a certainly a stranger in Canaan, yet he had bought from Ephron his own burial place among them, a piece of land, to be his hereditary burial plot. Christ did not have this. And what use to Christ would His own tomb be for so short a time? He only had a little rest and brief slumber in it! But now He has His eternal hereditary possession above in heaven. However, He is made so poor and needy here on earth for our sake, that by His poverty we might be made rich. Besides all this, Christ died not for His own sins, but for the sins of others; thus it is fitting for Him to be granted a little burial place in which He may rest a little after finishing His blood-draining labor. Third, the tomb was also cut into a rock. This happened out of the particular providence of God, that all cause and occasion for lying and blaspheming might be taken away and cut off from His enemies. Therefore, although the palpable lie went abroad that His disciples had stolen His body while their guards were sleeping, yet the tomb put to shame the shameless liars; for it was *hewn into a great rock,* fortified above, below, and on every side by nature, yet the entrance and the stone of the tomb with the seal remained intact. How then should the disciples have broken in and stolen Christ? Such was the tomb of Jesus.

Now as Christ *died* according to the Scriptures, He is also *buried* according to the Scriptures, so that, just as Jonah was three days and three nights in the belly of the whale, Christ is three days and three nights in the cool bosom of the earth. Accordingly, He not only canceled out the record of our sinful debts with His precious blood, but above and beyond this, took it with Him into the tomb and buried it in the earth so that it will never come to light or be seen forever and ever, if only we leave it buried and do not willfully root it up again, which happens when we let sin come to life again and rule in our mortal body. At the same time, our burial sites and graves are also sanctified and hallowed, and we are to view and regard them precisely as our sleeping chambers and beds of rest, in which we rest and sleep deeply and safely until the appearing of our Savior Jesus Christ, no matter where and how we might be buried. For the earth is the Lord's, and every place is consecrated and hallowed as a burial place with the most holy body of Jesus. Now therefore, while our bodies may grow detestable, see corruption, moulder, and decompose, and while they may teem with maggots and worms and give off a foul odor so that everyone shrinks from them—as a consolation for these things, the body of Christ here lies without corruption, and He causes our corruptible bodies to be made like His incorruptible body, and to be eternally incorruptible. For our body, which is sowed in dishonor and laid in the dust of the earth, shall come forth again with unspeakable glory on that great Day, and rise unto heavenly life. With this we are to sweeten the bitterness of death, and to go willingly and gladly to sleep in our graves because of the glory to come.

Prayer

I thank Thee, Lord Jesus Christ, from the depths of my heart, for the doctrine of Thy holy burial, by which Thou givest me not only a certain testimony that Thou didst truly die for my sins, but also the glorious consolation that Thou didst carry all my sins, which Thy Father cast upon Thee, to be buried with Thee, and didst truly assuage Thy Father's wrath. For just as the storm on the sea relented and ceased as soon as Jonah was cast overboard and swallowed by the fish, so the tempestuous and fierce wrath of Thy Father is truly assuaged and pacified, because Thou wast plucked away out of the land of the living and buried. O Lord Jesus, help me also, that, since Thou hast hallowed my grave with Thy holy body, I may not recoil when I think of it! Teach me, my Lord, to remember that I am earth, and shall return to the earth. Inscribe indelibly in my heart the consolation that my grave is no pit of devils, but a sweet sleeping chamber and soft bed of rest in which Thou also didst lie and rest until the third day, that I may learn to go to sleep and rest with joy, until Thou shalt gloriously waken my body on that Day and bring it, transfigured with heavenly glory, into Thy joy. Amen.

Mel.: Der Tag ist hin, mein Jesu, bei mir bleibe (p. 323)

Now of the tomb I need be fearful never,
Since in the tomb Thou too didst lie, my Savior;
  Thy tomb makes mine a sleeping chamber blest,
  A place of sweet repose and bed of rest.

My Savior, with Thee I'm already buried,
Since soul and body to Thy fount were carried
  In Baptism, which upon Thy death relies;
  Now let me with Thee also daily rise!

DEVOTION 65

Jesus Rests in the Tomb during the Sabbath

Mel.: O Traurigkeit, o Herzeleid

So rest, my Rest!
Thou ever Blest!
  Thy grave with sinners making,
    By Thy precious death from sin
  My dead soul awaking.

After Thy strife,
Life of my life,
  Thou'rt in the tomb reposing,
    Round Thee now a rock-hewn grave,
  Rock of Ages, closing.

How cold art Thou,
My Savior, now!
  Thy fervent love hath driven
    Thee into the cold, dark grave,
  That I might gain heaven.

He was taken from anguish and from judgment, and who shall declare the length of his life? For he was cut off out of the land of the living, when for the transgression of my people was he stricken. And he was buried as the wicked, and died as a rich man, although he had done no man violence, neither was there deceit in his mouth.

Isaiah 53:8–9

DEVOTION 65

And Mary Magdalene and Mary of Joses were sitting over against the sepulcher, and other women also, which had followed after Jesus from Galilee, beheld where and how His body was laid. And they returned, and prepared spices and ointments, and rested the sabbath day according to the commandment.
Matthew 27:61; Mark 15:47; Luke 23:55–56

A wearied body desires only rest, and as Job says, a servant longeth after the shadow, and a hireling, that his labor may be done (Job 7:2). Before this, the soul of Christ had toiled hard and His body had suffered many things and had much and great labor in our iniquities (Isa. 43:24). Now therefore, since all labor and the great work of our redemption was finished, He desires rest, to which He is therefore brought in the grave.

This rest He is also readily granted by His friends and by the women that mourn for Him, and they retire to their homes, having made good and sufficient inspection of His grave. Now they take thought for very costly ointment with which they mean to embalm Him after the great sabbath. How sorrowfully they must have viewed the place of His burial it is easy to imagine; for they did not yet understand the fruit thereof, and the effect of the death of Christ. Therefore their hope was dead and all their joys lay buried with Him.

But Christ in the grave also keeps His sabbath and day of rest, because He rested after the work of creation that first sabbath, and thus the seventh day. For the word *sabbath* means the sort of rest of which a man has need after he has done some great work. And although God does not rest as though He were wearied from the great work of creation (for how shall He seek rest for whom no labor is tiring?), He nevertheless rested in the sense that He created no further creature after the heavens and earth and all their works were finished. But it is far different in the work of our redemption. This was exhausting for Christ, even to the exhausting of His blood. He had spent all His powers and abilities upon it. Truly, then, a good rest was needed.

But here the Lord Jesus also sleeps on the sabbath of the Jews in token that it was to be valid no more, but was hereby to be ended and discontinued, even as Christians have also done away with the Jews' sabbath, and as Paul teaches in Colossians 2:16 that no man need worry his conscience about the holidays, new moons, or sabbaths appointed by the Jews. In Christian freedom, we Christians have transposed our sabbath to Sunday, for on that day the true Easter Sun, Jesus Christ, rose again, and by His salutary resurrection consecrated and hallowed the that day to the true worship of God. We are also to spend it in holy devotion and godly conduct, that God may not be angered at us and reject us and our feasts as He did the Jews, but that His name may be hallowed among us also and His kingdom come to us also. Then the Lord and Founder of the sabbath shall also have His sabbath and rest in us, in the hallowed temple and chapel of our heart, until He shall at last make the seventh day of the world an eternal sabbath, when we will begin in truth to go from "one sabbath to another" (Isa. 66:23) and to "dwell in proud rest" (Isa. 32:18). And whenever that sabbath may dawn—whether it be at even or at midnight or at cockcrow or in the morning—let us wait with sighs and wishes that God in His grace would at last give the six workdays of this world a Saturday of rest, and from this valley of sorrow fetch us home to Himself, and bid us keep unto Him the eternal sabbath of joy.

Prayer

O Lord Jesus! Thou liest now in the tomb and takest Thy rest after working Thyself weary, yea, even unto death, for my sake. For what Thou hast done and suffered Thou hast done and suffered for my good. Thy bonds are my unbinding, Thy reproach is my honor, Thy mourning is my joy, Thy stripes are my salvation, Thy wounds are my payment, Thy curse is my blessing, Thy death is my life. O my Lord Jesus, let me gratefully recognize these benefits and so take them to heart that, in testimony of my gratitude, I may go with the women and prepare a pleasing ointment from the loveliest spices in honor of Thee. Let me therefore take sincere readiness unto repentance, a confident faith, and tender kindness toward my neighbors, to make a fragrant balm for a sweet and pleasant savor before Thee, my God. Yea, Lord Jesus, I do not doubt that if these precious spices are prepared in the night of this life, and the longer the better, then on the joyous morning of the Resurrection I will go not with the women into Thy tomb of death, but with Thee into everlasting Life, where after the sad season of fasting and the Passiontide of this wretched life, my body and soul shall rejoice forever and keep hereafter the great and glorious Easter Day and Sabbath of joy. Amen, Lord Jesus, so be it! Amen.

Mel.: O Traurigkeit, o Herzeleid

Breath of all breath!
I know, from death
  Thou wilt my dust awaken;
    Wherefore should I dread the grave,
  Or my faith be shaken?

To me the tomb
Shall be a room,
  Where I lie down on roses;
    Who by faith hath conquered death,
  Sweetly there reposes.

The body dies—
Naught else—and lies
  In dust, until victorious
    From the grave it shall arise
  Beautiful and glorious.

Meantime I will,
My Savior, still
  Deep in my bosom lay Thee,
    Ever musing on Thy death:
  Leave me not, I pray Thee!

DEVOTION 66

Jesus' Sepulcher Is Sealed by the Enemies and a Watch Is Set

Mel.: Nun laßt uns den Leib begraben

Lord Jesus, our Redeemer blest,
Who in Thy tomb didst take Thy rest,
  Grant that we all may rest in Thee
  And let our life God-pleasing be.

All needful strength and courage, Lord,
Won by Thy blood, to us afford.
  And bring us into heaven's light,
  To God Thy Father's glorious sight.

O Lamb of God, our thanks to Thee,
Who slaughtered wast upon the Tree!
  May Thy dear pains for sinners prove
  An entrance to the life above.

Destroy this temple, and on the third day I will raise it up. — The evil and adulterous generation seeketh after a sign, and there shall no sign be given to it, but the sign of the prophet Jonas. For as Jonas was three days and three nights in the whale's belly, so shall the Son of Man be three days and three nights in the midst of the earth.
                                                       John 2:19; Matthew 12:39–40

The next day, that followed the day of the preparation, the chief priests and Pharisees came together unto Pilate, saying, Sir, we remember that that deceiver said, while He was yet alive, After three days I will rise again. Command therefore that the sepulcher be made sure until the third day, lest His disciples come [by night] and steal Him away, and say unto the people, He is risen from the dead: so the last deceit shall be worse than the first. Pilate said unto them, Ye have a watch: go your way, make it as sure as ye can. So they went, and made the sepulcher sure, sealing the stone, and setting a watch.

Matthew 27:62–66

The chief priests and Pharisees are worried that they might see Christ come to life again. Therefore they do not even spare the holy sabbath of the Passover, but assemble themselves, take counsel together against the Lord and against His Anointed, come together unto Pilate, swear before him concerning the preachings of Christ, claiming that He said that He would rise again after three days, and beseech the governor to grant them soldiers from the Roman garrison to make the sepulcher sure until the third day, that it might be seen whether this "deceiver" would still get out. They have so forgotten the universal maxim, *"De mortuis nil nisi bene,"* that is, "Speak no ill of the dead," that they disparage Jesus in the sepulcher as a "deceiver." Yea, by this they only proclaim their own name. They deceived Pilate and the poor people. Thus is the Word of God malleable to them, and they bend and twist it as they please according to their whim. Christ had told them to destroy the "temple," and in three days He would raise it up again. This He said of the temple of His body, as they well understood. And yet they censured Him before the high council as having spoken of the extraordinary Temple in Jerusalem. Now they turn it again, and relate it once more to His resurrection from the dead. They therefore despise and strike themselves with their own words, and throw dust in the eyes of Pilate with their false accusations, speaking all manner of evil against Jesus with palpable lies and insinuated falsehood. Accordingly, when any Christians are made to bear such disgrace, they are to take to heart this consolation: "Blessed are ye, when men shall revile you, and persecute you, and shall say all manner of evil against you falsely, for My sake. . . . great is your reward in heaven" (Matt. 5:11–12). So it was with the disciples here; for as the Jews disparage Christ before Pilate as a deceiver, so His disciples are also made out to be deceivers when the chief priests employ as a significant reason: "Lest His disciples come by night and steal Him away, and say unto the people, He is risen from the dead: so the last deceit shall be worse than the first."

But the effort is in vain, the worry wasted. They do not prosper according to their wishes, nor does it proceed according to their will, but rather the more they hope to suppress it, the more they are made to promote and disseminate among the people what really happened with the Jews and their leaders. In spite of all, Christ must rise again the third day. "The Lord of Sabaoth hath purposed; who shall disannul it?" (Isa. 14:27). Yea, the more they hope to suppress it, the more they are made to promote and disseminate it among the people; for it is by making the sepulcher sure and setting soldiers about it to watch it that they first learn of the resurrection of Christ from their own people, when the latter come into the city with a great cry and report to the chief priests all that had happened. Likewise, the more impressively they secure the sepulcher and seal it, so that even the watchmen themselves cannot get to the body of Jesus, the more impressively the power of His resurrection is manifested. Thus Christ for a while is weary and weak, suffers all manner of mischief to be perpetrated against Him, even as the ungodly desire, but at last is too strong for them and casts them down, so that they lie defeated and confounded. The ungodly, however, are truly the martyrs of the devil, who ceaselessly afflicts them with terror and fright, and hardens their heart so that they fiercely resist God, until at last they suffer utter failure and destruction in their wickedness and hardness of heart.

Now therefore, just as the Lord Jesus lies quiet in the sepulcher while the Jews scamper and scurry, conspire and collude, and rage and rave, we should do likewise when the Gospel is resisted and suppressed. The matter belongs to Christ; it is His glory and doctrine that are attacked. He sets His own as a seal upon His heart (Song of Songs 8:6). He "hath also sealed us, and given the earnest of the Spirit in our hearts" (2 Cor. 1:22). And "the foundation of God standeth sure, having this seal, The Lord knoweth them that are His" (2 Tim. 2:19). Therefore we should commit it to Him and let Him see to it, and meanwhile be still and hope in Him; then shall we be strong.

Prayer

O my sweet Lord Jesus! To Thee, to Thee, be eternal praise and glory for Thy bitter suffering and death, for Thy distress and torment, which Thou didst so patiently suffer for our sake! I beseech Thee, let not all these things be lost to me, a poor sinner. Grant that I may, until my death, acknowledge and adore with a thankful heart Thy love and the eternal benefit of this precious redemption, and in this alone rejoice and take comfort. Give me grace so to ponder without ceasing Thy Passion and death, that all wicked passions in me may be extinguished and destroyed, and all virtues may take root and multiply, that I, being dead to sin, may live unto righteousness, and following Thine example left for us, may walk in Thy footsteps, endure evil with patience, and suffer wrong with a good conscience. Hear me for the sake of Thy most holy, bitter sufferings, for the sake of Thy torments and agonies endured by Thee, for the sake of Thy death and the shedding of Thy blood. Amen, O my—my—*my* crucified Lord Jesus Christ! Amen, Amen!

Mel.: Nun laßt uns den Leib begraben

Lord Jesus, we give thanks to Thee
That Thou hast died to set us free;
  Made righteous through Thy precious blood,
  We now are reconciled to God.

By virtue of Thy wounds we pray,
True God and Man, be Thou our Stay,
  Our Comfort when we yield our breath,
  Our Rescue from eternal death.

Defend us, Lord, from sin and shame;
Help us by Thine almighty name
  To bear our crosses patiently,
  Consoled by Thy great agony:

And thus the full assurance gain
That Thou to us wilt true remain
  And not forsake us in our strife
  Until we enter into life.

INDEX OF HYMNS & SOURCES

1a "Prange, Welt, mit deinem Wissen" (J. Job, 1724), sts. 1, 5; tr. A. Hoppe.
1b "Prange, Welt, mit deinem Wissen" (J. Job, 1724), sts. 7, 8, tr. st. 7, A. Hoppe, st. 8, M. Carver; see *Walther's Hymnal* #90.
2a "Jesu, deine Passion," (S. von Birken, 1676), sts. 1, 3; tr. A. Crull.
2b "So gehst du nun, du Gotteslamm, mit Freuden" (E. Liebich, d. 1780), sts. 1, 3–4; tr. M. Carver.
3a "O falsche Treu, ach Heuchelei" (E. C. Homburg, 1659), sts. 1–2; tr. M. Carver.
3b "Wo Gott der Herr nicht bei uns hält" (J. Jonas, 1524), sts. 5, 7; tr. C. Winkworth.
4a "O Jesu Christ, mein schönstes Licht" (P. Gerhardt, 1653), sts. 1, 5, 9; tr. composite; see *Walther's Hymnal* #256.
4b "Der am Kreuz ist meine Liebe" (J. Greding, 1676), sts. 1–2; tr. *Hymnal for Ev. Luth. Missions* 1905.
5a "Christus, der uns selig macht" (M. Weiß, 1531), st. 8; tr. *Moravian Hymn-Book* 1819, alt.
5b "Gott der Vater, wohn uns bei" (M. Luther, 1524), st. 3; tr. R. Massie, alt.
6a "Auf, Seele, sei gerüst" (Georg Heine, ca. 1693), sts. 1–3; tr. M. Carver.
6b "Erschienen ist der herrlich Tag" (Nicolaus Herman, 1560), sts. 10–12; tr. st. 10, G. Walker; sts. 11–12, M. Carver; see *Walther's Hymnal* #103.
7a "Jesus Christus, unser Heiland" (M. Luther, 1524), sts. 1–2, 4; tr. composite.
7b "Herr Jesu Christ, du hast bereit" (S. Kinner, 1638), sts. 6–8; tr. E. Cronenwett, alt.
8a "O Jesu Christ, mein schönstes Licht" (P. Gerhardt, 1666), sts. 14, 16, tr. composite; see *Walther's Hymnal* #256.
8b "Du Herr des Himmels und der Erden" (B. Schmolck, d. 1737), sts. 1–3; tr. M. Carver.
9a "Trübe Wolken meiner Seelen" (B. Schmolck, d. 1737), sts. 5–6; tr. M. Carver.
9b "Wo soll ich fliehen hin" (Johann Heermann, 1630), sts. 2, 4, 11; tr. *Mor. H.-B.* 1795ff.
10a "Liebe, die du mich zum Bilde" (Johann Scheffler, 1657), sts. 3–5; tr. M. Carver, in *Lutheran Prayer Companion* #62.
10b "O tiefe Demut, wer kann dich ermessen" (Johann Heermann, 1630), sts. 12, 16–17; tr. M. Carver.
11a "Ach bleib mit deiner Gnade" (Josua Stegmann, 1630), sts. 1, 5–6; tr. A. Crull.
11b "Ach Gott, verlaß mich nicht" (Salomo Franck, d. 1725), sts. 2–3; tr. A. Crull.
12a "Bin ich, Herr Jesu, der dich liebet" (J. A. Grammlich, 1727), sts. 1–2, 6; tr. M. Carver.
12b "Sei Gott getreu, halt seinen Bund" (Michael Franck, 1657), sts. 1, 6; tr. M. Carver, 2012, in *Walther's Hymnal* #284.
13a "Christus der uns selig macht / ward ein Knecht" (Hanover, 1745), sts. 1–2, 6; tr. M. Carver.
13b "Christus der uns selig macht / ward ein Knecht" (Hanover, 1745), sts. 8–9; tr. M. Carver.
14a "Schöpfer dieser ganzen Welt" (B. Schmolck, d. 1737), sts. 5, 7; tr. M. Carver.
14b "Lasset uns mit Jesu ziehen" (S. von Birken, 1652), sts. 2–3; tr. J. A. Rimbach.
15a "Herr Jesu, habe Acht auf mich" (C. von Pfeil, 1782), sts. 1–2; tr. M. Carver.

15b "Fließt, ihr Augen, fließt von Thränen" (L. Laurentii, 1700), sts. 2, 12; tr. composite.
16a "So gehst du nun, mein Jesu, hin" (K. F. Nachtenhöfer, 1651), sts. 1, 3; tr. st. 1, A. T. Russell, alt., st. 3, M. Carver.
16b "Weg, Welt, mit deinen Freuden" (Anon., ca. 1718), sts. 1, 2, 8; tr. M. Carver.
17a "Meine Seel, jetzt ist es Zeit" (S. von Birken, 1653), sts. 1, 3; tr. M. Carver.
17b "Wenn ich gedenk, Herr Jesu Christ" (J. Leon, d. 1597), sts. 1–5; tr. M. Carver.
18a "Kommt her und schaut, kommt" (Dresden, 1694), sts. 1–4; tr. M. Carver, in *Walther's Hymnal* #80.
18b "Der Tod kommt an, da soll ich ringen" (P. H. Weissensee, 17th c.), sts. 1–2; tr. M. Carver.
19a "O du Liebe meiner Liebe" (E. von Senitz, d. 1679), sts. 1–2, tr. composite.
19b "Mache dich, mein Geist, bereit" (J. B. Freystein, 1695), sts. 1, 4, 8; tr. C. Winkworth, alt. / E. Cronenwett, alt.
20a "Halt im Gedächtnis Jesum Christ" (C. Günther, ca. 1700), sts. 1, 2, 5; tr. sts. 1–2, J. T. Mueller, st. 5, M. Carver.
20b "Rett, o Herr Jesu, rett dein Ehr" (Johann Heermann, 1630), sts. 1, 4–5; tr. M. Loy, alt.
21a "Mein Heiland! Es ist deine Sache" (P. F. Hiller, d. 1769), sts. 1–2, 5; tr. M. Carver.
21b "Jesu, meine Freude" (J. Franck, ca. 1653), sts. 2–3; tr. M. Carver.
22a "O mit was betrübtem Herzen" (J. C. Arnschwanger, 1680), sts. 1–2; tr. M. Carver.
22b "Sei getreu bis in das Ende" (B. Prätorius, 1659), st. 2; tr. A. B. Warner, st. 7, M. Carver, in *Walther's Hymnal* #283.
23a "Heiland, deine Menschenliebe" (J. J. Rambach, 1735), sts. 1–2; tr. M. Carver.
23b "Kommt her zu mir, spricht Gottes Sohn" (G. Grünwald, 1530), sts. 12, 15–16; tr. composite, in *Walther's Hymnal* #276.
24a "Wo ist wohl ein so treuer Hirte" (C. F. Förster, 1800), sts. 1–2; tr. M. Carver.
24b "Wie treu, mein guter Hirte" (G. Adolph, d. 1754), sts. 9–11; tr. M. Carver.
25a "Seid geküßt, ihr Jesus-Bande" (J. A. Grammlich, 1727), sts. 1–2, 4; tr. M. Carver.
25b "Jesu, der du wollen büßen" (Anon., Gotha, 1699), st. 3; tr. M. Carver, in *Walther's Hymnal* #78.
26a "Jesu, du Gottes Lämmelein" (Anon., ca. 1640), sts. 1–3; tr. M. Carver.
26b "Ach, was sind wir ohne Jesum" (P. Lackmann, 1704), sts. 1, 4, 6; tr. M. Carver, in *Walther's Hymnal* #264.
27a "Fließt, ihr Augen, fliest von Thränen" (L. Laurentii, 1700), sts. 4–5; tr. M. Carver.
27b "Herr Jesu, treuster Heiland, sei gepriesen" (J. Neunherz, d. 1737), st. 1–2, 13–14; tr. M. Carver.
28a "Herr, ich habe mißgehandelt" (Johann Franck, d. 1677), sts. 1–3, 5; tr. sts. 1–3, C. Winkworth, alt., st. 5, M. Carver.
28b "Mein Heiland nimmt die Sünder an" (L. F. Lehr, 1731), sts. 6–7; tr. st. 6, A. Hoppe, st. 7, M. Carver, in *Walther's Hymnal* #242, *Lutheran Prayer Companion*, p. 322.
29a "Jesu, der du meine Seele" (Anon., Gotha, 1699), st. 3; tr. M. Carver, in *Walther's Hymnal* #78.
29b "Schwing dich auf zu deinem Gott" (Paul Gerhardt, 1653), sts. 5, 10; tr. J. Kelly.
30a "O Gottes Sohn von Ewigkeit" (J. Breithaupt, 1687), st. 1–2, 7; tr. M. Carver.
30b "O Gottes Sohn von Ewigkeit" (J. Breithaupt, 1687), st. 13; tr. M. Carver.
31a "Jesu, meines Lebens Leben" (E. C. Homburg, 1659), st. 1; tr. C. Winkworth, alt.
31b "Jesu, meines Lebens Leben" (E. C. Homburg, 1659), st. 2–3; tr. C. Winkworth, alt.
32a "Treuer Wächter Israel" (J. Heermann, 1644), sts. 3–4, 6, 10; tr. M. Carver, in *Lutheran Prayer Companion* #96.

INDEX OF HYMNS & SOURCES

32b "Ach wir armen Sünder" (H. Bonnus, 1547), st. 7; tr. M. Carver.
33a "Ach wir armen Sünder" (H. Bonnus, 1547), sts. 1–2; tr. M. Carver.
33b "Fließt, ihr Augen, fließt von Thränen" (L. Laurentii, 1700), st. 5; tr. M. Carver.
34a "Wohl dem Menschen, der nicht wandelt" (P. Gerhardt, 1653), sts. 1, 4; tr. J. Kelly.
34b "Mitten wir im Leben sind" (M. Luther, 1524), st. 3; tr. M. Carver.
35a "Was willst du, armer Erdenkloß" (J. Heermann, 1630), sts. 5–6, 12; tr. M. Carver, in *Walther's Hymnal* #288.
35b "O Gott, du frommer Gott" (J. Heermann, 1630), sts. 8–9; tr. st. 8 *Hymnal for Ev. Luth. Missions* 1886, st. 9, C. Winkworth, alt.
36a "Allein auf Gottes Wort will ich" (J. Walther, ca. 1555), sts. 3–5; tr. st. 3. C. A. Miller, sts. 4–5, M. Carver, in *Lutheran Prayer Companion* #33.
36b "Mein Gott, das Herze bring ich dir" (J. C. Schade, 1699), sts. 10, 17, 19; tr. M. Carver, in *Lutheran Prayer Companion* #44.
37a "So freudig darf mein Jesus sagen" (B. Schmolck, d. 1737), sts. 1–3, 7; tr. M. Carver.
37b "O König aller Ehre" (M. Behem, 1606), sts. 3–5; tr. C. Winkworth, alt.
38a "Jesus schwebt mir in Gedanken" (Unkn.), sts. 1–2; tr. M. Carver.
38b "Wer ist wohl wie du?" (J. A. Freylinghausen, 1704), sts. 1–2, 5–6; tr. composite, cf. *Lutheran Prayer Companion* #53.
39a "O Lamm, das keine Sünde je" (J. A. Freylinghausen, 1704), sts. 2–3, 9; tr. M. Carver.
39b "Herzliebster Jesu, was hast du verbrochen" (J. Heermann, 1630), sts. 4–7; tr. C. Winkworth.
40a "Komme mit betrübten Blicken" (Anon., ca. 1650), sts. 1–2; tr. M. Carver.
40b "Sei gegrüßt, du Ehrenkönig" (J. A. Grammlich, 1727), sts. 1–5; tr. M. Carver.
41a "Seht, welch ein Mensch ist das" (B. Schmolck, 1704), sts. 2, 4–5; tr. A. Warner, alt.
41b "Jesus, meines Lebens Leben" (E. C. Homburg, 1659), sts. 3–4; tr. C. Winkworth, 1851.
42a "O Durchbrecher aller Bande" (G. Arnold, 1697), sts. 10–11; tr. E. F. Bevan.
42b "Wer ist wohl, wie du?" (J. A. Freylinghausen, 1704), sts. 3–5; tr. composite, cf. *Lutheran Prayer Companion* #53.
43a "Herzliebster Jesu, was hast du verbrochen" (J. Heermann, 1630), sts. 1, 3–5; tr. C. Winkworth, alt.
43b "Herr Jesu Christ, dein theures Blut" (J. Olearius, 1671), sts. 1–4; tr. C. H. L. Schuette.
44a "Ein Lämmlein geht und trägt die Schuld" (P. Gerhardt, 1653), sts. 1–3; tr. *Ev. Luth. Hymn-Book* 1918.
44b "Mir nach, spricht Christus, unser Herr" (J. Scheffler, 1668), sts. 1, 6–7; tr. C. W. Schaeffer, alt.
45a "So gehst du nun, mein Jesu, hin" (M. C. Nachtenhöfer, 1651), sts. 1, 3, 5; tr. st. 1, A. T. Russell, alt., sts. 3, 5, M. Carver.
45b "Fließt, ihr Augen, fließt von Thränen" (L. Laurentii, 1700), sts. 9–10; tr. composite.
46a "Herr Jesu Christe, treuer Heiland werth" (V. Schmuck, 1617), sts. 1–3; tr. M. Carver.
46b "O du Liebe meiner Liebe" (E. von Senitz, d. 1679), sts. 1, 3, 5; tr. composite.
47a "O, so hängt denn meine Liebe" (J. A. Grammlich, 1727), sts. 1–4; tr. M. Carver.
47b "O, so hängt denn meine Liebe" (J. A. Grammlich, 1727), sts. 6–7; tr. M. Carver.
48a "O Welt, sieh hier dein Leben" (P. Gerhardt, 1653), sts. 1–2; tr. J. Kelly.
48b "O Welt, sieh hier dein Leben" (P. Gerhardt, 1653), sts. 9–10, 12–14; tr. J. Kelly.
49a "Dem König, welcher Blut und Leben" (E. G. Woltersdorf, 1750), sts. 1–3; tr. M. Carver.
49b "Valet will ich dir geben" (V. Herberger, 1613), sts. 3, 5; tr. M. Carver.

50a "Der am Kreuz ist meine Liebe / und sonst …" (J. E. Greding, 1723), sts. 1–3, 5b; tr. sts. 1, 3, J. T. Mueller, alt., sts. 2, 5, M. Carver.
50b "O Jesu Christ, dein theures Blut" (J. Olearius, 1671), sts. 1–2; tr. M. Carver.
51a "O Haupt voll Blut und Wunden" (P. Gerhardt, 1659), sts. 5–7; tr. J. Kelly.
51b "Hör an, mein Herz, die sieben Wort" (P. Gerhardt, 1659), st. 5; tr. J. Kelly, alt.
52a "O Lamm gottes unschuldig" (N. Decius, 1523), sts. 1–3, expanded by Anon.; tr. A. T. Russell, alt.
52b "Jesu, meines Lebens Leben" (E. C. Homburg, 1659), sts. 4, 7; tr. C. Winkworth, alt.
53a "So wahr ich lebe, spricht dein Gott" (J. Heermann, 1630), sts. 1–2, 7; tr. J. C. Jacobi, alt.
53b "Höchster König, Jesu Christ" (A. Gryphius, 1659), sts. 1–3, 6; tr. M. Carver, in *Walther's Hymnal* #217.
54a "Jesu Leiden, Pein und tod" (P. Stockmann, d. 1636), sts. 23, 34; tr. st. 23, M. Carver, st. 24, Mor. H.-B 1854.
54b "Mein Gott, du wirst mich nicht verlassen" (J. G. Kästner, 1768, alt.), as revised by E. R. Stier, 1835, sts. 1–3; tr. M. Carver.
55a "Seelenbräutigam" (A. Drese, ca. 1690), sts. 7–8, 13; tr. sts. 7–8, M. Carver, 2012, st. 13, E. Cronenwett.
55b "Jesu, der du wollen büssen" (Gotha, 1699), st. 9; tr. M. Carver.
56a "Jesus Christus hat vollbracht" (P. F. Hiller, d. 1769), sts. 1, 6, 2–3; tr. M. Carver.
56b "Es ist vollbracht, so ruft das Gotteslamm" (F. Gude, 1765), sts. 1–10; tr. M. Carver.
57a "Ich danke dir für deinen Tod" (J. Scheffler, 1657), sts. 1–3; tr. M. Carver.
57b "O Haupt voll Blut und Wunde" (P. Gerhardt, d. 1659), sts. 8–10; tr. J. W. Alexander.
58a "Ach stirbt denn so mein allerliebstes Leben?" (G. W. Sacer, 1661), sts. 1–2, 4–5; tr. M. Carver.
58b "Reißt, ihr Felsen, Erde, bebe" (Hanover, 1745), sts. 1, 7; tr. M. Carver.
59a "Seele, geh auf Golgatha" (B. Schmolck, d. 1737), sts. 1–4; tr. sts. 1–3, A. Hoppe, alt., st. 4, M. Carver.
59b "Christus, der uns selig macht" (M. Weiß, 1531), st. 8; tr. *Mor. H.-B.* 1819, alt.
60a "Meine Seel, ermuntre dich" (J. C. Schade, 1699); sts. 1–3, 9; tr. sts. 1–3, A. Hoppe, st. 9, M. Carver.
60b "Unter Jesu Kreuze stehn" (P. F. Hiller, 1767), sts. 1–2, 9; tr. M. Carver.
61a "Die Seele Christi heilge mich" (J. Scheffler, d. 1677), sts. 1–5; tr. M. Loy, alt.
61b "O Jesu Christ, meins Lebens Licht" (M. Böhme, 1608), sts. 7–8, 11, 15; tr. sts. 8, 15, C. Winkworth, alt., sts. 7, 11, *Ev. Luth. Hymn-Book* 1893.
62a "Mein Jesus ruht, wie war sein Kampf so groß" (Anon., 1727), sts. 1–2; tr. M. Carver.
62b "O Traurigkeit" (J. Rist, 1641), sts. 4–6; tr. C. Winkworth, alt.
63a "Ach stirbt denn so mein" (G. W. Sacer, 1661), sts. 6–8; tr. M. Carver.
63b "O Traurigkeit" (J. Rist, 1641), sts. 1–2, 7–8; tr. C. Winkworth, alt.
64a "O Lamm, das meine Schuldenlast (J. A. Freylinghausen, 1704), sts. 1–2, 4; tr. M. Carver.
64b "O Lamm, das meine Schuldenlast (J. A. Freylinghausen, 1704), sts. 7–8; tr. M. Carver.
65a "So ruhest du, o meine Ruh" (S. Frank, 1685), sts. 1–3; tr. R. Massie, alt.
65b "So ruhest du, o meine Ruh" (S. Frank, 1685), sts. 4–7; tr. R. Massie, alt.
66a "Der du, Herr Jesu, Ruh und Rast" (G. Werner, 1638), sts. 1–3; tr. M. Carver.
66b "Wir danken dir, Herr Jesu Christ" (C. Vischer, ca. 1598), sts. 1–4; tr. A. Crull.

MELODY APPENDIX

1. Ach Gott, erhör mein Seufzen und Wehklagen

2. Ach, wir armen Sünder

MELODY APPENDIX

3. Der am Kreuz ist meine Liebe

4. Der Tag ist hin, mein Jesu, bei mir bleibe

5. *O Jesu, Gottes Lämmelein*

6. *Singen wir aus Herzensgrund*